HALF A CENTURY

BY

JANE GREY SWISSHELM.

SOURCE BOOK PRESS

HALF A CENTURY.

BY

JANE GREY SWISSHELM.

* * * "God so willed:
Mankind is ignorant! a man am I:
Call ignorance my sorrow, not my sin!"

* * "O, still as ever friends are they
Who, in the interest of outraged truth
Deprecate such rough handling of a lie!"
ROBERT BROWNING.

Second Edition.

CHICAGO:
JANSEN, McCLURG & COMPANY.
1880.

STEREOTYPED, PRINTED AND BOUND
BY
THE CHICAGO LEGAL NEWS COMPANY.

PREFACE.

It has been assumed, and is generally believed, that the Anti-slavery struggle, which culminated in the Emancipation Proclamation of 1862, originated in Infidelity, and was a triumph of Skepticism over Christianity. In no way can this error be so well corrected as by the personal history of those who took part in that struggle; and as most of them have passed from earth without leaving any record of the education and motives which underlay their action, the duty they neglected becomes doubly incumbent on the few who remain.

To supply one quota of the inside history of the great Abolition war, is the primary object of this work; but scarcely secondary to this object is that of recording incidents characteristic of the Peculiar Institution overthrown in that struggle.

Another object, and one which struggles for precedence, is to give an inside history of the hospitals during the war of the Rebellion, that the American people may not forget the cost of that Government so often imperiled through their indifference.

A third object, is to give an analysis of the ground which produced the Woman's Rights agitation, and the causes which limited its influence.

A fourth is, to illustrate the force of education and the mutability of human character, by a personal narrative of one who, in 1836, would have broken an engagement rather than permit her name to appear in print, even in the announcement of marriage; and who, in 1850, had as much newspaper notoriety as any man of that time, and was singularly indifferent to the praise or blame of the Press;—of one who, in 1837, could not break the seal of silence set upon her lips by "Inspiration," even so far as to pray with a man dying of intemperance, and who yet, in 1862, addressed the Minnesota Senate in session, and as many others as could be packed in the hall, with no more embarrassment than though talking with a friend in a chimney corner.   J. G. S.

CONTENTS.

(5)

6   CONTENTS.

HALF A CENTURY.

CHAPTER I.

I FIND LIFE.

Those soft pink circles which fell upon my face and
hands, caught in my hair, danced around my feet, and
frolicked over the billowy waves of bright, green grass
—did I know they were apple blossoms? Did I know
it was an apple tree through which I looked up to the
blue sky, over which white clouds scudded away toward
the great hills? Had I slept and been awakened by
the wind to find myself in the world?

It is probable that I had for some time been familiar with that tree, and all my surroundings, for I had
been breathing two and a half years, and had made
some progress in the art of reading and sewing, saying catechism and prayers. I knew the gray kitten
which walked away; knew that the girl who brought
it back and reproved me for not holding it was Adaline, my nurse; knew that the young lady who stood
near was cousin Sarah Alexander, and that the girl to
whom she gave directions about putting bread into a
brick oven was Big Jane; that I was Little Jane, and
that the white house across the common was Squire
Horner's.

(7)

There was no surprise in anything save the loveli-
ness of blossom and tree; of the grass beneath and the
sky above; and this first indelible imprint on my memory seems to have found this inner something I call
me, as capable of reasoning as it has ever been.

While I sat and wondered, father came, took me in
his loving arms and carried me to mother's room,
where she lay in a tent-bed, with blue foliage and blue
birds outlined on the white ground of the curtains,
like the apple-boughs on the blue and white sky. The
cover was turned down, and I was permitted to kiss a
baby-sister, and warned to be good, lest Mrs. Damp-
ster, who had brought the baby, should come and take
it away. This autocrat was pointed out, as she sat in
a gray dress, white 'kerchief and cap, and no other po-
tentate has ever inspired me with such reverential
awe.

My second memory is of a "great awakening" to
a sense of sin, and of my lost and undone condition.
On a warm summer day, while walking alone on the
common which lay between home and Squire Horner's
house, I was struck motionless by the thought that I
had forgotten God. It seemed probable, considering
the total depravity of my nature, that I had been
thinking bad thoughts, and these I labored to recall,
that I might repent and plead with Divine mercy for
forgiveness. But alas! I could remember nothing
save the crowning crime—forgetfulness of God.

I seemed to stand outside, and see myself a mere
mite, in a pink sun-bonnet and white bib, the very
chief of sinners, for the probability was I had been
thinking of that bonnet and bib. It was quite certain

that God knew my sin; and ah, the crushing horror that I could, by no possibility conceal aught from the All-seeing Eye, while it was equally impossible to win its approval. The Divine Law was so perfect that I could not hope to meet its requirements—the Divine Law-giver so alert that no sin could escape detection.

Under that cloud of doom the sunshine grew dark, and I did not dare to move until a cheery voice called out something about my pretty bonnet, and gave me a sense of companionship in this dreadful, dreadful world. Rose, a large native African, had spoken to me from her place in Squire Horner's kitchen, and I went home full of solemn resolves and sad forebodings.

This is probably what evangelists would call my conversion, and it came in my third summer. There was a fire in the grate when mother showed Dr. Robt. Wilson, our family physician, a pair of wristbands and collar I had stitched for father, and when they spoke of me as not being three years old—but then I had in my mind the marks of that "great awakening."

To me, no childhood was possible under the training this indicates, yet in giving that training, my parents were loving and gentle as they were faithful. Believing in the danger of eternal death, they could but guard me from it, by the only means of which they had any knowledge.

Before the completion of that momentous third year of life, I had learned to read the New Testament readily, and was deeply grieved that our pastor played "patty cake" with my hands, instead of hearing me recite my catechism, and talking of original sin. Dur-

ing that winter I went regularly to school, where I
was kept at the head of a spelling-class, in which were
young men and women. One of these, Wilkins Mc-
Nair, used to carry me home, much amused, no doubt,
by my supremacy. His father, Col. Dunning McNair,
was proprietor of the village, and had been ridiculed
for predicting that, in the course of human events,
there would be a graded, McAdamized road, all the way
from Philadelphia to Pittsburg, and that if he did not
live to see it his children would. He was a neighbor
and friend of Wm. Wilkins, afterwards Judge, Secretary of War, and Minister to Russia, and had named
his son for him. When his prediction was fulfilled
and the road made, it ran through his land, and on it
he laid out the village and called it Wilkinsburg. Mr.
McNair lived south of it in a rough stone house—the
manor of the neighborhood—with half a dozen slave
huts ranged before the kitchen door, and the gateway
between his grounds and the village, as seen from the
upper windows of our house, was, to me, the boundary
between the known and the unknown, the dread por-
tal through which came Adam, the poor old ragged
slave, with whom my nurse threatened me when I did
not do as she wished. He was a wretched creature,
who made and sold hickory brooms, as he dragged his
rheumatic limbs on the down grade of life, until he
found rest by freezing to death in the woods, where he
had gone for saplings.

I was born on the 6th of December, 1815, in Pittsburg, on the bank of the Monongahela, near its confluence with the Allegheny. My father was Thomas
Cannon, and my mother Mary Scott. They were

both Scotch-Irish and descended from the Scotch Reformers. On my mother's side were several men and
women who signed the "Solemn League and Covenant," and defended it to the loss of livings, lands and
life. Her mother, Jane Grey, was of that family
which was allied to royalty, and gave to England her
nine day's queen.

This grandmother I remember as a stately old lady,
quaintly and plainly dressed, reading a large Bible or
answering questions by quotations from its pages.
She was unsuspicious as an infant, always doubtful
about "actual transgressions" of any, while believing
in the total depravity of all. Educated in Ireland as
an heiress, she had not been taught to write, lest she
should marry without the consent of her elder brother
guardian. She felt that we owed her undying gratitude for bestowing her hand and fortune on our grandfather, who was but a yoeman, even if "he did have
a good leasehold, ride a high horse, wear spurs, and
have Hamilton blood in his veins." She made us familiar with the battle of the Boyne and the sufferings
in Londonderry, in both of which her great-grand-
father had shared, but was incapable of that sectarian
rancor, which marks so many descendents of the men
who met on those fields of blood and fought for their
convictions.

In April, 1816, father moved from Pittsburg out to
the new village of Wilkinsburg; took with him a large
stock of goods, bought property, built the house in
which I first remember him, and planted the apple
tree which imprinted the first picture on my memory.
But the crash which followed the last war with Eng-

land brought general bankruptcy; the mortgages on Col. McNair's estate made the titles valueless, and this, with the fall of his real estate in Pittsburg, reduced father to poverty, from which he never recovered.

CHAPTER II.

PROGRESS IN CALVINISM—HUNT GHOSTS—SEE LA FAYETTE.

—AGE, 6-9.

My parents were members of the Covenanter Congregation, of which Dr. John Black was pastor for forty-five years. He was a man of power, a profound logician, with great facility in conveying ideas. To his pulpit ministrations I am largely indebted for whatever ability I have to discriminate between truth and falsehood; but the church was in Pittsburg, and our home seven miles away, so we seldom went to meeting. The rules of the denomination forbade " occasional hearing." Father and mother had once been "sessioned" for stopping on their way home to hear the conclusion of a communion service in Dr. Bruce's church, which was Seceder. So our Sabbaths were usually spent in religious services at home. These I enjoyed, as it aided my life-work of loving and thinking about God, who seemed, to my mind, to have some special need of my attention. Nothing was done on that day which could have been done the day before, or could be postponed till the day after. Coffee grinding was not thought of, and once, when we had no flour for Saturday's baking, and the buckwheat cakes were baked the evening before and warmed on Sabbath morning, we were all troubled about the violation of the day.

There was a Presbyterian "meeting-house" two miles east of Wilkinsburg, where a large, wealthy congregation worshipped. Rev. James Graham was pastor, and unlike other Presbyterians, they never "profaned the sanctuary" by singing "human compositions," but confined themselves to Rouse's version of David's Psalms, as did our own denomination. This aided that laxness of discipline which permitted Big Jane, Adaline and brother William to attend sometimes, under care of neighbors. Once I was allowed to accompany them.

I was the proud possessor of a pair of red shoes, which I carried rolled up in my 'kerchief while we walked the two miles. We stopped in the woods; my feet were denuded of their commonplace attire and arrayed in white hose, beautifully clocked, and those precious shoes, and my poor conscience tortured about my vanity. The girls also exchanged theirs for morocco slippers. We concealed our walking shoes under a mossy log and proceeded to the meeting-house.

It was built in the form of a T, of hewn logs, and the whole structure, both inside and out, was a combination of those soft grays and browns with which nature colors wood, and in its close setting of primeval forest, made a harmonious picture. At one side lay a graveyard; birds sang in the surrounding trees, some of which reached out their giant arms and touched the log walls. Swallows had built nests under the eaves outside, and some on the rough projections inside, and joined their twitter to the songs of other birds and the rich organ accompaniment of wind and trees.

There were two sermons, and in the intermission, a church sociable, in fact if not in name. Friends who lived twenty miles apart, met here, exchanged greetings and news, gave notices and invitations, and obeyed the higher law of kindness under protest of their Calvinistic consciences. In this breathing-time we ate our lunch, went to the nearest house and had a drink from the spring which ran through the stone milk-house. It was a day full of sight-seeing and of solemn, grand impressions.

Of the two sermons I remember but one, and this from the text "Many are called but few are chosen," and the comments were Calvinism of the most rigid school. On our way home, my brother William— three years older than I—was very silent and thoughtful for some time, then spoke of the sermon, of which I entirely approved, but he stoutly declared that he did not believe it; did not believe God called people to come to him while he did not choose to have them come. It would not be fair, indeed, he thought it would be mean.

That evening, when we were saying the shorter catechism, the question, "What are the decrees of God?" came to me, and after repeating the answer, I asked father to explain it—not that I needed any explanation, but that William might be enlightened; for I was anxious about his soul, on account of his skepticism. Enlightened he could not be, and even to father expressed his doubts and disapprobation. We renewed the discussion when alone, and during all his life I labored with him; but soon found the common refuge of orthodox minds, in feeling that those espe-

cially loved by them will be made exceptions in the
general distribution of wrath due to unbelief.

One day I went with him to hunt the cow. We
came to a wood just north of the village, where the
wind roared and shook the trees so that I was quite
awe-stricken; but he held my hand and assured me
there was no danger, until he suddenly drew me back,
exclaiming:

" Oh see!" as a great tree came crashing down across
the path before us, and so near that it must have fallen
on us if he had not seen it and stepped back. Even
then he refused to go home without the cow, and taking up a daddy-long-legs, he inquired of it where she
was, and started in the direction indicated, when we
were arrested by the voice of Big Jane, who had come
to search for us.

On reaching home, we found a new baby-sister, Elizabeth. Soon after her birth, in April, 1821, father
moved back to Pittsburg, and lived on Sixth street,
opposite Trinity Church, on property belonging to my
maternal grandfather. There was no church there at
that time, but a thickly peopled graveyard, which adjoined that of the First Presbyterian Church, on the
corner of Sixth and Wood. These were above the
level of the street, and were protected by a worm-fence
that ran along the top of a green bank on which we
played and gathered flowers.

Grandmother took me sometimes to walk in these
graveyards at night, and there talked to me about God
and heaven and the angels. I was sufficiently interested in these, but especially longed to see the ghosts,
and often went to look for them. We had a bachelor

uncle who delighted in telling us tales of the supernatural, and he peopled these graveyards with ghosts,
in which I believed as implicitly as in the Revelations
made to John on the Isle of Patmos, which were my
favorite literature.

When the congregation concluded to abandon the
"Round Church," which stood on the triangle between
Liberty, Wood and Sixth streets, and began to dig for
a foundation for Trinity, where it now stands, there
was great desecration of graves. One day a thrill of
excitement and stream of talk ran through the neighborhood, about a Mrs. Cooper, whose body had been
buried three years, and was found in a wonderful state
of preservation, when the coffin was laid open by the
diggers. It was left that the friends might remove it,
and that night I felt would be the time for ghosts. So
I went over alone, and while I crouched by the open
grave, peering in, a cloud passed, and the moon poured
down a flood of light, by which I could see the quiet
sleeper, with folded hands, taking her last, long rest.

It was inexpressibly grand, solemn and sad. There
were no gaslights, no paved street near, no one stir-
ring. Earth was far away and heaven near at hand,
but no ghost came, and I went home disappointed.
Afterwards I had a still more disheartening adventure.

I had gone an errand to cousin Alexander's, on Fifth
street, stayed late, and coming home, found Wood
street deserted. The moon shone brightly, but on the
graveyard side were heavy shadows, except in the open
space opposite the church. I was on the other side,
and there was the office of the Democratic paper, and
over the door the motto "Our country, right or

wrong." This had long appeared to be an uncanny spot, owing to the wickedness of this sentiment, and I was thinking of the possibility of seeing Auld Nick guarding his property, when my attention was attracted to a tall, white figure in the bright moonlight, outside the graveyard fence.

I stopped an instant, in great surprise, and listened for footsteps, but no sound accompanied the motion. It did not walk, but glided, and must have risen out of the ground, for only a moment before there was nothing visible. I clasped my hands in mute wonder, but my ghost was getting away, and to make its acquaintance I must hurry. Crossing the street I ran after and gained on it. It passed into the shadow of the engine house, on across Sixth street, into the moonlight, then into the shadow, before I overtook it, when lo! it was a mortal woman, barefoot, in a dress which was probably a faded print. Most prints faded then, and this was white, long and scant, making a very ghostly robe, while on her head she carried a bundle tied up in a sheet. She had, of course, come out of Virgin alley, where many laundresses lived, and had just passed out of the shadow when I saw her. We exchanged salutations, and I went home to lie and brood over the unreliable nature of ghosts.

I was trying to get into a proper frame of mind for saying my prayers, but I doubt if they were said that night, as we were soon aroused by the cries of fire. Henry Clay was being burned, in effigy, on the corner of Sixth and Wood streets, to show somebody's disapproval of his course in the election of John Quincy Adams. The Democratic editor, McFarland, was tried

2

and found guilty of the offense, and took revenge in ridiculing his opponents.   Charles Glenn, a fussy old gentleman, member of our church, was an important witness for the prosecution, and in the long, rhyming account published by the defendant, he was thus re- membered:

" Then in came Glenn, that man of peace,
    And swore to facts as sleek as grease;
    By all his Uncle Aleck's geese,
        McFarland burnt the tar-barrel.'

It was before this time that Lafayette revisited Pittsburg, and people went wild to do him honor. The schools paraded for his inspection, and ours was ranged along the pavement in front of the First Pres- byterian church, the boys next the curb, the girls next the fence, all in holiday attire, and wearing blue badges.   The distinguished visitor passed up between them, leaning on the arm of another gentleman, bow- ing and smiling as he went.   When he came to where I stood, he stepped aside, laid his hand on my head, turned up my face and spoke to me.

I was too happy to know what he said, and in all the years since that day, that hand has lain on my brow as a consecration.

CHAPTER III.

FATHER'S DEATH.——AGE, 6-12.

IN the city we went regularly to meeting, and Dr. Black seemed always to talk to *me*, and I had no more difficulty in understanding his sermons, than in mas-

tering the details of the most simple duty. The first
of which I preserve the memory was about Peter, who
was made to illustrate the growth of crime. He began
with boasting; then came its natural fruit, cowardice, in
following his master afar off; next falsehood, and from
this he proceeded to perjury. It did seem that a
disciple of Christ could go no further; but for falsehood and perjury there might be excuse in the hope
of reward, and Peter found a lower deep, for "he began
to curse and to swear." A profane swearer is without
temptation, and serves the devil for the pure love of
the service. What more could Peter do to prove that
he knew not Jesus?

In the communion service is a ceremony called
"fencing the tables," which consists of an appeal to the
consciences of intended communicants. Dr. Black began with the first commandment and forbade those
living in its violation to come to the table, and so proceeded through the decalogue. When he came to the
eighth, he straightened himself, placed his hands behind him, and with thrilling emphasis said, "I debar
from this holy table of the Lord, all slave-holders and
horse-thieves, and other dishonest persons," and without another word passed to the ninth commandment.

Soon after we returned to the city, sister Mary died
of consumption, and father's health began to fail. I
have preserved the spinning wheel on which mother
converted flax yarn into thread, which she sold to aid
in the support of the family, but soon the entire burden fell on her, for father's illness developed into consumption, from which he died in March, 1823.

In spite of all the testamentary precautions he could

take, whatever of his estate might have been available
for present support, was in the hands of lawyers, and
mother was left with her children and the debts. There
were the contents of his shop and warehouse, some
valuable real estate in Pittsburg, which had passed out
of his possession on a claim of ground-rent, and a
village home minus a title.

William was a mechanical genius, so mother set him
to making little chairs, which he readily sold, but he
liked better to construct fire engines, which were quite
wonderful but brought no money. He had a splendid
physique, was honorable and faithful, and if mother
had been guided by natural instinct in governing him,
all would have been well; but he never met the requirements of the elders of the church, who felt it their
duty to manage our family affairs. So he was often
in trouble, and I, who gloried in him, contrived to
shield him from many a storm.

At this time there was a fashionable *furor* for lace
work. Mother sent me to learn it, and then procured
me pupils, whom I taught, usually sitting on their
knee. But lace work soon gave way to painting on
velvet. This, too, I learned, and found profit in selling
pictures. Ah, what pictures I did make. I reached
the culminating glory of artist life, when Judge
Braden, of Butler, gave me a new crisp five dollar bill
for a Goddess of Liberty. Indeed, he wanted me to
be educated for an artist, and was far-seeing and generous enough to have been my permanent patron, had
an artistic education, or any other education, been possible for a Western Pennsylvania girl in that dark
age—the first half of the nineteenth century.

Mother made a discovery in the art of coloring leg-horn and straw bonnets, which brought her plenty of work, so we never lacked comforts of life, although grandfather's executors made us pay rent for the house we occupied.

CHAPTER IV.

GO TO BOARDING-SCHOOL.—AGE, 12.

During my childhood there were no public schools in Pennsylvania. The State was pretty well supplied with colleges for boys, while girls were permitted to go to subscription schools. To these we were sent part of the time, and in one of them Joseph Caldwell, afterwards a prominent missionary to India, was a schoolmate. But we had Dr. Black's sermons, full of grand morals, science and history.

In lieu of colleges for girls, there were boarding-schools, and Edgeworth was esteemed one of the best in the State. It was at Braddock's Field, and Mrs. Olever, an English woman of high culture, was its founder and principal. To it my cousin, Mary Alexander, was sent, but returned homesick, and refused to go back unless I went with her. It was arranged that I should go for a few weeks, as I was greatly in need of country air; and, highly delighted, I was at the rendezvous at the hour, one o'clock, with my box, ready for this excursion into the world of polite litera-ture. Mary was also there, and a new scholar, but Father Olever did not come for us until four o'clock. He was a small, nervous gentleman, and lamps were already lighted in the smoky city when we started to drive twelve miles through spring mud, on a cloudy, cheerless afternoon. We knew he had no confidence in his power to manage those horses, though we also knew he would do his best to save us from harm; but as darkness closed around us, I think we felt like babes in the woods, and shuddered with vague fear as much as with cold and damp. When we reached the "Bullock Pens," half a mile west of Wilkinsburg, there were many lights and much bustle in and around the old yellow tavern, where teamsters were attending to their weary horses. Here we turned off to the old mud road, and came to a place of which I had no previous knowledge—a place of outer darkness and chattering teeth.

We met no more teams, saw no more lights, but seemed to be in an utterly uninhabited country. Then, after an hour of wearisome jolting and plunging, we discovered that the darkness had not been total, for the line of the horizon had been visible, but now it was swallowed up. We knew we were in a wood, by the rush of the wind amid the dried white oak leaves —knew that the road grew rougher at every step— that our driver became more nervous as he applied the brake, and we went down, down.

Still the descent grew steeper. We stopped, and Father Olever felt for the bank with his whip to be sure we were on the road. Then we heard the sound of rushing, angry waters, mingled with the roar of the wind, and he seemed to hesitate about going on, but we could not very well stay there, and he once more put his horses in motion, while we held fast and prayed

silently to the great Deliverer.   After stopping again
and feeling for the bank, lest we should go over the
precipitous hillside, which he knew was there, he proceeded until, with a great plunge, we were in the angry waters, which arose to the wagon-bed, and roared
and surged all around us.   The horses tried to go on,
when something gave way, and our guardian concluded
further progress was impossible, and began to hallo at
the top of his voice.

For a long time there was no response; then came
an answering call from a long distance.   Next a light
appeared, and that, too, was far away, but came toward us.   When it reached the brink of the water,
and two men with it, we felt safe.   The light-bearer
held it up so that we saw him quite well, and his peculiar appearance suited his surroundings.   He was
more an overgrown boy than a man, beardless, with a
long swarthy face, black hair and keen black eyes.
He wore heavy boots outside his pantaloons, a blouse
and slouch hat, spoke to his companion as one having
authority, and with a laugh said to our small gentleman:

"Is this where you are?" but gave no heed to the
answer as he waded in and threw off the check lines,
saying: "I wonder you did not drown your horses."

He next examined the wagon, paying no more attention to Father Olever's explanations than to the water
in which he seemed quite at home, and when he had
finished his inspection he said:

"They must go to the house," and handing the light
to the driver he took us up one by one and carried us
to the wet bank as easily as a child carries her doll.

He gave some directions to his companion, took the light and said to us:

"Come on," and we walked after him out into the limitless blackness, nothing doubting. We went what seemed a long way, following this brigand-looking stranger, without seeing any sign of life or hearing any sound save the roar of wind and water, but on turning a fence corner, we came in sight of a large two-story house, with a bright light streaming out through many windows, and a wide open door. There was a large stone barn on the other side of the road, and to this our conductor turned, saying to us: "Go on to the house." This we did, and were met at the open door by a middle-aged woman, shading with one hand the candle held in the other. This threw a strong light on her face, which instantly reminded me of an eagle. She wore a double-bordered white cap over her black hair, and looked suspiciously at us through her small keen, black eyes, but kindly bade us come in to a low wainscoted hall, with broad stairway and many open doors. Through one of these and a second door we saw a great fire of logs, and I should have liked to sit by it, but she led us into a square wainscotted room on the opposite side, in which blazed a coal fire almost as large as the log heap in the kitchen.

She gave us seats, and a white-haired man who sat in the corner, spoke to us, and made me feel comfortable. Up to this time all the surroundings had had an air of enchanted castles, brigands, ghosts, witches. The alert woman with the eagle face, in spite of her kindness, made me feel myself an object of doubtful character, but this old man set me quite at ease. We were no more than well warmed when the wagon drove to the door, and the boy-man with the lantern appeared, saying,

"Come on."

We followed him again, and he lifted us into the wagon, while the mistress of the house stood on the large flag-stone door-step, shading her candle-flame, and giving directions about our wraps.

"Coming events cast their shadows before," when they are between us and the light; but that night the light must have been between them and me; for I bade good-bye to our hostess without any premonition we should ever again meet, or that I should sit alone, as I do to-night, over half a century later, in that same old wainscoted room, listening to the roar of those same angry waters and the rush of the wind wrestling with the groaning trees, in the dense darkness of this low valley.

When we had been carefully bestowed in the wagon, our deliverer took up his lantern, saying to Father Olever:

"Drive on."

He was obeyed, and led the way over a bridge across another noisy stream, and along a road where there was the sound of a waterfall very near, then up a steep, rocky way until he stopped, saying,

"I guess you can get along now."

To Father Olever's thanks he only replied by a low, contemptuous but good-humored laugh, as he turned to retrace his steps. All comfort and strength and hope seemed to go with him. We were abandoned to our fate, babes in the woods again, with only God for our reliance. But after a while we could see the horizon, and arrived at our destination several minutes before midnight, to find the great mansion full of glancing lights and busy, expectant life.

The large family had waited up for Father Olever's return, for he and his wagon were the connecting link between that establishment and the outside world. He appeared to great advantage surrounded by a bevy of girls clamoring for letters and messages. To me the scene was fairy-land. I had never before seen anything so grand as the great hall with its polished stairway. We had supper in the housekeeper's room, and I was taken up this stairway, and then up and up a corkscrew cousin until we reached the attic, which stretched over the whole house, one great dormitory called the " bee-hive." Here I was to sleep with Helen Semple, a Pittsburg girl, of about my own age, a frail blonde, who quite won my heart at our first meeting.

Next day was Sabbath, and I was greatly surprised to see pupils walk on the lawn. This was such a desecration of the day, but I made no remark. I was too solemnly impressed by the grandeur of being at Braddock's Field to have hinted that anything could be wrong. But for my own share in the violation I was painful'v penitent.

This was not new, for there were a long series of years in which the principal business of six days of every week, was repentance for the very poor use made of the seventh, and from this dreary treadmill of sin and sorrow, no faith ever could or did free me. I never could see salvation in Christ apart from salvation from sin, and while the sin remained the salvation was doubtful and the sorrow certain.

On the afternoon of that first Sabbath, a number of young lady pupils came to the Bee-hive for a visit, and as I afterwards learned to inspect and name the two new girls, when I was promptly and unanimously dubbed "Wax Doll." After a time, one remarked that they must go and study their "ancient history lesson." I caught greedily at the words, ancient history. Ah, if I could only be permitted to study such a lesson! No such progress or promotion seemed open to me; but the thought interfered with my prayers, and followed me into the realm of sleep. So when that class was called next forenoon, I was alert, and what was my surprise, to hear those privileged girls stumbling over the story of Samson? Could it be possible that was ancient history? How did it come to pass that every one did not know all about Samson, the man who had laid his head on Delilah's wicked lap, to be shorn of his strength. If there is any thing in that account, or any lesson to be drawn from it, with which I was not then familiar, it is something I have never learned. Indeed, I seemed to have completed my theological education before I did my twelfth year.

One morning, Mrs. Olever sent for me, and told me she had learned my mother was not able to send me to school, but if I would take charge of the lessons of the little girls, she would furnish me board and tuition. This most generous offer quite took my breath away, and was most gladly accepted; but it was easy work, and I wondered my own studies were so light. I was allowed to amuse myself drawing flowers, which were quite a surprise, and pronounced better than anything the drawing master could do—to recite poetry, for the benefit of the larger girls, and to play in the orchard with my pupils.

With the other girls, I became interested in hairdressing. I had read "The Children of the Abbey," and Amanda's romantic adventures enchanted me; but she was quite outside my life. Now I made a nearer acquaintance with her. She changed her residence; so had I. She had brown ringlets; I too should have them. So one Friday night, my hair was put up in papers, and next morning, I let loose an amazing shower of curls.

The next thing to do was to go off alone, and sit reading in a romantic spot. Of course I did not expect to meet Lord Mortimer! Miss Fitzallen never had any such expectations. I was simply going out to read and admire the beauties of nature. When I had seated myself, in proper attitude, on the gnarled root of an old tree, overhanging a lovely ravine, I proceeded to the reading part of the play, and must of course be too much absorbed to hear the approaching footsteps, to which I listened with bated breath. So I did not look up when they stopped at my side, or until a pleasant voice said:

"Why you look quite romantic, my dear."

Then I saw Miss Olever, the head teacher, familiarly called "Sissy Jane." In that real and beautiful presence Miss Fitzallen retired to her old place, and oh, the mortification she left behind her! I looked up, a detected criminal, into the face of her who had brought to me this humiliation, and took *her* for a model. My folly did not prevent our being sincere friends during all her earnest and beautiful life.

She passed on, and I got back to the Bee-hive, when I disposed of my curls, and never again played heroine.

CHAPTER V.

LOSE MY BROTHER.—Age, 12–15.

Measured by the calendar, my boarding-school life was six weeks; but measured by its pleasant memories, it was as many years. Mother wrote for me to come home; and in going I saw, by sunlight, the scene of our adventure that dark night going out. It was a lovely valley, walled in by steep, wooded hills. Two ravines joined, bringing each its contribution of running water, and pouring it into the larger stream of the larger valley—a veritable "meeting of the waters" —in all of nature's work, beautiful exceedingly.

The house, which stood in the center of a large, green meadow, through which the road ran, was built in two parts, of hewn logs, with one great stone chimney on the outside, protected by an overshot in the roof, but that one in which the log-heap burned that night was inside. One end had been an Indian fort when Gen. Braddock tried to reach Fort Pitt by that road. The other end and stone barn had been built by its present proprietor. A log mill, the oldest in Allegheny county, stood below the barn, and to it the French soldiers had come for meal from Fort Duquesne. The stream crossed by the bridge was the

mill-race, and the waterfall made by the waste-gate.
It was the homestead of a soldier of the Revolution,
one of Washington's lieutenants—the old man we had
seen. The woman was his second wife. They had a
numerous family, and an unpronounceable name.

At home I learned that, on account of a cough, I
had been the object of a generous conspiracy between
mother and Mrs. Olever, and had been brought home
because I was worse. Our doctors said I was in the
first stage of consumption, that Elizabeth was to reach
that point early in life, and that our only hope lay in
plenty of calomel. Mother had lost her husband and
four vigorous children; there had been no lack of calomel, and now, when death again threatened, she resolved to conduct the defense on some new plan.

She had gained legal possession of our village home,
and moved to it. Our lot was large and well supplied
with choice fruit, and the place seemed a paradise after our starved lives in the smoky city. My apple
tree still grew at the east end of the house. There
was a willow tree mother had planted, which now swept
the ground with its long, graceful branches. There
were quantities of rose and lilac bushes, a walled
spring of delicious water in the cellar, and a whole
world of wealth; but the potato lot looked up in despair—a patch of yellow clay. Mother put a twelve
years' accumulation of coal ashes on it, and thus proved
them valuable both as a fertilizer and a preventive of
potato-rot, though at first her project met general opposition.

William did the heavy work and was proud of it.
He was in splendid health, for his insubordination

had, from a very early age, saved him from drugging either mental or physical. The lighter gardening became part of my treatment for consumption. By having me each day lie on the floor on my back without a pillow, and gentle use of dumb-bells, mother straightened my spine and developed my chest—my clothes being carefully adapted to its expansion. Dancing was strictly forbidden by our church, but mother was educated in Ireland and danced beautifully. She had a class of girls and taught us, and with plenty of fresh air, milk and eggs, effectually disposed of hereditary consumption in her family. But while attending to us, she must also make a living, so she bought a stock of goods on credit, opened a store, and soon had a paying business. In this I was her special assistant. But the work supplied to William did not satisfy the holy men of the church, who furnished us advice. He still made fire engines, and a brook in a meadow presented irresistible temptation to water-wheels and machinery. One of his tilt-hammers made a very good ghost, haunting the meadow and keeping off trespassers. He had a foundry, where he cast miniature cannon, kettles and curious things, and his rifle-practice was a neighborhood wonder. He brought water from the cellar, and did other chores which Pennsylvania rules assigned to women, and when boys ridiculed him, he flogged them, and did it quite as effectually as he rendered them the same service when they were rude to a girl. He was a universal favorite, even if he did hate catechism and love cake.

So mother's conscience was worked upon until she

bound him to a cabinet maker in the city. To him, the restraint was unendurable, and he ran away. He came after dark to bid me good-bye, left love for mother and Elizabeth, and next morning left Pittsburg on a steamboat, going to that Eldorado of Pittsburg boys—" down the river."

For some time letters came regularly from him, and he was happy and prosperous. Then they ceased, and after two years of agonizing suspense, we heard that he had died of yellow fever in New Orleans. To us, this was dreadful, irreparable, and was wholly due to that iron-bedstead piety which permits no natural growth, but sets down all human loves and longings as of Satanic origin.

Soon after our removal to the village, grandfather's estate was advertised for sheriff's sale. Mother had the proceedings stayed, the executors dismissed, and took out letters of administration, which made it necessary for her to spend some portion of every month in the city. This threw the entire charge of house and store on me. As soon, therefore, as possible, she sent me to the city to school, where I realized my aspiration of studying ancient history and the piano, and devoured the contents of the text-book of natural philosophy with an avidity I had never known for a novel.

In April, 1830, I began to teach school, the only one in Wilkinsburg, and had plenty of pupils, young men and women, boys and girls, at two dollars and one dollar and a half a term. Taught seven hours a day, and Saturday forenoon, which was devoted to Bible reading and catechism. I was the first, I believe, in Allegheny Co., to teach children without beating

them. I abolished corporeal punishment entirely, and
was so successful that boys, ungovernable at home,
were altogether tractable. This life was perfectly
congenial, and I followed it for nearly six years.
Mother started a Sabbath School, the only one in the
village, and this, too, we continued for years.

One of the pupils was a girl of thirteen, daughter
of a well-to-do farmer, who lived within a mile of the
village. Her father had been converted at a camp-
meeting and was a devout Methodist. The first day
she attended, I asked her the question:

"How many Gods are there?"

She thought a moment, and then said, with an air
of satisfaction:

"Five."

I was shocked, and answered in the language of the
catechism:

"O Margaret! 'There is but one only living and
true God.'"

She hung her head, then nodded it, and with the
emphasis of a judge who had weighed all the evidence, said:

"I am sure I ha' hearn tell o' more nur one of em."

A young theological student came sometimes to stay
over Sabbath and assist in the school. He led in
family worship, and had quite a nice time, until one
evening he read a chapter from the song of songs
which was Solomon's, when I bethought me that he
was very much afraid of toads. I began to cultivate
those bright-eyed creatures, so that it always seemed
probable I had one in my pocket or sleeve. The path
of that good young man became thorny until it di-
verged from mine.

3

I was almost fifteen, when I overheard a young lady say I was growing pretty. I went to my mirror and spent some moments in unalloyed happiness and triumph. Then I thought, "Pretty face, the worms will eat you. All the prettiest girls I know are silly, but you shall never make a fool of me. Helen's beauty ruined Troy. Cleopatra was a wretch. So if you are pretty, *I* will be master, remember that."

CHAPTER VI.

JOIN CHURCH AND MAKE NEW ENDEAVORS TO KEEP SABBATH.——AGE, 15.

IN the year 1800, the Covenanter church of this country said in her synod: "Slavery and Christianity are incompatible," and never relaxed her discipline which forbade fellowship with slave-holders—so I was brought up an abolitionist. I was still a child when I went through Wilkins' township collecting names to a petition for the abolition of slavery in the District of Columbia. Here, in a strictly orthodox Presbyterian community, I was everywhere met by the objections: "Niggers have no souls," "The Jews held slaves," "Noah cursed Canaan," and these points I argued from house to house, occasionally for three years, and made that acquaintance which led to my being sent for in cases of sickness and death, before I had completed my sixteenth year. In this, I in some measure took the place long filled by mother, who was often a substitute for doctor and preacher.

Looking back at her life, I think how little those

know of Calvinists who regard them merely as a class of autocrats, conscious of their own election to glory, and rejoicing in the reprobation of all others; for I have never known such humble, self-distrustful people as I have found in that faith. Mother, whose life was full of wisdom and good works, doubted, even to the last, her own acceptance with God. She and I believed that "a jealous God," who can brook no rivals, had taken away our loving husband and father; our strong and brave son and brother, because we loved them too much, and I was brought up to think it a great presumption to assume that such a worm of the dust as I, could be aught to the Creator but a subject of punishment.

During the spring of 1831, mother said to me:

"Sabbath week is our communion, and I thought you might wish to join the church."

I was startled and without looking up, said:

"Am I old enough?"

"If you feel that the dying command of the Savior, 'do this in remembrance of me' was addressed to you, you are old enough to obey it."

Not another word was said and the subject was never again broached between us, but here a great conflict began. That command was given to me, but how could I obey it without eating and drinking damnation to myself? Was mine a saving faith, or did I, like the devils, believe and tremble? I had been believing as long as I could remember, but did not seem to grow in the image of God.

The conflict lasted several days. Sleep left me. The heavens were iron and the earth brass. I turned to

Erskine to learn the signs of saving faith, but found
only reason to suspect self-deception. I could not submit to God's will—could not be willing that William
should be lost—nay, I was not willing that any one
should be lost. I could not stay in heaven, and know
that any one was enduring endless torments in some
other place! I must leave and go to their relief. It
was dreadful that Abraham did not even try to go to
poor Dives, or to send some one. My whole soul flew
into open revolt; then oh! the total depravity which
could question "the ways of God to man." I hated
Milton. I despised his devils; had a supreme contempt for the "Prince of the Power of the Air;" did
not remember a time when I was afraid of him. God
was "my refuge and my shield, in straits a present
aid." If he took care of me, no one else could hurt
me; if he did not, no one else could; and to be accepted by him was all there was or could be worth caring
for; but how should I find this acceptance with my
heart full of rebellion?

One afternoon I became unable to think, but a white
mist settled down over hell. Even those contemptible
devils were having their tongues cooled with blessed
drops of water. The fires grew dim, and it seemed as
if there was to be a rain of grace and mercy in that
region of despair. Then I preferred my petition, that
God would write his name upon my forehead, and
give me that "new name" which should mark me as
his; that he would bring William into the fold, and
do with me as he would. I would be content to spend
my whole life in any labor he should appoint, without
a sign of the approval of God or man, if, in the end,

I and mine should be found among those "who had washed their robes, and made them white in the blood of the Lamb."

I fell asleep—slept hours—and when the sun was setting, woke in perfect peace. My proposition had been accepted, and wonderful grace, which had given what I had not dared to ask, assurance of present acceptance. I should have all the work and privation for which I had bargained—should be a thistle-digger in the vineyard; should be set to tasks from which other laborers shrank, but in no trial could I ever be alone, and should at last hear the welcome "well done."

I arose as one from a grave to a joyous resurrection; but kept all these things in my heart. Personal experiences being altogether between God and the soul, were not considered fit subjects for conversation, and when I came before the session applying for church membership, no mention was made of them, except as a general confession of faith.

Rev. Andrew Black addressed the table at which I sat in my first communion, and said:

"The Lord's Supper has been named the Eucharist, after the oath taken by a Roman soldier, never to turn his back upon his leader. You, in partaking of these emblems, do solemnly vow that you will never turn your back upon Christ, but that you will follow him whithersoever he goeth. Let others do as they will, you are to follow the Lamb, through good and through evil report, to a palace or to a prison; follow him, even if he should lead you out of the church."

This was in perfect harmony with my private agree-

ment, and no other act of my life has been so solemn
or far-reaching in its consequences, as that ratification
of my vow, and it is one I have least cause to repent.

However, it brought a new phase to an old trouble.
How should I follow Christ? I could not do as he
had done. I could not go to meeting every Sabbath,
and society every Friday; and if I did, was that following Christ who never built a meeting-house, or
conducted any service resembling those now held? I
read the life of Jonathan Edwards, and settled back
into the old Sabbath-keeping rut. Resolving to do
my best, I prayed all week, for grace to keep the next
Sabbath. I rose early that trial-morning, prayed as
soon as my eyes were open, read a chapter, looked out
into the beautiful morning, thought about God and
prayed—spent so much time praying, that Elizabeth
had breakfast ready when I went down stairs. While
I ate it, I held my thoughts to the work of the day,
worshiping God; but many facts and fancies forced
themselves in and disturbed my pious meditations.
After breakfast, I went back to my room to continue
my labor; but mother soon came and said:

"Do you intend to let Elizabeth do all the work?"

I dropped my roll of saintship, and went and washed
the dishes. Had I been taught that he who does any
honest work serves God and follows Christ, what a
world of woe would have been spared me.

CHAPTER VII.

THE DELIVERER OF THE DARK NIGHT.—AGE, 19-21.

QUILTINGS furnished the principal amusement, and
at these I was in requisition, both for my expertness

with the needle, and my skill in laying out work; but
as I had no brother to come for me, I usually went
home before the evening frolic, which consisted of
plays. Male and female partners went through the
common quadrille figures, keeping time to the music
of their own voices, and making a denoument every
few moments by some man kissing some woman, perhaps in a dark hall, or some woman kissing some man,
or some man kissing all the women, or *vice versa*.
Elders and preachers often looked on in pious appro-
bation, and the church covered these sports with the
mantle of her approval, but was ready to excommuni-
cate any one who should dance. Promiscuous dancing was the fiery dragon which the church went out
to slay. Only its death could save her from a fit of
choler which might be fatal, unless, indeed, the dancing were sanctified by promiscuous kissing. If men
and women danced together without kissing, they
were in immediate danger of eternal damnation; but
with plenty of kissing, and rude wrestling to overcome
the delicacy of women who objected to such desecration, the church gave her blessing to the quadrille.

My protest against these plays had given offense,
and I chose to avoid them; but one evening the host
begged me to remain, saying he would see that I was
not annoyed, and would himself take me home. The
frolic was only begun, when he came and asked permission to introduce a gentleman, saying: "If you do
not treat him well, I will never forgive you."

There was no need of this caution, for he presented
a man whose presence made me feel that I was a very
little girl and should have been at home. He was

over six feet tall, well formed and strongly built, with
black hair and eyes, a long face, and heavy black
whiskers. He was handsomely dressed, and his manner that of a grave and reverend seignor. A Russian
count in a New York drawing room, then, when
counts were few, could not have seemed more foreign
than this man in that village parlor, less than two
miles from the place of his birth.

He was the son of the old revolutionary soldier,
with the unpronounceable name, who lived in the beautiful valley. This I knew at once, but did not, for
some time, realize that it was he who rescued us from
the black waters on that dark night, carried us to safety and light, and left us again in darkness. This incident, so much to me, he never could distinguish
among the many times he had "helped Olever and his
seminary girls out of scrapes," and he never spoke of
these adventures without that same laugh which I
noticed when Father Olever thanked him.

He had elected me as his wife some years before
this evening, and had not kept it secret; had been assured his choice was presumptuous, but came and took
possession of his prospective property with the air of
a man who understood his business. I next saw him
on horseback, and this man of giant strength in full
suit of black, riding a large spirited black horse, became my "black knight."

My sister hated him, and my mother doubted him,
or rather doubted the propriety of my receiving visits
from him. His family were the leading Methodists of
the township; his father had donated land and built a
meeting-house, which took his name, and his house

was the headquarters of traveling preachers. There
was a camp-meeting ground on the farm; his mother
"lived without sin," prayed aloud and shouted in
meeting, while the income and energy of the family
were expended in propagating a faith which we believed false. A marriage with him would be incon-
gruous and bring misery to both. These objections
he overruled, by saying he was not a member of any
church, would never interfere with my rights of conscience, would take or send me to my meeting when
possible, and expect me to go sometimes with him.
He proposed going up the Allegheny to establish
saw-mills, and if I would go into the woods with him,
there should be no trouble about religion. So there
seemed no valid objection, and two years after our introduction we were married, on the 18th of Novem-
ber, 1836.

Then all was changed. I offended him the day after by shedding tears when I left home to go for a visit
to his father's house, and his sister had told him that
I cried while dressing to be married. These offenses
he never forgave, and concluded that since I cared so
little for him, he would not leave his friends and go
up the Allegheny with me. His services were indispensable at home, since his brother Samuel had
gone into business for himself, and the next brother
William was not seventeen, and could not take charge
of the farm and mills. His mother was ready to take
me into the family,—although the house was not large
enough to accommodate us comfortably—the old shop
in the yard could be fitted up for a school-room. I
could teach and he could manage the estate.

In this change, he but followed that impulse which
led the men of England, centuries ago, to enact, that
" marriage annuls all previous contracts between the
parties," and which now leads men in all civilized
countries to preserve such statutes. It is an old adage,
"All is fair in love as in war," but I thought not of
general laws, and only felt a private grievance.

By a further change of plan, I was to get religion
and preach. Wesley made the great innovation of
calling women to the pulpit, and although it had afterwards been closed to them generally, there were still
women who did preach, while all were urged to take
part in public worship. My husband had been converted after our engagement and shortly before our
marriage, and was quite zealous. He thought me won-
derfully wise, and that I might bring souls to Christ
if I only would. I quoted Paul: "Let women keep silence in churches, and learn of their husbands at
home." He replied, "Wives, obey your husbands."
He laughed at the thought of my learning from him
and said: "What shall I teach you? Will you come
to the mill and let me show you how to put a log on
the carriage?"

It was a very earnest discussion, and the Bible was
on both sides; but I followed the lead of my church,
which taught me to be silent. He quoted his preachers,
who were in league with him, to get me to give myself to the Lord, help them save souls, by calling on
men everywhere to repent; but I was obstinate. I
would not get religion, would not preach, would not
live in the house with his mother, and stayed with my
own. His younger brothers came regularly to me for

lessons with my sister, and I added two idiotic children bound to his sister's husband, to whose darkened minds I found the key hidden from other teachers. His brothers I adopted from the first, in place of the one I had lost, and they repaid my love in kind; but books soon appeared as an entering wedge between their souls and religion, which formed the entire mental pabulum of the family.

I believe there was not at that time a member of the Pittsburg Conference who was a college graduate, few who had even a good, common school education, while two of those who preached in our meeting-house and were frequent guests in the family, were unable to read.

My husband's father was old and feeble, and had devised his property to his wife, to be divided at her death between her sons. My husband, as her agent, would come into possession of the whole, and they thought I might object to the "prophet's chamber;" but it required no worldly motive to stimulate these fiery zealots to save a sinner from the toils of Calvinism. It is probable many of them would have laid down his life for his religion, and when they got on the track of a sinner, they pursued him as eagerly as ever an English parson did a fox, but it was to save, not to kill. In these hot pursuits, they did not stand on ceremony, and in my case, found a subject that would not run. My kith and kin had died at the stake, bearing testimony against popery and prelacy; had fought on those fields where Scotchmen charged in solid columns, singing psalms; and though I was wax at all other points, I was granite on "The Solemn League

and Covenant." With the convictions of others I did
not interfere, but when attacked would "render a reason." My assailants denounced theological semina-
ries as " preacher-factories "—informed me that "neither Dr. Black nor any of his congregation ever had
religion," and that only by getting it could any one be
saved. My husband became proud of my defense,
and the boys grew disrespectful to their religious
guides. Their mother became anxious about their
souls, so the efforts for my conversion were redoubled.

From the first the preachers disapproved of my being permitted to go to my meeting, and especially to
my husband accompanying me. He refused to go, on
the ground that he had not been invited to commune,
and as I sank in the deep waters of affliction, I did so
need the pulpit teachings of my old pastor, which
seemed to lift me and set my feet upon a rock. One
day I walked the seven miles and back, when the
family carriage went to take two preachers to an appointment; three horses stood in the old stone barn,
and my husband at home with his mother. This gave
great offense as the advertisement of a grievance, and
was never repeated.

During all my childhood and youth, I had been
spoiled by much love, if love can spoil. I was non-
resistant by nature, and on principle, believed in the
power of good. Forbearance, generosity, helpful service, would, should, must, win my new friends to love
me.

Getting me into the house with my mother-in-law,
was so important a part of the plan of salvation, that

to effect it, I was left without support or compensation for my services as teacher, tailor, dress-maker, for my husband's family. He visited me once or twice a week, and ignored my mother's presence, while she felt that in this, as in any church-joining conflict, only God could help me, and stood aloof.

To me the sun was darkened, and the moon refused her light. I knew "that jealous God" who claimed the supreme love of his creatures, was scourging me for making an idol and bowing down before it—for loving my husband. I knew it was all just and clung to the Almighty arm, with the old cry, "Though he slay me, yet will I trust in him." To my husband I clung with like tenacity, and could not admit that my suffering was through any fault of his.

The summer after my marriage, mother went for a long visit to Butler, and left us in possession of her house. My husband bought a village property, including a wagon-maker's shop, employed a workman and sent him to board with me. He also made some additions to a dwelling on it, that we might go there to live, and the workmen boarded with me, while my mother-in-law furnished provisions and came or sent a daughter to see that I did not waste them. Her reproofs were in the form of suggestions, and she sought to please me by saying she had " allowed James " to get certain things for me; but he did not visit me any oftener than when mother was at home, and when she returned in the autumn, the potatoes were frozen in the ground, the apples on the trees, and the cow stood starving at the stable door.

Then I learned that I had been expected to secure

the fall crops on mother's lot, and this was not unreasonable, for I had married a Pennsylvania farmer, and their wives and sisters and daughters did such work often, while the "men folks" pitched horseshoes to work off their surplus vitality. Lack of strength was no reason why a woman should fail in her duty, for when one fell at her post, there was always another to take her place.

Up to this time mother had left me to settle my troubles, but now, she told me I must turn and demand justice; that generosity was more than thrown away; that I never could live with my husband and bear his neglect and unkindness and that of his family. I must leave him, defend myself, or die. That I should have been expected to gather apples and dig potatoes, filled her with indignation. She advised me to stay with her and refuse to see him, but I shuddered to think it had come to this in one short year, and felt that all would yet be well. So I went to live in the house he provided for me, his mother furnished my supplies, and he came once a week to see me.

Here let me say, that in my twenty years of married life, my conflicts were all spiritual; that there never was a time when my husband's strong right arm would not be tempered to infantile gentleness to tend me in illness, or when he hesitated to throw himself between me and danger. Over streams and other places impassible to me, he carried me, but could not understand how so frail a thing could be so obstinate.

CHAPTER VIII.

FITTING MYSELF INTO MY SPHERE.—AGE, 22, 23.

DURING all my girlhood I saw no pictures, no art
gallery, no studio, but had learned to feel great contempt for my own efforts at picture-making. A
traveling artist stopped in Wilkinsburg and painted
some portraits; we visited his studio, and a new world
opened to me. Up to that time portrait painting had
seemed as inaccessible as the moon—a sublimity I no
more thought of reaching than a star; but when I saw
a portrait on the easel, a palette of paints and some
brushes, I was at home in a new world, at the head of
a long vista of faces which I must paint; but the new
aspiration was another secret to keep.

Bard, the wagon-maker, made me a stretcher, and
with a yard of unbleached muslin, some tacks and
white lead, I made a canvas. In the shop were white
lead, lampblack, king's yellow and red lead, with oil
and turpentine. I watched Bard mix paints, and concluded I wanted brown. Years before, I heard of
brown umber, so I got umber and some brushes and
begun my husband's portrait. I hid it when he was
there or I heard any one coming, and once blistered it
badly trying to dry it before the fire, so that it was a
very rough work; but it was a portrait, a daub, a like-
ness, and the hand was his hand and no other. The
figure was correct, and the position in the chair, and,
from the moment I began it, I felt I had found my
vocation.

What did I care for preachers and theological arguments? What matter who sent me my bread, or
whether I had any? What matter for anything, so
long as I had a canvas and some paints, with that long
perspective of faces and figures crowding up and begging to be painted. The face of every one I knew
was there, with every line and varying expression, and
in each I seemed to read the inner life in the outer
form. Oh, how they plead with me! What graceful
lines and gorgeous colors floated around me! I forgot God, and did not know it; forgot philosophy, and
did not care to remember it; but alas! I forgot to get
Bard's dinner, and, although I forgot to be hungry, I
had no reason to suppose he did. He would willing-
ly have gone hungry, rather than give any one trouble;
but I had neglected a duty. Not only once did I do
this, but again and again, the fire went out or the
bread ran over in the pans, while I painted and
dreamed.

My conscience began to trouble me. Housekeeping
was "woman's sphere," although I had never then
heard the words, for no woman had gotten out of it,
to be hounded back; but I knew my place, and scorned
to leave it. I tried to think I could paint without neglect of duty. It did not occur to me that painting
was a duty for a married woman! Had the passion
seized me before marriage, no other love could have
come between me and art; but I felt that it was too
late, as my life was already devoted to another object
—housekeeping.

It was a hard struggle. I tried to compromise, but
experience soon deprived me of that hope, for to paint

was to be oblivious of all other things.   In my doubt, I met one of those newspaper paragraphs with which men are wont to pelt women into subjection: "A man does not marry an artist, but a housekeeper." This fitted my case, and my doom was sealed.

I put away my brushes; resolutely crucified my divine gift, and while it hung writhing on the cross, spent my best years and powers cooking cabbage. "A servant of servants shall she be," must have been spoken of women, not negroes.

Friends have tried to comfort me by the assurance that my life-work has been better done by the pen, than it could have been with the pencil, but this cannot be.   I have never cared for literary fame; have avoided, rather than sought it; have enjoyed the abuse of the press more than its praise; have held my pen with a feeling of contempt for its feebleness, and never could be so occupied with it as to forget a domestic duty, while I have never visited a picture gallery, but I have bowed in deep repentance for the betrayal of a trust.

Where are the pictures I should have given to the world?   Where my record of the wrongs and outrages of my age; of the sorrows and joys; the trials and triumphs, that should have been written amid autumn and sunset glories in the eloquent faces and speaking forms which have everywhere presented themselves, begging to be interpreted?   Why have I never put on canvas one pair of those pleading eyes, in which are garnered the woes of centuries?

Is that Christianity which has so long said to one-half of the race, "Thou shalt not use any gift of the

4

Creator, if it be not approved by thy brother; and unto man, not God, thou shalt ever turn and ask, ' What wilt thou have me to do ?' "

It was not only my art-love which must be sacrificed to my duty as a wife, but my literary tastes must go with it. "The husband is the head of the wife." To be head, he must be superior. An uncultivated husband could not be the superior of a cultivated wife. I knew from the first that his education had been limited, but thought the defect would be easily remedied as he had good abilities, but I discovered he had no love for books. His spiritual guides derided human learning and depended on inspiration. My knowledge stood in the way of my salvation, and I must be that odious thing—a superior wife—or stop my progress, for to be and appear were the same thing. I must be the mate of the man I had chosen; and if he would not come to my level, I must go to his. So I gave up study, and for years did not read one page in any book save the Bible. My religious convictions I could not change, but all other differences should disappear.

Mother moved to the city in the spring of 1838, and my health was rapidly failing. I had rebelled against my mother-in-law, returned her supplies, and refused to receive anything from her. This brought on a fearful crisis, in which my husband threatened suicide; but I was firm, and he concluded to rent the mills and take me away. This he did. His father lived but a few months, and died on the second anniversary of our marriage. He lies buried in the ground he donated as "God's acre," with only this inscription at his head: "John Swisshelm, aged 86." No sign that he was one of the world's heroes—yet, when our revolution broke out, his parents had but two children. The oldest enlisted and was killed, when John caught up his rifle, took his place, and kept it until the close of the war. He spent the winter in Valley Forge, and once, in the darkest time, discovered Washington on his knees in a lonely thicket, praying aloud for his country. This gave him hope, when hope was well-nigh dead, and he followed his commander across the Jerseys, one of the two thousand who wrote in blood, from their shoeless feet, their protest against British rule on the soil they thus consecrated to Freedom.

CHAPTER IX.

HABITATIONS OF HORRID CRUELTY.——AGE, 23, 24.

ON the 6th of June, 1838, the white frost lay on the west side of Pittsburg roofs as we steamed away from her wharf, bound for Louisville, where my husband proposed going into a business already established by his brother Samuel.

On the boat, all the way down the river, the general topic of conversation was the contrast between the desolate slave-cursed shores of Kentucky, and the smiling plenty of the opposite bank; but Louisville was largely settled by Northern people, and was to prove an oasis in the desert of slavery.

It lay at the head of the Falls of the Ohio, and the general government had lately expended large sums in building a canal around them. Henry Clay was in the zenith of his power, slavery held possession

of the national resources, Louisville might count on
favors, and she was to be Queen City of the West.
There was an aspiring little place which fancied
itself a rival, a little boat-landing, without natural advantages, called Cincinnati, where they killed hogs;
but it was quite absurd to think of her competing
with the great metropolis at the head of the canal.

I was quite surprised to find there were a good
many houses and folks in Cincinnati; but our boat
did not stop long, and we soon reached our Eldorado.
Before we effected a landing at the crowded wharf, I
fell to wondering if a Pittsburg drayman could take a
Louisville dray, its load, its three horses and ragged
driver, pile them on his dray, and with his one horse
take them to their destination—and I thought he
could.

Samuel met us, and as we went in a hack to the
boarding place he had engaged. I wondered what had
happened that so many men were off work in the
middle of the forenoon. Who or what could they
be, those fellows in shining black broadcloth, each
with a stove-pipe hat on the side of his head, his
thumbs in the armholes of a satin vest, displaying a
wonderful glimmer of gold chain and diamond stud,
balancing himself first on his heels and then on his
toes, as he rolled a cigar from one side of his mouth
to the other? How did they come to be standing
around on corners and doorsteps by the hundred, like
crows on a cornfield fence?

It was some time before I learned that this was the
advance guard of a great army of woman-whippers,
which stretched away back to the Atlantic, and around

the shores of the Gulf of Mexico, and that they were out on duty as a staring brigade, whose business it was to insult every woman who ventured on the street without a male protector, by a stare so lascivious as could not be imagined on American free soil. I learned that they all lived, in whole or in part, by the sale of their own children, and the labor of the mothers extorted by the lash. I came to know one hoary-haired veteran, whose entire support came from the natural increase and wages of nineteen women, one of whom, a girl of eighteen, lived with him in a fashionable boarding-house, waited on him at table, slept in his room, and of whose yearly wages one hundred and seventy-five dollars were credited on his board bill.

I learned that none of the shapely hands displayed on the black vests, had ever used other implement of toil than a pistol, bowie-knife or slave-whip; that any other tool would ruin the reputation of the owner of the taper digits; but they did not lose caste by horse-whipping the old mammys from whose bosoms they had drawn life in infancy.

Our boarding-house was on Walnut street, one block west of the theatre, and looked toward the river. On the opposite side of the street stood a two-story brick house, always closed except when a negress opened and dusted the rooms. I never saw sadness or sorrow until I saw that face; and it did not appear except about her work, or when she emerged from a side gate to call in two mulatto children, who sometimes came out on the pavement.

This house belonged to a Northern " mudsill," who

kept a grocery, and owned the woman, who was the
mother of five children, of whom he was the father.
The older two he had sold, one at a time, as they became saleable or got in his way. On the sale of the
first, the mother "took on so that he was obliged to
flog her almost to death before she gave up." But he
had made her understand that their children were to
be sold, at his convenience, and that he "would not
have more than three little niggers about the house at
one time."

After that first lesson she had been "reasonable."

Our hostess, a Kentucky lady, used to lament the
loss of two boys—"two of the beautifulest boys!"

They were the sons of her bachelor uncle, who had
had a passion for Liza, one of his father's slaves, a
tall, handsome quadroon, who rejected his suit and was
in love with Jo, a fellow slave. To punish both, the
young master had Jo tied up and lashed until he fainted, while Liza was held so that she must witness the
torture, until insensibility came to her relief. This
was done three times, when Jo was sold, and Liza herself bound to the whipping-post, and lashed until she
yielded, and became the mother of those two beautiful
boys.

"But," added her biographer, "she never smiled after Jo was sold, took consumption and died when her
youngest boy was two months old. They were the
beautifulest boys I ever laid eyes on, and uncle sot
great store by them. He could n't bear to have them
out of his sight, and always said he would give them
to me. He would have done it, I know, if he had
made a will; but he took sick sudden, raving crazy,

and never got his senses for one minute. It often took three men to hold him on the bed. He thought he saw Jo and Liza, and died cursing and raving."

She paused to wipe away a tear, and added: "The boys were sold down South. Maybe your way, up North, is best, after all. I never knew a cruel master die happy. They are sure to be killed, or die dreadful!"

She had an old, rheumatic cook, Martha, who seldom left her basement kitchen, except when she went to her Baptist meeting, but for hours and hours she crooned heart-breaking melodies of that hope within her, of a better and a happier world.

She had a severe attack of acute inflammation of the eyelids, which forcibly closed her eyes, and kept them closed; then she refused to work.

Her wages, one hundred and seventy-five dollars a year, were paid to her owner, a woman, and these went on; so her employer sent for her owner, and I, as an abolitionist, was summoned to the conference, that I might learn to pity the sorrows of mistresses, and understand the deceitfulness of slaves.

The injured owner sat in the shaded parlor, in a blue-black satin dress, that might almost have stood upright without assistance from the flesh or bones inside; with the dress was combined a mass of lace and jewelry that represented a large amount of money, and the mass as it sat there, and as I recall it, has made costly attire odious.

This bedizzoned martyr, this costumer's advertisement, sat and fanned as she recounted her grievances. Her entire allowance for personal expenses, was the wages of nine women, and her husband would not give her another dollar. They, knowing her necessities, were so ungrateful!—nobody could think how ungrateful; but in all her sorrows, Martha was her crowning grief. She had had two husbands, and had behaved so badly when the first was sold. Then, every time one of her thirteen children were disposed of, she "did take on so;" nobody could imagine "how she took on!"

Once, the gentle mistress had been compelled to send her to the workhouse and have her whipped by the constable; and that cost fifty cents; but really, this martyr and her husband had grown weary of flogging Martha. One hated so to send a servant to the public whipping-post; it looked like cruelty—did cruelty lacerate the feelings of refined people, and it was so ungrateful in Martha, and all the rest of them, to torture this fine lady in this rough way.

As to Martha's ingratitude, there could be no doubt; for, to this, our hostess testified, and called me to witness, that she had sent her a cup of tea every day since she had complained of being sick; yes, "a cup of tea with sugar in it," and yet the old wretch had not gone to work.

When they had finished the recital of their grievances they came down to business. The owner would remit two week's wages; after that it was the business of the employer to pay them, and see that they were earned. If it were necessary now to send Martha to the whipping-post, the lady in satin would pay the fifty cents; but for any future flogging, the lady in lawn must be responsible to the City of Louisville.

We adjourned to the kitchen where old Martha

stood before her judge, clutching the table with her
hard hands, trembling in every limb, her eyelids
swollen out like puff-balls, and offensive from neglect,
her white curls making a border to her red turban, receiving her sentence without a word. As a sheep before her shearers she was dumb, opening not her
mouth. Those wrinkled, old lips, from which I had
heard few sounds, save those of prayer and praise, were
closed by a cruelty perfectly incomprehensible in its
unconscious debasement. Our hostess was a leading
member of the Fourth St. M. E. Church, the other
feminine fiend a Presbyterian.

I promised the Lord then and there, that for life, it
should be my work to bring "deliverance to the cap-
tive, and the opening of the prison to them that are
bound," but all I could do for Martha, was to give her
such medical treatment as would restore her sight and
save her from the whipping-post, and this I did.

While I lived on that dark and bloody ground, a
man was beaten to death in an open shed, on the corner of two public streets, where the sound of the
blows, the curses of his two tormentors, and his shrieks
and unavailing prayers for mercy were continued a
whole forenoon, and sent the complaining air shud-
dering to the ears of thousands, not one of whom
offered any help.

A brown-haired girl, Maria, the educated, refined
daughter of a Kentucky farmer, was lashed by her
brutal purchaser, once, and again and again for chastity, where hundreds who heard the blows and shrieks
knew the cause. From that house she was taken to
the work-house and scourged by the public execu-

tioner, backed by the whole force of the United States
government. Oh! God! Can this nation ever, ever
be forgiven for the blood of her innocent children?

Passing a crowded church on a Sabbath afternoon,
I stepped in, when the preacher was descanting on
the power of religion, and, in illustration, he told of
two wicked young men in that state, who were drinking and gambling on Sunday morning, when one said :

"I can lick the religion out of any nigger."

The other would bet one hundred dollars that he had
a nigger out of whom the religion could not be licked.
The bet was taken and they adjourned to a yard.
This unique nigger was summoned, and proved to be
a poor old man. His master informed him he had a
bet on him, and the other party commanded him to
"curse Jesus?" on pain of being flogged until he did.
The old saint dropped on his knees before his master,
and plead for mercy, saying:

"Massa! Massa! I cannot curse Jesus! Jesus
die for me! He die for you, Massa. I no curse him;
I no curse Jesus!"

The master began to repent. In babyhood he had
ridden on those old bowed shoulders, then stalwart and
firm, and he proposed to draw the bet, but the other
wanted sport and would win the money. Oh! the
horrible details that that preacher gave of that day's
sport, of the lashings, and faintings, and revivals, with
washes of strong brine, the prayers for mercy, and the
recurring moan!

"I no curse Jesus, Massa! I no curse Jesus; Jesus
die for me, Massa; I die for Jesus?"

As the sun went down Jesus took him, and his merciful master had sold a worthless nigger for one hundred dollars. But, the only point which the preacher made, was that one in favor of religion. When it could so support a nigger, what might it not do for one of the superior race?

For months I saw every day a boy who could not have been more than ten years old, but who seemed to be eight, and who wore an iron collar with four projections, and a hoop or bail up over his head. This had been put on him for the crime of running away; and was kept on to prevent a repetition of that crime. The master, who thus secured his property, was an Elder in the Second Presbyterian church, and led the choir.

The principal Baptist preacher owned and hired out one hundred slaves; took them himself to the the public mart, and acted as auctioneer in disposing of their services. The time at which this was done, was in the Christmas holidays, or rather the last day of the year, when the slaves' annual week of respite ended.

A female member of the Fourth St. Methodist church was threatened with discipline, for nailing her cook to the fence by the ear with a ten-penny nail. The preacher in charge witnessed the punishment from a back window of his residence. Hundreds of others witnessed it, called by the shrieks of the victim; and his reverence protested, on the ground that such scenes were calculated to injure the church.

CHAPTER X.

KENTUCKY CONTEMPT FOR LABOR.——AGE, 23, 24.

To A white woman in Louisville, work was a dire disgrace, and one Sabbath four of us sat suffering from thirst, with the pump across the street, when I learned that for me to go for a pitcher of water, would be so great a disgrace to the house as to demand my instant expulsion.

I grew tired doing nothing. My husband's business did not prosper, and I went to a dressmaker and asked for work. She was a New England woman, and after some shrewd questions, exclaimed:

"My dear child, go home to your mother! What does your husband mean? Does he not know you would be insulted at every step if you work for a living? Go home—go home to your mother!"

I was homesick, and the kindness of the voice and eyes made me cry. I told her I could not leave my husband.

"Then let him support you, or send you home until he can! I have seen too many like you go to destruction here. Go home."

I said that I could never go to destruction, but she interrupted me:

"You know nothing about it. You are a mere baby. They all thought as you do. Go home to your mother!"

"But I never can go to destruction! No evil can befall me, for He that keepeth Israel slumbers not nor sleeps."

She concluded to give me work, but said:

"I will send it by a servant. Don't you come here."

I never thrust my anti-slavery opinions on any one, but every Southerner inquired concerning them, and I gave true answers. There were many boarders in the house, and one evening when there were eighteen men in the parlor, these questions brought on a warm discussion, when one said :

"You had better take care how you talk, or we will give you a coat of tar and feathers."

I agreed to accept such gratuitous suit, and a Mississippi planter, who seemed to realize the situation, said gently :

"Indeed, madam, it is not safe for you to talk as you do."

When reminded of constitutional guarantees for freedom of speech, and his enjoyment of it in my native State, he replied :

"There is no danger in Pennsylvania from freedom of speech, but if people were allowed to talk as you do here, it would overthrow our institutions."

There were mobs in the air. The mayor closed a Sunday-school, on the ground that in it slaves were taught to read. The teacher, a New England woman, denied the charge, and claimed that only free children had been taught, while slaves were orally instructed to obey their masters, as good Presbyterians, who hoped to escape the worm that never dies. Her defense failed, but seemed to establish the right of free colored people to a knowledge of the alphabet, but there was no school for them, and I thought to establish one.

Jerry Wade, the Gault House barber, was a mulatto, who had bought himself and family, and acquired considerable real estate. In the back of one of his houses, lived his son with a wife and little daughter. We rented the front, and mother sent me furniture. This was highly genteel, for it gave us the appearance of owning slaves, and Olivia, young Wade's wife, represented herself as my slave, to bring her and her child security. As a free negro, she labored under many disadvantages, so begged me to claim her.

In this house I started my school, and there were no lack of pupils whose parents were able and willing to pay for their tuition, but ruffians stood before the house and hooted at the "nigger school." Threatening letters were sent me, and Wade was notified that his house would be burned or sacked, if he permitted its use for such purpose. In one day my pupils were all withdrawn.

After this, I began to make corsets. It was a joy to fit the superb forms of Kentucky women, and my art-love found employment in it, but my husband did not succeed, and went down the river.

A man came to see if I could give work to his half-sister, for whose support he could not fully provide. She was a Fitzhugh,—a first Virginia family. Her father had died, leaving a bankrupt estate. She had learned dressmaking, and had come with him to Louisville to find work, but she was young and beautiful, and he dare not put her into a shop, but thought I might protect her, so she came to live with me.

One evening an old and wealthy citizen called about work I was doing for his wife, became interested in me, as a stranger who had seen little of Louisville, and tendered the use of his theatre-box and carriage to the young lady and myself. I declined, with thanks. When he had taken leave, Miss Fitzhugh sprang to her feet, and with burning cheeks and flashing eyes, demanded to know if I knew that that man had insulted us both. I did not know, but she did, and would tell Edward, who should cowhide him publicly. I told her that if Edward attempted that, he would probably lose his life, and we would certainly be dragged into a police court. Even if we had been insulted, it only proved that the old man thought we were like himself —that we were told in the Psalms that wicked men thought God was like themselves, and did approve their sin, and he did not have them cowhided. After a moment's reflection she sat down, exclaiming:

"Well, you are the strangest woman I ever did see!"

We never again saw the man, and I hope the incident helped the honest Edward in his loving task of protecting the fiery Fitzhugh.

My husband's trip down the river was a failure, and he went back home. Remembering he had heard me say I could do so much better at corset-making if I could buy goods at wholesale, he sold his Wilkinsburg property and turned the proceeds into dry goods. To me this seemed very unwise, but I tried to make the best of it, and we took a business house on Fourth street. I cut and fitted dresses, and with a tape-line could take a measure from which I could make a perfect fit without trying on. I soon had more work than I could do, and took two new girls, but the goods were dead stock. My husband was out of employment, and tried to assist in my business. He was out most of the day, and in the evening wanted to retire early. I was busy all day, and could not go out alone after dark, so came to be a prisoner.

One warm evening I was walking back and forth in front of our house, though I knew it a great risk, when a man overtook me, cleared his throat as if to speak, and passed on to the lamp-post, which had made one limit of my walk. I did not shorten my path, and when I came up to the post he again cleared his throat as if to speak, and next time stepped out, lifted his hat, and remarked:

"A very pleasant evening, Miss."

I stopped, looked at him, and said:

"It is a very pleasant evening; had you not better walk on and enjoy it?"

He bowed low, and answered:

"I beg your pardon, madam. I was mistaken."

"Pardon for what, sir? It *is* a very pleasant evening; please to pass on."

He did, and I walked till I was tired, thinking of all the sacrifices I had made to be my husband's housekeeper and keep myself in woman's sphere, and here was the outcome! I was degrading him from his position of bread-winner. If it was my duty to keep his house, it must be his to find me a house to keep, and this life must end. I would go with him to the poorest cabin, but he must be the head of the matrimonial firm. He should not be my business assistant. I would not be captain with him for lieutenant. How to extricate myself I did not see, but extricated I would be.

We needed a servant. A Kentucky " gentleman," full six feet three, with broad shoulders and heavy black whiskers, came to say: " I have a woman I can let you have ! A good cook, good washah and ionah, fust rate housekeepah! I 'll let you have ah for two hundred dollahs a yeah; but I 'll tell you honest, you 'll have to hosswhipah youahself about twice a week, for that wife of youahs could nevah do anything with ah."

While he talked I looked. His suit was of the finest black broadcloth, satin vest, a pompous display of chain, seals, studs and rings, his beaver on the back of his head, his thumbs in the arms of his vest, and feet spread like the Colossus of Rhodes.

This new use for Pennsylvania muscle seemed to strike my husband as infinitely amusing, for he burst out laughing, and informed the " gentleman " that he did not follow the profession of whipping women, and must decline his offer. But I wanted to be back on free soil, out of an atmosphere which killed all manhood, and furnished women-whippers as a substitute for men.

CHAPTER XI.

REBELLION.—AGE, 24.

During the late spring and early summer, my letters from home spoke often of mother's failing health, and in July one came from her saying her disease had been pronounced cancer, and bidding me come to her. The same mail brought a letter from Dr. Joseph Gazzam, telling me she was certainly on her death-bed,

5

and adding: "Let nothing prevent your coming to your mother at once."

I was hurt by this call. Was I such a monster that this old family friend thought it necessary to urge me to go to my dying mother? Stunned and stupified with grief, I packed my trunk.

My husband came in at noon, and I handed him the letters. He read them and expressed surprise and sorrow, and I told him to hurry to the wharf and see when the first boat started. He thought I should not go until I heard again. It might not be so bad. Then, after reflecting, said, why go at all, if there was no hope? Of what use could I be? If there was hope, he would agree to my going, but as there was none, he must object. In fact, he did not see how I could think of leaving him with those goods on his hands. How could I be so ready to drop all and not think of the consequences, for what could he do with that stock of dry goods. My mother pretended to be a Christian, but would take me away from my duty. I, too, read the Bible, but paid little heed to its teachings. He brought that book and read all of Paul's directions to wives, but rested his case on Ephesians, v, 22: "Wives submit yourselves unto your own husbands as unto the Lord. For the husband is head of the wife even as Christ is head of the church; therefore, as the church is subject unto Christ, so let the wives be to their own husbands in everything."

While he continued his comments, I buried my head in pillows, saying, "Lord what wilt thou have me to do?"

Milton epitomized Paul when he made Eve say to

Adam, "Be God thy law, thou mine;" but was that the mind and will of God? Had he transferred his claim to the obedience of half the human family? Was every husband God to his wife? Would wives appear in the general judgment at all, or if they did, would they hand in a schedule of marital commands?

If the passage meant anything it meant this: One might as well try to be, and not to be, at the same time, as own allegiance to God and the same allegiance to man. I was either God's subject or I was not. If I was not, I owed him no obedience. Christ as head of the church was her absolute lawgiver, and thus saith the Lord, was all she dare demand. Was I to obey my husband in that way? If so, I had no business with the moral law or any other law, save his commands. Christian England had taken this view, and enacted that a wife should not be punished for any crime committed by command, or in presence of her husband, "because, being altogether subject to him, she had no will of her own;" but this position was soon abandoned, and this passage stamped as spurious. Every Christian church had so stamped it, for all encouraged wives to join their communion with or without the consent of their husbands. Thousands of female martyrs had sealed their testimony with their blood, opposing the authority of their husbands, and had been honored by the church. As for me, I must take that passage alone for my Bible, or expunge it.

Then and there I cast it from me forever, as being no part of divine law, and thus unconsciously took the first step in breaking through a faith in plenary inspiration.

I next turned to the book in general for guidance: "Wives, obey your husbands;" "Children obey your parents;" "Honor thy father and thy mother." What a labyrinth of irreconcilable contradictions! God, in nature, spoke with no uncertain sound, "Go home to your mother," and my choice was made while my husband talked.

I said that if he did not see about a boat I would. When he told me that he had a legal right to detain me, and would exercise it, I assured him the attempt would be as dangerous as useless, for I was going to Pittsburg.

He went out, promising to engage my passage, but staid so long that I went to the wharf, where respectable women were not seen alone, saw a boat with a flag out for Pittsburg, engaged a berth, and so left Louisville.

CHAPTER XII.

THE VALLEY OF THE SHADOW OF DEATH.—AGE, 24, 25.

MOTHER was suffering when I reached her, as I had not dreamed of. After a consultation, Drs. Gazzam and Fahnestock thought she could not live more than four weeks; but Spear said she might linger three months. This blanched the cheek of each one. Three months of such unremitting pain, steadily on the increase, was appalling; but mother faced the prospect without a murmur, willing to bear by God's grace what He should inflict, and to wait His good time for deliverance. I was filled with self-reproach, for I should have been with her months before.

In a few days my mother-in-law and one of her daughters came to see how long I proposed to stay, why I had left James with the goods, and when I would go and take charge of them. They had had a letter from him, and he was in great trouble. She was gentle and grave—inquired minutely about our nursing, but thought it expensive—dwelt at length on the folly of spending time and money in caring for the sick when recovery was impossible. Mother could not see them, and they were offended, for they proposed helping to take care of her, that I might return to my duty.

Some time after the visit of my mother-in-law, her son-in-law—who was a class-leader and a man of prominence in the community—came with solemn aspect, took my hand, sighed, and said:

"I heard you had left James with the goods." Here he sighed again, wagged his head, and added:

"But I could n't believe it!" and without another word turned and walked away.

They chose to regard mother's illness as a personal grievance. "The way of the transgressor is hard;" and she, having sinned against the saints, must bear her iniquity, and thus suffer the just reward of her deeds.

I had frequent letters from my husband, and he was waiting on the wharf, watching every boat for my appearance. I told him before leaving Louisville, that I never would return—never again would try to live in a slave State, and advised him to sell the goods at auction, and with the money start a sawmill up the Allegheny river, and I would go to him. This advice

he resented. At length he grew tired waiting, and
came for me. It is neither possible nor necessary here
to describe the trouble which ensued, but I would not
nor did not leave mother, and she at last remembered
the protection to which she was entitled by the city
government.

With all mother's courage, her moans were heart-
breaking. No opiate then known could bring one half-
hour of any sleep in which they ceased, and in her
waking hours the burden of her woe found vent in a
low refrain:

"My Father! is it not enough?"

Our principal care was to guard her from noise.
The click of a knife or spoon on a plate or cup in the
adjoining room, sent a thrill of pain to her nerve cen-
tres. Only two friends were gentle enough to aid
Elizabeth and me in nursing her, as she murmured,
constantly: "If my husband were only here!"

She could bear no voice in reading save Gabriel Adams' and my own. I read to her comforting passages
of Scripture, and said prayers which carried her soul
up to the throne, and fell back on mine in showers of
dust and ashes. A great black atheism had fallen on
me. There was no justice on earth, no mercy in
heaven.

Her house was in Pittsburg, on Sixth street, a little
cottage built for her father and mother when they
were alone. It stood back in a yard, and rough men
in passing stepped lightly—children went elsewhere
with their sports—friends tapped on the gate, and we
went out to answer inquiries and receive supplies—
prayers were offered for her in churches, societies and

families.   The house was a shrine consecrated by suffering and sorrow.

The third month passed, and still she lingered.   For seven weeks she took no nourishment but half a cup of milk, two parts water, per day.   Then her appetite returned and her agony increased, but still with no lament save: "My Father!   Is it not enough?"

In the sixth month, January 17th, 1840, relief came. As I knelt for her last words, she said: "Elizabeth?"

I replied, "She is here, dear mother, what of her?" Summoning strength she said:

"Let no one separate you!" then looked up and said, "It is enough," and breathed no more.

As her spirit rose, it broke the cloud, and the divine presence fell upon me.   The room, the world was full of peace.   She had been caught up out of the storm; and "he who endureth unto the end shall be saved."

By her request, I and a dear friend, Martha Campbell, prepared her body for burial, and we wrapped her in a linen winding-sheet, as the body of Christ was buried—no flowers, no decorations; only stern, solemn Death.

On the last day of father's life he had said to her, "Mary you are human, and must have faults, but whatever they are I never have seen them."

She had been his widow seventeen years, and by her desire we opened his grave and laid her body to mingle its dust with his, who had been her only love in the life that now is, and with whom she expected to spend an eternity.

CHAPTER XIII.

"LABOR—SERVICE OR ACT."—AGE, 25.

MOTHER'S will left everything to trustees, for the use
of Elizabeth and myself.   She had wished my husband
to join her in a suit for the recovery of father's city
property, and he refused, but signed a deed with me
conveying my interest to her.   This claim she also
willed to her trustees for my use.   He felt himself
wronged and became angry, but had one remedy.
Being the owner of my person and services, he had
a right to wages for the time spent in nursing mother,
and would file his claim against her executors.

I do not know why I should have been so utterly
overwhelmed by this proposal to execute a law passed
by Christian legislators for the government of Christian people—a law which had never been questioned
by any nation, or state, or church, and was in full
force all over the world.   Why should the discovery
of its existence curdle my blood, stop my heart-beats,
and send a rush of burning shame from forehead to
finger-tip?   Why should I have blushed that my husband was a law-abiding citizen of the freest country
in the world?   Why blame him for acting in harmony
with the canons of every Christian church—aye, of that
one of which I was a member, and proud of its history
as a bulwark of civil liberty?   Was it any fault of his
that "all that she (the wife) can acquire by her labor-
service or act during coverture, belongs to her husband?"   Certainly not.   Yet that law made me shrink
and think of mother's warning, given so long ago.

But marriage was a life-contract, and God required me to keep it to the end, and said, "When thou passeth through the fire I will be with thee, and the floods shall not overflow thee." I could not bear to have a bill sent to mother's executors for my wages, but I could compromise, and I did.

He returned to Louisville, sold the goods, went on a trading-boat, and joined Samuel in Little Rock. While he was there Samuel died—died a Presbyterian, and left this message for me:

"Tell sister Jane I will meet her in heaven."

This my husband transmitted to me, and was deeply grieved and much softened by his brother's death.

Rev. Isaiah Niblock, of Butler, Pa., a distant relative and very near friend, asked me to take charge of the Butler Seminary and become his guest. My salary would be twenty-five dollars a month, and this was munificent. Elizabeth went to Pittsburg to school, and I to Butler, where my success was complete and I very happy. Among my pupils were two daughters of my old patron, Judge Braden. One of these, little Nannie, was full of pleasant surprises, and "brought down the house" during examination, by reciting a country girl's account of her presentation at court, in which occurs this stanza:

> "And there the King and I were standing
>   Face and face together;
> I said, 'How is your Majesty?
>   It's mighty pleasant weather!'"

By Nannie's way of giving the lines, they were so fixed on my memory as to be often mingled with solemn reveries in after years.

Petitions were presented in the Pennsylvania Legislature for the abolition of capital punishment. Senator Sullivan, chairman of the committee to which
they were referred, wrote to Mr. Niblock for the scripture view. He was ill and requested me to answer,
which I did, and Mr. Sullivan drew liberally from my
arguments in his report against granting the petitions.
The report was attacked, and I defended it in several
letters published in a Butler paper—anonymously—
and this was my first appearance in print, except a
short letter published by George D. Prentiss, in the
Louisville *Journal*, of which I remember nothing,
save the strangeness of seeing my thoughts in print.

CHAPTER XIV.

SWISSVALE.——AGE, 26, 27.

IN April, 1842, my husband took possession of the
old home in the valley, and we went there to live.
There were large possibilities in the old house, and
we soon had a pleasant residence. I had the furniture mother left me, and a small income from her
estate. The farm I named "Swissvale," and such is
the name thereof. When the Pennsylvania railroad
was built it ran through it, but not in sight of the
house, and the station was called for the homestead.

In the summer of '42 I began to write stories and
rhymes, under the *nom de plume* of "Jennie Deans,"
for *The Dollar Newspaper* and *Neal's Saturday
Gazette*, both of Philadelphia. Reece C. Fleeson published an anti-slavery weekly in Pittsburg, *The Spirit*

of Liberty, and for this I wrote abolition articles and essays on woman's right to life, liberty, and the pursuit of happiness. My productions were praised, and my husband was provoked that I did not use my own name. If I were not ashamed of my articles, why not sign them? He had not given up the idea that I should preach. Indeed, he held me accountable for most of the evils in the world, on the ground that I could overthrow them if I would.

Elizabeth was married in June, and went to Ohio. In the autumn, my husband's mother and the boys came to live with us, to which I made no objection, for "honor thy father and mother" was spoken as much to him as to me. Maybe I had some spiritual pride in seeing that she turned from her converted daughters, who were wealthy and lived near, to make a home with unregenerate me. She liked my housekeeping, and " grandmother," as I always called her, with her white 'kerchiefs and caps, sitting by the fireplace plying her knitting-needles, became my special pride.

My husband had converted the Louisville goods into one panther, one deer, two bears, and a roll of " wildcat " money. It was not very good stock with which to begin life on a farm, but the monotony was relieved by a hooking, kicking cow, and a horse which broke wagons to splinters.

Tom, the panther, was domiciled in the corner made by the old stone chimney and the log wall of the house, close to the path which led to the garden. The bears were chained in the meadow behind the house and Billy, the deer, ranged at will. Tom and the bears ate pigs and poultry so fast that we gave up trying to raise any, while Billy's visits to the garden did not improve the vegetables. I tried to establish some control over Tom, as a substitute for the fear he felt for his master, who was not always within call, and who insisted that Tom could be tamed so as to serve the place of a watch-dog. Tom had been quite obedient for Tom, and my terror for him had abated.

I was interested in the heathen of India, and was president of a society which met in Pittsburg. Coming home from a meeting, I was thrown out of a buggy and so badly hurt that I was kept in bed six weeks. When I began to go out on crutches, I started to go to the garden, and forgot Tom until I heard him growl. He lay flat, with his nose on his paws, his tail on the ground straight as a ramrod, save a few inches at the tip, which wagged slowly, his eyes green and fiery, and I not three feet from his head, and just in reach, even if his chain held; but I had seen it break in one of those springs which he was now preparing to make. There was no help near! He would spring for my head and shoulders. If these were out of his way, he could not hold me by my dress which was a thin muslin wrapper. He was not likely to leap until something moved, and might lie there sometime. I had heard that a panther will not jump under the gaze of a human eye, so I looked steadily into his, while I talked to him.

"Tom! Tom! Down sir," and so tried to recall his knowledge of me.

Fortunately my feet were a little in advance of my crutches, and while I looked and talked, holding my body motionless, I was planting my crutches and throwing my weight on my well foot. I heard the girl coming out of the house and knew the time had come. With all my strength I swung myself back-ward as he made the leap. His hot breath rushed into my face, his fiery eyes glared close to mine, but his chain was too short. Then I knew I had no mis-sion for taming panthers. From the first I had feared that he would kill some child, and it was impossible to prevent them trooping to see him. After my own narrow escape I protested so strongly against keeping him, that my husband consented to sell him to a me-nagerie; but those which came were supplied with panthers, and, although he was a splendid specimen, full nine feet long, no sale was found for him.

That adventure supplied memory with a picture, which for long years breathed and never was absent. If it was not before me it was in some corner, and I knew Tom was crouched to spring on me; his fiery eyes glared, the tip of his tail wagged, and he was waiting, only waiting for me to move. Often when I woke at night, he was on my bed or in a corner of the room. He was hidden in fence corners and behind bushes on the road-side, and Mary's little lamb was never half so faithful as my phantom panther.

My husband could not understand the fear I felt, nor realize the danger of keeping him. He enjoyed his own mastery over him, and with a box on the side of the head he made Tom whine and crouch like a spaniel. I have often wondered that in all the accounts I have ever read of fights with wild animals, no one ever planted a good fist-blow under the ear of his four-legged antagonist, and so stretch it out stiff to await his leisure in disposing of it.

CHAPTER XV.

WILLOWS BY THE WATER-COURSES.—AGE, 27.

PENNSYLVANIA customs made it unmanly for a man or boy to aid any woman, even mother or wife, in any hard work with which farms abounded at that time. Dairy work, candle and sausage making were done by women, and any innovation was met with sneers. I stubbornly refused to yield altogether to a time-honored code, which required women to perform out-door drudgery, often while men sat in the house, and soon had the sympathy of our own boys; for it was often impossible to obtain any domestic help, though Pittsburg "charitable" people supported hundreds of women in idleness who might have had homes and wages in farm-houses.

Much of the natural beauty of Swissvale had been destroyed by pioneer improvements, which I sought in some degree to replace. I loved the woods, and with my little grubbing-hoe transplanted many wild and beautiful things. This my mother-in-law did not approve, as her love for the beautiful was satisfied by a flower border in the garden. One day she said:

"James, I would not have that willow in that corner. The roots will get into the race. It is the real basket willow, and if you cut it into stubs and stick them in the swamp, you can sell enough willow to buy all your baskets."

I replied:

"Grandmother, you forget that is my tree; I want it to drape that bare knoll. The roots will run below the bed of the race. The boys can get plenty of stubs at Flemming's."

She only replied by a "humph!" and next day I discovered my tree had been sawed into pieces and planted in the swamp. Words would not restore it, and I wasted none; but next morning rose early, and, hatchēt in hand, went to the parent tree, climbed on a fence and cut off a limb, which I dragged home, feeling glad that anything had brought me a walk on such a glorious morning. I planted the main stock in that corner, then put about a hundred twigs in the swamp for basket willow. In a few days my second tree disappeared, and I brought another, for a tree there was indispensable, and I hoped to make my husband see as I did, and thought I had won his consent to willows. So I went up and down the race and runs, putting in twigs, and thinking of the "willows by the watercourses," and Israel's lament:

> " By Babel's streams we sat and wept
> When Zion we thought on,
> In midst thereof we hanged our harps
> The willow trees upon."

I was banished from my Zion, never permitted to hear the teachings of my old pastor,'for which my soul panted as the thirsty hart for the water brooks, and in my Babylon I wanted willows. Some of my plantings were permitted to remain, and Swissvale is now noted for its magnificent willows; but that main tree was chopped up and burned. In its stead I planted a young chestnut, where it still stands, a thing of beauty and joy to the boys.

CHAPTER XVI.

THE WATERS GROW DEEP.—AGE, 29.

THE plans for my conversion seemed to be aided by our coming to the farm, as I fitted up the "prophet's chamber" to entertain my husband's friends in his house. There were two preachers in the circuit. The eldest, a plain, blunt man, began on his first visit to pelt me with problems about "man-made ministers" and Calvinism. I replied by citing the election of Abraham, Jacob, and the entire Jewish nation, and by quoting the 8th chapter of Romans, until he seemed to despair and came no more, for they could not accept my hospitality while I refused their religion. The other circuit rider was young, handsome and zealous, and was doing a great work in converting young girls. On his first visit I thought him rude. On his second, he inquired at table:

"Is this the place where they put onions into everything?"

I replied that we used none in tea or coffee. When I joined him and my husband in the parlor, he waived his hand around the room to point out its decorations and said:

"Brother James tells me that this is all your work. It is quite wonderful, and now, sister, what a pity it is that you will not turn your attention to religion. You seem to do everything so well."

He motioned as if to lay his hand on my shoulder. I drew back and said:

"Excuse me, sir, but I am not your sister; and as for your religion you remind me with it of Doctor Jaynes and his hair tonic."

"How so, sister?"

"Again pardon, but I am not your sister. Doctor Jaynes uses a large part of his column to persuade us that it is good to have good hair. No one disputes that, and he should prove that his tonic will bring good hair. So you talk of the importance of religion. No one disputes this, and it is your business to prove that the nostrum you peddle is religion. I say it is not. It is a system of will worship. Religion is obedience to God's law. You teach people that they can, and do, obey this law perfectly, while they do not know it. Your church has no bibles in her pews, few in her families, and these unread. Preachers and all, not one in twenty can repeat the ten commandments. You are blind leaders of the blind, and must all fall into the ditch, destroyed for lack of knowledge!"

That week he proposed to abandon the Swissvale meeting-house, and build one in Wilkinsburg, giving as a reason the impossibility of keeping up a congregation with me on the farm.

Next Conference sent Rev. Henderson as presiding elder, who brought in a new era. He slept in the "prophet's chamber," admired my pretty rooms, and said nothing about my getting religion. The circuit preacher was of the same mind, an earnest, modest, young man, wrestling with English grammar, who on his first visit sought my help about adverbs, while my mother-in-law looked on in evident displeasure.

6

To her this was the dawn of that new day, in which the Methodist church rivals all others in her institutions of learning. The good time of inspiration was slipping away. What wonder that she clutched it as Jacob did his angel? There in that house she had for long years been an oracle to inspired men, and now to see God's Spirit displaced by Kirkham's grammar was rank infidelity. The Wilkinsburg meeting-house was being built, and that one which had been to her all that the temple ever was to Solomon, would be left to the owls and bats—her Zion desolate. Those walls, made sacred by visions of glory and shouts of triumph, would crumble to ruin in the clinging silence. How could she but think that the influence was evil which could bring such result?

The new building was consecrated with much ceremony. The two Hendersons staid with us, and on Sabbath morning consulted me as to the best way of taking up subscriptions. Mother-in-law looked on till she could bear it no longer, and said:

"Brother Henderson, if you mean to be in time for love feast, you must not stay fooling there."

Both men sprang to their feet, hurried away and never returned.

General Conference at its session in Baltimore, in 1840, passed the "Black Gag" law, which forbade colored members of the church to give testimony in church-trials against white members, in any state where they were forbidden to testify in courts. Four members of the Pittsburg Conference voted for it, and when my husband returned from the dedication, I learned that three of them had figured prominently in the exercises, and he had refused to commune on account of their ministrations.

Everything went smoothly for ten days, when my husband came to our room, where I sat writing, threw himself on the bed and poured out such a torrent of accusations as I had not dreamed possible, and of which I refrain from giving any adequate description. I looked up and saw that he was livid with rage. His words appeared the ravings of a mad man, yet there was method in them, and no crime in the calendar with which they did not charge me. Butter money was not accounted for, pickles and preserves missing, things about the house were going to destruction, the country was full of falsehoods and I had told them all. It was all a blur of sound and fury, but in it stood out these words:

"You ruined Samuel, and now you are trying to ruin the boys and those two fool preachers. People know it, too, and I am ashamed to show my face for the talk."

When he seemed to have finished, I asked:

"How long since you learned my real character?"

This spurred him to new wrath, and he exclaimed:

"There now, that's the next of it. You will go and tell that I've abused you. It's not me. I never suspected your honesty, but my mother, yes, my poor old mother. I would not care, if you could only behave yourself before my mother!"

I sat leaning my elbows on my table with my head in my hands, and the words "ruined Samuel" became a refrain. I thought of the danger out of which I had plucked him while in Louisville, of the force

with which I had grappled him with hooks of steel,
as he hung on the outer edge of that precipice of dis-
sipation, while I clung to the Almighty Arm for help.
I thought of the tears and solemnity with which this
man had given to me the dying message of that rescued brother. Earth seemed to be passing away, and
to leave no standing room. I was teaching school in the
abandoned meeting-house. It was noon recess and I
must hurry or be late. I passed into the hall and out
of the house, with the thought "I cross his threshold
now for the last time;" but I must remain near and
finish my school, when I would be present to meet
those monstrous charges before the world. My reveries did not interfere with my school duties, and when
they were over I sat in the old meeting-house or
walked its one aisle, with the quiet dead lying all
around me, thinking of that good fight which I
should fight, ere I finished my course, and lay down
to rest as they did. But the sun went down, the long
twilight drew on the coming night, and I was home-
less. Where should I go?

I thought of the Burkhammers, whose little son
lay among the dead beside me. I had tended him in
his last illness and prepared his body for burial. They
were German tenants of Judge Wilkins, and to reach
their house I must pass through the dark valley over
which now lay a new pall. There were lights in the
house as I passed, and Tom rattled his chain and gave
forth one of those shrieks which pierced the air for a
mile. I was glad to know that he was not loose, and
that it was only my phantom which crouched in every
available place, ready to spring. The bears bellowed

a response to his shriek, but I did not hasten. The stream, so loud and angry on that night of my first entrance into this vale of tears, was now low, and sang a lullaby of angelic music as I crossed it on stepping stones. On the hillside it was almost as dark as that night when Father Olever stopped and felt for the bank with his whip.

The Burkhammers asked no questions, and I went to sleep without giving any account of my strange visit, but about midnight I awoke myself and the whole family by my sobs. They gathered around my bed, and I must tell. What I said I do not know, but the old man interrupted me with:

"Oh tamm Jim. You stay here mit us. My old woman und me, we has blenty. We dakes care of you. Nopody never said nodding bad about you. Everypody likes you, caus you is bleasant mit everypody."

As he talked he drew his sleeve across his eyes, while his wife and daughter comforted me. I would board there and finish my school, then go to Butler and take the seminary, or a place in the common school.

I saw no one as I passed my late home next morning. In school the first exercise was bible, reading verse about with the pupils. The xxv (25) chapter of Matthew came in order, and while reading its account of the final judgment, I saw as by a revelation why this trouble had been sent to me, and a great flood of light seemed thrown across my path before me.

Christ's little ones were sick and in prison, and I had not visited them! Old Martha, standing before her judges, rose up to upbraid me! I was to have followed the Lamb, and had been making butter to add to an estate larger now than the owner could use. No wonder she thought I stóle the money. I, who had failed to rebuke man-stealing, might steal anything. That meeting-house which I had been helping to build by entertaining its builders and aiding them about subscriptions, it and they were a part of a great man-thieving machine. I had been false to every principle of justice; had been decorating parlors when I should have been tearing down prisons! *I*, helping Black Gagites build a church!

> "When thou a thief didst see
> Thou join'st with him in sin.'"

Thinking, reaching out for the path to that bastile which I must attack, I went on with my school duties until my husband walked in and asked why I had not been at home. I was worn with intense strain, and at the word home, burst into a passion of tears. I told the pupils to take their books, and leave, there would be no more school, and I could hear them go around on tip-toe and whisper. Twice a pair of little arms were thrown around me, and the sound of the retreating footsteps died away when my husband laid his hand all trembling on my head. I threw it off and begged him to go away, his presence would kill me. He would not go, and I went out into the woods. He followed, and said he had never charged me with an evil thought, much less an action, was the most loving of husbands and the most injured in that I had thought he had found fault with me. He might have spoken a hasty word, but was it right to lay it up against him?

I still begged him to leave—that I should die if he did not. He went, and I crossed the fields to the house of Thomas Dickson, thinking that from it I could get to the city by the river road and fly any where.

Mrs. Dickson made me go to bed, as I was able to go no where else, and here my husband's brother-in-law found me. He had come as peace-maker, and could not think what it all meant; some angry words of James about his mother, who would now go back to live with him. The Dicksons joined him with entreaties. If my husband had injured me, he was very, very sorry, was quite overwhelmed with grief for the pain he had cost me. Then they brought down the lever of scripture and conscience: "If thy brother offend thee seventy times seven," and I yielded.

My husband came and I went home with him that evening, expecting that my mother-in-law was installed in her new home on the hill; but she met and kissed me at the door, and I did not care. Nothing could add to the shudder of going into the house, and she seemed so grieved and frightened that my heart was touched, and I was sorry for her that we had ever met.

CHAPTER XVII.

MY NAME APPEARS IN PRINT.—AGE, 29.

It was the third morning after my return, that my head would not leave the pillow. Dr. Carothers came and blistered me from head to feet, and for three weeks I saw no one but my attendants and my phantom

panther. He never left me. There was one corner of
the room in which he stayed most, and sometimes
there was not room for his tail to wag, and then he
moved forward where I could not see his head. This
troubled me, for then I could not hold him with my
eyes. At night they were two balls of green fire; but
they had always been, only when I was well I could
turn my head away, now I could not move it. I knew
most of the time it was a shadow from my brain, but
was glad to hear Tom's chain rattle and feel sure it
was not his very self.

They nursed me carefully, and I lay thinking of the
"little ones sick and in prison." Old Martha came
and plead with me. I saw Liza and Maria under the
lash for the crime of chastity, and myself the accom-
plice of their brutal masters. I pictured one of them
a member of the M. E. Church, appealing to that church
for redress and spurned under the "Black Gag," and
I? why I had been helping men who voted for it to
build a meeting-house! What was Peter's denial compared to mine?

The case arranged itself in my mind. I had writing materials brought, and there, with my head fast
on the pillow, I wrote a hexameter rhyme half a column long, arraigning by name those Black Gag preachers, painting the scene, and holding them responsible.
I signed my initials, and sent it to Mr. Fleeson, with
a note telling him to give my name if it was inquired
for.

Our "Spirit" did not come that week; but soon my
husband came to my room with a copy of "The Pittsburg Gazette," in which was an editorial and letter

full of pious horror and denunciation of that article, and giving my name as the author; so that we knew Mr. Fleeson had published the name in full. This was my first appearance in print over my own signature, and while I was shocked, my husband was delighted, even though he knew a libel suit was threatened. I soon went to Pittsburg, saw William Elder and John A. Wills, the only anti-slavery lawyers in the city. They said the article was actionable, for it had brought those men into contempt. Elder added: "They are badly hurt, or they would not cry out so loud."

Both tendered their gratuitous services for my defense. In a civil suit we could prove the truth of the charge, and they could get nothing, for my husband owned no property—everything belonged to his mother—and my trustees could not be held for my misdeeds. Their action would doubtless be criminal, and I would probably be imprisoned. I went home and wrote a reply to the *Gazette*, which it refused to publish, but it appeared in the *Spirit*. I reiterated, urged and intensified my charges against these false priests, until they were dumb about their injuries and libel suit, but of that original article I never could get a copy. Every one had been sold and resold, and read to rags, before I knew it was in print.

I continued to write for the "Spirit," but still there did not seem to be anything I could do for the slave. As soon as I was able to be about the house, I fell into my old round of drudgery, but with hope and pride shut out of it. Once my burden pressed so that I could not sleep, and rose at early dawn, and sat looking over the meadow, seeing nothing but a dense, white fog. I leaned back, closed my eyes and thought how like it was to my own life. When I looked again, oh, the vision of glory which met my sight!

The rising sun had sent, through an opening in the woods, a shaft of light, which centred on a hickory tree that stood alone in the meadow, and was then in the perfection of its golden autumn glory. It dripped with moisture, blazed and shimmered. The high lights were diamond tipped, and between them and the deepest shadow was every tint of orange and yellow, mingled and blended in those inimitable lines of natural foliage. Over it, through it, and around it, rolled the white fog, in great masses, caressing the earth and hanging from the zenith like the veil of the temple of the Most High. All around lay the dark woods, framing in the vision like serried ranks encompassing a throne, to which great clouds rolled, then lifted and scudded away, like couriers coming for orders and hastening to obey them.

John's New Jerusalem never was so grand! No square corners and forbidding walls. The gates were not made of several solid pearls, but of millions of pearletts, strung on threads of love, offering no barriers through which any soul might not pass. My Patmos had been visited and I could dwell in it, work and wait; but I would live in it, not lie in a tomb, and once more I took hold of life.

I organized a society at which we read, had refreshments and danced—yea, broke church rules and practiced promiscuous dancing minus promiscuous kissing. Of course this was wicked. I roamed the woods,

brought wild flowers and planted them, set out berry
bushes, and collected a large variety of roses and lilies.

CHAPTER XVIII.

MEXICAN WAR.—AGE, 30–32.

JAMES G. BIRNEY was the presidential candidate of
the "Liberty Party" in 1844, as he had been in '40.
During the campaign I wrote under my initials for
The Spirit of Liberty, and exposing the weak part
of an argument soon came to be my recognized forte.
For using my initials I had two reasons—my dislike
and dread of publicity and the fear of embarrassing the
Liberty Party with the sex question. Abolitionists
were men of sharp angles. Organizing them was like
binding crooked sticks in a bundle, and one of the
questions which divided them was the right of women
to take any prominent part in public affairs.

In that campaign, the great Whig argument against
the election of Polk was, that it would bring on a
war with Mexico for the extension of slavery, and
when the war came, Whigs and Liberty Party men
vied with each other in their cry of "Our Country,
right or wrong!" and rushed into the army over every
barrier set up by their late arguments. The nation
was seized by a military madness, and in the furore,
the cause of the slave went to the wall, and *The
Spirit of Liberty* was discontinued. Its predecessor,
The Christian Witness, had failed under the suc-
cessive management of William Burleigh, Dr. Elder,
and Rev. Edward Smith, three giants in those days,

and there seemed no hope that any anti-slavery paper could be supported in Pittsburg, while all anti-slavery matter was carefully excluded from both religious and secular press. It was a dark day for the slave, and it was difficult to see hope for a brighter. To me, it seemed that all was lost, unless some one were especially called to speak that truth, which alone could make the people free, but certainly I could not be the messenger.

For years there had run through my head the words, "Open thy mouth for the dumb, plead the cause of the poor and needy." The streams sang them, the winds shrieked them, and now a trumpet sounded them, but the words could not mean more than talking in private. I would not, could not, believe they meant more, for the Bible in which I read them bid me be silent. My husband wanted me to lecture as did Abby Kelley, but I thought this would surely be wrong. The church had silenced me so effectuately, that even now all my sense of the great need of words could not induce me to attempt it; but if I could "plead the cause" through the press, I must write. Even this was dreadful, as I must use my own name, for my articles would certainly be libelous. If I wrote at all, I must throw myself headlong into the great political maelstrom, and would of course be swallowed up like a fishing-boat in the great Norway horror which decorated our school geographies; for no woman had ever done such a thing, and I could never again hold up my head under the burden of shame and disgrace which would be heaped upon me. But what matter? I had no children to dishonor; all save one who had ever loved me were dead, and she no longer needed me, and if the Lord wanted some one to throw into that gulf, no one could be better spared than I.

The Pittsburg Commercial Journal was the leading Whig paper of western Pennsylvania, Robert M. Riddle, its editor and proprietor. His mother was a member of our church, and I thought somewhere in his veins must stir anti-slavery blood. So I wrote a letter to the *Journal*, which appeared with an editorial disclaimer, "but the fair writer should have a hearing." This letter was followed by another, and they continued to appear once or twice a week during several months.

I do not not remember whom I attacked first, but from first to last my articles were as direct and personal as Nathan's reproof to David. Of slavery in the abstract I knew nothing. There was no abstraction in tying Martha to a whipping-post and scourging her for mourning the loss of her children. The old Kentucky saint who bore the torture of lash and brine all that bright Sabbath day, rather than "curse Jesus," knew nothing of the abstraction of slavery, or the fine-spun theories of politeness which covered the most revolting crimes with pretty words. This great nation was engaged in the pusillanimous work of beating poor little Mexico—a giant whipping a cripple. Every man who went to the war, or induced others to go, I held as the principal in the whole list of crimes of which slavery was the synonym. Each one seemed to stand before me, his innermost soul laid bare, and his idiosyncrasy I was sure to strike with sarcasm, ridicule solemn denunciations, old truths from Bible and

history and the opinions of good men. I had a reckless abandon, for had I not thrown myself into the
breach to die there, and would I not sell my life at its
full value?

My style I caught from my crude, rural surroundings, and was familiar to the unlearned, and I was not
surprised to find the letters eagerly read. The *Journal*
announced them the day before publication, the news-
boys cried them, and papers called attention to them,
some by daring to indorse, but more by abusing Mr.
Riddle for publishing such unpatriotic and "incen-
diary rant." In quoting the strong points, a venal
press was constrained to "scatter the living coals of
truth." The name was held to be a *nom de plume*, for
in print it looked so unlike the common pronuncia-
tion of that of one of the oldest families in the county
that it was not recognized. Moreover, it mus t be a
disguise adopted by some man. Wiseacres said, one
of the county judges. No western Pennsylvania woman had ever broken out of woman's sphere. All lived
in the very centre of that sacred enclosure, making
fires by which husbands, brothers and sons sat reading
the news; each one knowing that she had a soul, because the preacher who made his bread and butter by
saving it had been careful to inform her of its existence as preliminary to her knowledge of the indispensable nature of his services.

But the men whom I ridiculed and attacked knew
the hand which held the mirror up to nature, and also
knew they had a legal remedy, and that to their fines
and imprisonment I was as indifferent as to their opinions. One of these, Hon. Gabriel Adams, had taken

me by the hand at father's funeral, led me to a stranger
and introduced me as:

"The child I told you of, but eight years old, her
father's nurse and comforter."

He had smoothed my hair and told me not to cry;
God would bless me for being a good child. He was
a member of the session when I joined church; his
voice in prayer had soothed mother's hard journey
through the dark valley; and now, as mayor of the
city, had ordered its illumination in honor of the battle of Buena Vista, and this, too, on Saturday evening, when the unholy glorification extended into the
Sabbath. Measured by the standards of his profession as an elder in the church, whose highest judica-
tory had pronounced slavery and Christianity incompatible; no one was more vulnerble than he, and of
none was I so unsparing, yet as I wrote, the letter was
blistered with tears; but his oft repeated comment
was:

"Jane is right," and he went out of his way to take
my hand and say, "You were right."

Samuel Black, a son of my pastor, dropped his place
as leader of the Pittsburg bar and rushed to the war.
My comments were thought severe, even for me, yet
the first intimation I had that I had not been cast
aside as a monster, came from his sister, who sent me
a message that her father, her husband and herself, approved my criticism. Samuel returned with a colonel's commission, and one day I was about to pass him
without recognition, where he stood on the pavement
talking to two other lawyers, when he stepped before
me and held out his hand. I drew back, and he said:

"Is it possible you will not take my hand?"

I looked at it, then into his manly, handsome face, and answered:

"There is blood on it; the blood of women and children slain at their own altars, on their own hearthstones, that you might spread the glorious American institution of woman-whipping and baby-stealing."

"Oh," he exclaimed, "This is too bad! I swear to you I never killed a woman or a child."

"Then you did not fight in Mexico, did not help to bombard Buena Vista."

His friends joined him, and insisted that I did the Colonel great wrong, when he looked squarely into my face and, holding out his hand, said:

"For sake of the old church, for sake of the old man, for sake of the old times, give me your hand."

I laid it in his, and hurried away, unable to speak, for he was the most eloquent man in Pennsylvania. He fell at last at the head of his regiment, while fighting in the battle of Fair Oaks, for that freedom he had betrayed in Mexico.

When Kossuth was on his starring tour in this country, he used to create wild enthusiasm by "Your own late glorious struggle with Mexico;" but when he reached that climax in his Pittsburg speech a dead silence fell upon the vast, cheering audience.

The social ostracism I had expected when I stepped into the political arena, proved to be Bunyan lions. Instead of shame there came such a crop of glory that I thought of pulling down my barns and building greater, that I might have where to store my new goods. Among the press notices copied by the *Journal* was this:

"The *Pittsburg Commercial Journal* has a new contributor who signs her name 'Jane G. Swisshelm,' dips her pen in liquid gold, and sands her paper with the down from butterflies' wings."

This troubled me, because it seemed as though I had been working for praise; still the pretty compliment gratified me.

CHAPTER XIX.

TRAINING SCHOOL.

Paul fought with beasts at Ephesus, as a part of his training for that "good fight" with principalities and powers and iniquity in high places, and I think that Tom and the bears helped to prepare me for a long conflict with the southern tiger. I had early come to think that Tom would kill some of the children who trooped to see him, and that I should be responsible as I alone saw the danger. This danger I sought to avert, but how to dispose of the beautiful creature I could not conjecture. There was usually a loaded gun in the house, but I was almost as much afraid of it as of Tom. All our neighbors were delighted with him and loath to have him killed. I had once tried to poison a cat but failed, and I would not torture Tom. I wanted Dr. Palmer to give me a dose for him, but he declined. I tried in vain to get some one to shoot him. Then I thought of striking the great beast on the head with a hatchet, while he had hold of some domestic animal. The plan seemed feasible, but I kept my own council and my hatchet, and practiced with it until I could

7

hit a mark, and thought I could bury the sharp blade in Tom's skull.

One day, all the men were in the meadow making hay, and I alone getting dinner. John McKelvey came with his great dog, Watch. He went up into the meadow, and Watch staid in the kitchen. I started to go to the garden for parsley, and found Tom crouched to spring on a cow. He made the leap, came short of the cow, which ran away bellowing with terror, and Tom had but touched the ground when Watch sprang upon him. It was a sight for an amphitheatre. The two great creatures rolled in a struggle, which I knew must be fatal to Watch, but thought he could engage Tom's attention until I got my hatchet. I ran back for it, took the dinner-horn and blew a blast that would bring one man, and I did not want a thousand. Then I ran back to the scene of conflict, horn in one hand, hatchet in the other, and lo! no conflict was there. No Tom! no dog! nothing but the torn and bloody ground. Horror of horrors, there was a broken chain! Tom loose! Tom free! Now some one would be murdered. I turned to look, and there on a log not a rod from me, he stood with head erect and tail drooping, his white throat, jaws and broken chain dripping with blood, and with my first thankfulness that he had not escaped, came admiration for the splendid sight: the bold, sweeping curves and graceful motion as he turned his head to listen. Then I learned panthers went by sound, not scent. I blew another blast on the horn and went toward him, for I must not lose sight of him. If he attacked me, could I defend myself with the hatchet? When they

found me I would be horrible to look upon, and it
would kill Elizabeth. Will my peas burn? The flies
will get into that pitcher of cream. If I am killed,
they will forget to put parsley in the soup. Tom
changed his weight from one fore-claw to the other,
and gnashed his teeth. "Here, the king and I are
standing face and face together; King Tom, how is
your majesty, it's mighty pleasant weather."

So ran my thoughts in the intense strain of that
waiting. It must be full ten minutes before Tom's
master could get to the house after that first blast, and
if he did not hear that, must be too late; but Tom kept
his place and my husband rushed by me, carrying the
pitchfork with which he had been at work, and I saw
no more until Tom was in his cage. Watch had
dragged himself to his master's feet to die, and I went
into the house and finished getting dinner, more than
ever afraid of Tom and more than ever at a loss to
know how to get rid of him. Yet he still lived and
rattled his chain by the garden path, but it was a year
before our next adventure.

One summer morning at sunrise I was shocked out
of sleep by shrieks and shouts and scurrying feet. I
sprang out of bed and rushed into the hall in time to
see Tom dash out of it into the dining-room, mother-
in-law and the girl disappearing up stairs and the two
hired men through the barn door. My husband soon
followed Tom, who had taken refuge under a large
heavy falling-leaf table, and seemed inclined to stay
there. This time his collar was broken and feeling
the advantage he paid no heed to the hand or voice of
his quandom master. He would not move, but

growled defiance, and the table protected him from a blow under the ear, so his late master became utterly nonplussed. If the cage were there, the great beast would probably go into it, but how get it there? The wealth of India would not have induced one of those men to come out of that barn, or one of those women to come down those stairs.

Something must be done, and I proposed to hold Tom while my husband brought the cage. He hesitated. I was not in good fighting trim, for my hair which was long and heavy had fallen loose, but preparation could avail nothing. The only hope lay in perfect coolness and a steady gaze. I knelt and took hold of Tom by the back of the neck, talked to him and thought that cage was long in coming. He shifted his weight and seemed about to get up. This meant escape, and I held him hard, commanding him to "lie down, sir." He blinked at me, seemed quite indifferent and alto_ gether comfortable. By and by, the man who had ceased to be master returned without the cage, utterly demoralized; and was here without a weapon, without a plan. I resigned my place and told him I would bring a rope. This I intended to do, and also my hatchet.

I had but gotten half way to the front door when there was a scuffle, the loud voice of my husband, shrieks up stairs, rattling of furniture and crashing of glass, and when I got back to the room I saw the tip of Tom's tail disappearing. He had gone through the window and taken the sash with him. He ran into his cage, and that was his last taste of liberty; but he lived a year after, chained in a corn crib. Every evening in the gloaming he would pace back and forth, raise his kingly head, utter his piercing shriek, then stop and hark for a response; walk again, shriek and listen, while the bears would bellow an answer.

The bears, too, were often exciting and interesting. Once I rescued a toddling child when running towards " big bear," and not more than two feet from where he stood waiting with hungry eyes. At another time, they both broke loose, on a bitter cold day when I was alone in the house. I defended myself with fire, meeting them at every door and window with a hickory brand. I wondered as they went round and round the house, if they would stop in the chimney corner, and make the acquaintance of Tom; but they took no notice of him, and after they had eaten several buckets of porridge, they concluded there was nothing in the house they wanted, so became good natured and went and climbed a tree.

Such schoolmasters must have imparted a flavor of savagery to my Mexican war letters, which attracted readers as Tom did visitors.

CHAPTER XX.

RIGHTS OF MARRIED WOMEN.

AFTER mother's death, I prosecuted to a successful issue a suit for the recovery of the house in which I was born. It stood on Water street, near Market, and our lawyer, Walter Lowrie, afterwards supreme judge, was to have given us possession of the property on the 1st of July, 1845, which would add eight hundred dollars a year to the income of my sister and myself. But on the 10th of April, the great fire swept away the building and left a lot bearing ground rent. Property rose and we had a good offer for the lease. Every one was willing to sell, but the purchasers concluded that both our husbands must sign the deed. To this no objection was made, and we met in William Shinn's office, when my husband refused to sign unless my share of the purchase money were paid to him.

Mother's will was sacred to me. The money he proposed to put in improvements on the Swissvale mills. These, in case of his death before his mother, would go to his brothers. I had not even a dower right in the estate, and already the proceeds of my labor and income from my separate estate were put upon it. I refused to give him the money, and on my way alone from the lawyer's office it occurred to me that all the advances made by humanity had been through the pressure of injustice, and that the screws had been turned on me that I might do something to right the great wrong which forbade a married woman to own property. So, instead of spending my strength quarreling with the hand, I would strike for the heart of that great tyranny.

I borrowed books from Judge Wilkins, took legal advice from Colonel Black, studied the laws under which I lived, and began a series of letters in the *Journal* on the subject of a married woman's right to hold property. I said nothing of my own affairs and confined myself to general principles, until a man in East Liberty furnished me an illustration, and with it I made the cheeks of men burn with anger and shame.

The case was that of a young German merchant who married the daughter of a wealthy farmer. Her father gave her a handsome outfit in clothes and furniture. She became ill soon after marriage, her sister took her place as house-keeper and nursed her till she died, after bequeathing the clothes and furniture to the sister; but the sorrowing husband held fast to the property and proposed to turn it into money. The father wanted it as souvenie of his lost child, and tried to purchase of him, but the husband raised the price until purchase was impossible, when he advertised the goods for sale at vendue. The father was an old citizen, highly respected, and so great contempt and indignation was felt, that at the vendue no one would bid against him, so the husband's father came forward and ran up the price of the articles. When her riding dress, hat and whip were held up, there was a general cry of shame. The incident came just in time for my purpose, so I turned every man's scorn against himself, said to them:

"Gentlemen, these are your laws! Your English ancestors made them! Your fathers brought them across the water and planted them here, where they flourish like a green bay tree. You robbed that wife of her right to devise her own property—that husband is simply your agent."

Lucretia Mott and Mary A. Grew, of Philadelphia, labored assiduously for the same object, and in the session of '47 and '48, the legislature of Pennsylvania secured to married women the right to hold property.

Soon after the passage of the bill, William A. Stokes said to me:

"We hold you responsible for that law, and I tell you now, you will live to rue the day when you opened such a Pandora's box in your native state, and cast such an apple of discord into every family in it."

His standing as a lawyer entitled his opinion to respect, and as he went on to explain the impossibility of reconciling that statute with the general tenor of law and precedent, I was gravely apprehensive. The public mind was not prepared for so great a change; there had been no general demand for it; lawyers did not know what to do with it, and judges shook their heads. Indeed, there was so much doubt and opposition that I feared a repeal, until some months after Col. Kane came to me and said:

"There is a young lawyer from Steubenville named Stanton who would like to be introduced to you."

I was in a gracious mood and consented to receive the young lawyer named Stanton. As he came into the room and advanced toward me, immediately I felt myself in the presence of a master mind, of a soul born to command. When introduced he gravely took my hand, and said:

"I called to congratulate you upon the passage of your bill. It is a change I have long desired to see."

We sat and talked on the subject some time, and my fears vanished into thin air. If this man had taken that law into favor it would surely stand, and as he predicted be "improved and enlarged." I have never been so forcibly impressed by any stranger. His compactness of body and soul, the clear outlines of face and figure, the terseness of his sentences, and firmness yet tenderness of his voice, were most striking; and as he passed down the long room after taking leave my thought was:

"Mr. Stanton you have started for some definite point in life, some high goal, and you will reach it."

This was prophetic, for he walked into the War Department of this nation at a time when it is probable no other man in it, could have done the work there which freedom demanded in her hour of peril, for this young man was none other than Edwin M. Stanton, the Ajax of the great Rebellion.

CHAPTER XXI.

THE PITTSBURG SATURDAY VISITER.

AFTER the war, abolitionists began to gather their scattered forces and wanted a Liberty Party organ. To meet this want, Charles P. Shiras started the *Albatross* in the fall of '47. He was the "Iron City Poet," author of "Dimes and Dollars" and "Owe no Man a Dollar." He was of an old and influential family, had considerable private fortune, was courted and flattered, but laid himself and gifts on the altar of Liberty. His paper was devoted to the cause of the slave and of the free laborer, and started with bright prospects. He and Mr. Fleeson urged me to become a regular contributor, but Mr. Riddle objected, and the *Journal* had five hundred readers for every one the *Albatross* could hope. In the one I reached the ninety and nine unconverted, while in the other I must talk principally to those who were rooted and grounded in the faith. So I continued my connec-

tion with the *Journal* until I met James McMasters,
a prominent abolitionist, who said sorrowfully: "Well,
the last number of the *Albatross* will be issued on
Thursday."

"Is it possible?"

"Possible and true! That is the end of its first
quarter, and Shiras gives it up. In fact we all do. No
use trying to support an abolition paper here."

While he spoke a thought struck me like a lightning
flash, and he had but finished speaking, when I replied:

"I have a great notion to start a paper myself."

He was surprised, but caught at the idea, and said:

"I wish you would. You can make it go if any-
body can, and we'll do all we can to help you."

I did not wait to reply, but hurried after my husband, who had passed on, soon overtook and told him
the fate of the *Albatross.* For this he was sorry,
for he always voted a straight abolition ticket. I repeated to him what I had said to Mr. McMasters,
when he said :

"Nonsense!" then reflected a little, and added,
"Well, I do not know after all but it would be a good
idea. Riddle makes lots of money out of your letters."

When we had talked about five minutes, he turned
to attend to business and I went to the *Journal* office.
found Mr. Riddle in his sanctum, and told him the
Albatross was dead; the Liberty Party without an
organ, and that I was going to start the *Pittsburg
Saturday Visiter;* the first copy must be issued Saturday week, so that abolitionists would not have time
to be discouraged, and that I wanted him to print my
paper.

He had pushed his chair back from his desk, and sat regarding me in utter amazement while I stated the case, then said:

" What do you mean? Are you insane? What does your husband say?"

I said my husband approved, the matter was all arranged, I would use my own estate, and if I lost it, it was nobody's affair.

He begged me to take time to think, to send my husband to him, to consult my friends. Told me my project was ruinous, that I would lose every dollar I put into it, and begged, entreated me to take time; but all to no purpose, when a bright idea came to him.

"You would have to furnish a desk for yourself, you see there is but one in this room, and there is no other place for you. You could not conduct a paper and stay at home, but must spend a good deal of time here!"

Then I suddenly saw the appalling prospect thus politely presented. I had never heard of any woman save Mary Kingston working in an office. Her father, a prominent lawyer, had employed her as his clerk, when his office was in their dwelling, and the situation was remarkable and very painful; and here was I, looking not more than twenty, proposing to come into the office of the handsome stranger who sat bending over his desk that he might not see me blush for the unwomanly intent.

Mr. Riddle was esteemed one of the most elegant and polished gentlemen in the city, with fine physique and fascinating manners. He was a man of the world, and his prominence had caused his name to become the target for many an evil report in the bitter personal conflicts of political life. I looked the facts squarely in the face and thought:

"I have been publicly asserting the right of woman to earn a living as book-keepers, clerks, sales-women, and now shall I shrink for fear of a danger any one must meet in doing as I advised? This is my Red Sea. It can be no more terrible than the one which confronted Israel. Duty lies on the other side, and I am going over! 'Speak unto the children of Israel that they go forward.' The crimson waves of scandal, the white foam of gossip, shall part before me and heap themselves up as walls on either hand."

So rapidly did this reflection pass through my mind, or so absorbed was I with it, that there had been no awkward pause when I replied:

"I will get a desk, shall be sorry to be in your way, but there is plenty of room and I can be quiet."

He seemed greatly relieved, and said cheerfully:

"Oh yes, there is plenty of room, I can have my desk moved forward and take down the shutters, when there will be plenty of light. Heretofore you have been Jove thundering from a cloud, but if you will come down to dwell with mortals we must make a place for you."

Taking down the shutters meant exposing the whole interior of the room to view, from a very public street; and after he had exhausted every plea for time to get ready, he engaged to have the first copy of the *Visiter* printed on the day I had set. He objected to my way of spelling the word, but finding I had Johnson for authority, would arrange the heading to suit.

I was in a state of exaltation all forenoon, and when I met my husband at dinner, the reaction had set in, and I proposed to countermand the order, when he said emphatically:

"You will do no such thing. The campaign is coming, you have said you will start a paper, and now if you do not, I will."

The coming advent was announced, but I had no arrangements for securing either advertisements or subscribers. Josiah King, now proprietor of the *Pittsburg Gazette* and James H. McClelland called at the *Journal* office and subscribed, and with these two supporters, the *Pittsburg Saturday Visiter*, entered life. The mechanical difficulty of getting out the first number proved to be so great that the forms were not on the press at 3 P. M. By five the streets were so blocked by a waiting crowd, that vehicles went around by other ways, and it was six o'clock, Jan. 20th, 1848, when the first copy was sold at the counter. I was in the editorial room all afternoon, correcting proof to the last moment, and when there was nothing more I could do, was detained by the crowd around the doors until it was after eleven.

Editors and reporters were gathered in the sanctum, and Mr. Riddle stood by his desk pointing out errors to some one who should have prevented them, when I had my wraps on ready to start. Mr. Fleeson, then a clerk on the *Journal*, stepped out, hat in hand, and bowing to the proprietor, said:

"Mr. Riddle, it is your privilege to see Mrs. Swiss_ helm to her lodgings, but as you seem to decline, I hope you will commission me."

Mr. Fleeson was a small man and Mr. Riddle had drawn himself to his full height and stood looking down at him, saying:

"I want it distinctly understood that Mrs. Swisshelm's relations in this office are purely those of business. If she requires anything of any man in it, she will command him and her orders shall be obeyed. She has not ordered my attendance, but has kept her servant here all the evening to see her to her friend's house, and this should be sufficient notice to any gentleman that she does not want him."

During the ten years we used the same editorial-room. Mr. Riddle was often absent on the days I must be there, and always secured plenty of light by setting away the shutters when I entered. He generally made it necessary for me to go to his house and settle accounts, and never found it convenient to offer his escort to any place unless accompanied by his wife.

The *Visiter* was three years old when he turned one day, examined me critically, and exclaimed:

"Why do you wear those hideous caps? You seem to have good hair. Mrs. Riddle says she knows you have, and she and some ladies were wondering only yesterday, why you do make yourself such a fright."

The offending cap was a net scarf tied under the chin, and I said, "You know I am subject to quinsy, and this cap protects my tonsils."

He turned away with a sigh, and did not suspect that my tonsils had no such protection outside the office, where I must meet a great many gentlemen and make it apparent that what I wanted of them was votes! votes!! Votes for the women sold on the auction block, scourged for chastity, robbed of their children, and that admiration was no part of my object.

Any attempt to aid business by any feminine attraction was to my mind revolting in the extreme, and certain to bring final defeat. In nothing has the church of Rome shown more wisdom than in the costume of her female missionaries. When a woman starts out in the world on a mission, secular or religious, she should leave her feminine charms at home. Had I made capital of my prettiness, I should have closed the doors of public employment to women for many a year, by the very means which now makes them weak, underpaid competitors in the great workshop of the world.

One day Mr. Riddle said:

"I wish you had been here yesterday. Robert Watson called. He wanted to congratulate us on the relations we have for so long maintained. We have never spoken of it, but you must have known the risk of coming here. He has seen it, says he has watched you closely, and you are an exception to all known law, or the harbinger of a new era in human progress."

Robert Watson was a retired lawyer of large wealth, who watched the world from his study, and philosophized about its doings; and when Mr. Riddle had given me this conclusion, the subject was never again referred to in our years of bargaining, buying and selling, paying and receipting.

CHAPTER XXII.

RECEPTION OF THE VISITER.

WHILE preparing matter for the first number of the *Visitor*, I had time to think that so far as any organization was concerned, I stood alone. I could not work with Garrison on the ground that the Constitution was pro-slavery, for I had abandoned that in 1832, when our church split on it and I went with the New School, who held that it was then anti-slavery. The Covenanters, before it was adopted, denounced it as a "Covenant with death and an agreement with hell." I had long ago become familiar with the arguments on that side, and I concluded they were fallacious, and could not go back to them even for a welcome into the abolition ranks.

The political action wing of the anti-slavery party had given formal notice that no woman need apply for a place among them. True, there was a large minority who dissented from this action, but there was division enough, without my furnishing a cause for contention. So I took pains to make it understood that I belonged to no party. I was fighting slavery on the frontier plan of Indian warfare, where every man is Captain-lieutenants, all the corporals and privates of his company. I was like the Israelites in the days when there was no king, and "every man did that which was right in his own eyes."

It seemed good unto me to support James G. Birney, for President, and to promulgate the principles of the platform on which he stood in the last election.

This I would do, and no man had the right or power to stop me. My paper was a six column weekly, with a small Roman letter head, my motto, "Speak unto the children of Israel that they go forward," the names of my candidates at the head of the editorial column and the platform inserted as standing matter.

It was quite an insignificant looking sheet, but no sooner did the American eagle catch sight of it, than he swooned and fell off his perch. Democratic roosters straightened out their necks and ran screaming with terror. Whig coons scampered up trees and barked furiously. The world was falling and every one had "heard it, saw it, and felt it."

It appeared that on some inauspicious morning each one of three-fourths of the secular editors from Maine to Georgia had gone to his office suspecting nothing, when from some corner of his exchange list there sprang upon him such a horror as he had little thought to see.

A woman had started a political paper! A woman! Could he believe his eyes? A woman! Instantly he sprang to his feet and clutched his pantaloons, shouted to the assistant editor, when he, too, read and grasped frantically at his cassimeres, called to the reporters and pressmen and typos and devils, who all rushed in, heard the news, seized their nether garments and joined the general chorus, "My breeches! oh, my breeches!" Here was a woman resolved to steal their pantaloons, their trousers, and when these were gone they might cry "Ye have taken away my gods, and what have I more?" The imminence of the peril called for prompt action, and with one accord they shouted, "On to the

8

breach, in defense of our breeches! Repel the invader or fill the trenches with our noble dead."

"That woman shall not have *my* pantaloons," cried the editor of the big city daily; "nor my pantaloons" said the editor of the dignified weekly; "nor my pantaloons," said he who issued manifestos but once a month; "nor mine," "nor mine," "nor mine," chimed in the small fry of the country towns.

Even the religious press could not get past the tailor shop, and "pantaloons" was the watchword all along the line. George D. Prentiss took up the cry, and gave the world a two-third column leader on it, stating explicitly, "She is a man all but the pantaloons." I wrote to him asking a copy of the article, but received no answer, when I replied in rhyme to suit his case:

> Perhaps you have been busy
> Horsewhipping Sal or Lizzie,
> Stealing some poor man's baby,
> Selling its mother, may-be.
> You say—and you are witty—
> That I—and, tis a pity—
> Of manhood lack but dress;
> But you lack manliness,
> A body clean and new,
> A soul within it, too.
> Nature must change her plan
> Ere you can be a man.

This turned the tide of battle. One editor said, "Brother George, beware of sister Jane." Another, "Prentiss has found his match." He made no reply, and it was not long until I thought the pantaloon argument was dropped forever.

There was, however, a bright side to the reception of

the *Visiter*. Horace Greeley gave it respectful recognition, so did N. P. Willis and Gen. Morris in the *Home Journal*. Henry Peterson's *Saturday Evening Post*, *Godey's Lady's Book*, Graham's and ' Sargent's magazines, and the anti-slavery papers, one and all, gave it pleasant greeting, while there were other editors who did not, in view of this innovation, forget that they were American gentlemen.

There were some saucy notices from "John Smith," editor of *The Great West*, a large literary sheet published in Cincinnati. After John and I had pelted each other with paragraphs, a private letter told me that she, who had then won a large reputation as John Smith, was Celia, who afterwards became my very dear friend until the end of her lovely life, and who died the widow of another dear friend, Wm. H. Burleigh.

In the second number of the *Visiter*, James H. McClelland, as secretary of the county convention, published its report and contributed an able article, thus recognizing it as the much needed county organ of the Liberty Party.

CHAPTER XXIII.

MY CROOKED TELESCOPE.

In the autumn of 1847, Dr. Robert Mitchell, of Indiana, Pa., was tried in Pittsburg, in the United States Court, before Judge Grier, for the crime of harboring fugitive slaves. In an old cabin ten miles from

Indiana, on one of the doctor's farms, some colored men had taken refuge and worked as harvest hands in the neighborhood. To it came the sheriff at midnight with a posse, and after as desperate a resistance as unarmed men could make, two were captured. On one of these was found a note:

"Kill a sheep and give Jerry the half.

"Rob't Mitchell."

The name of the man who had the note was Jerry. It was addressed to a farmer who kept sheep for the doctor, so it was conclusive evidence of the act charged, and the only defense possible was want of knowledge. There was no proof that Dr. Mitchell knew Jerry to be a slave, none, surely, that he knew him to be the property of plaintiff, who was bound to give notice of ownership before he could be entitled to damages from defendant.

This defense Judge Grier overruled, by deciding that no notice was required, the law presumed a guilty knowledge on the part of defendant.

Under this ruling Dr. Mitchell was fined $5,000, and the costs, which were $5,000 additional. His homestead and a magnificent tract of pine land lying on the northern slope of the Alleghenies, were sold by the sheriff of Indiana county to pay the penalty of this act of Christian charity; but the Dr. said earnestly, "I'll do it again, if they take every dollar I have."

This ruling was alarming, for under it, it was unsafe either to sell or give food or lodging to a stranger. The alarm was general, and even pro-slavery men regretted that this necessary act of justice should fall so heavily on so good and gentle a man. There was much unfavorable comment, but all in private, for the Pittsburg press quailed before Judge Grier, and libel laws were the weapon with which he most loved to defend the dignity of the bench. One editor he had kept in jail three months and ruined his business. Col. Hiram Kane was a brilliant writer, a poet and pungent paragraphist, and had at one time criticised some of Judge Grier's decisions, when by a libel suit the Judge had broken up his business and kept him in jail eighteen months. Public sentiment was on Kane's side, and he had an ovation on his release, when he became city editor of the *Journal*.

There was disappointment that I had not criticised Judge Grier's course in the first number of the *Visiter*, but this was part of my plan. In the second number I stated that there had been for a long time a great legal luminary visible in the Pennsylvania heavens, which had suddenly disappeared. I had been searching for him for several weeks with the best telescopes in the city, and had about given him up as a lost star, when I bethought me of Paddy, who had heated his gun-barrel and bent it around a tree so that he might be able to shoot around corners. Paddy's idea was so excellent that I had adopted it and made a crooked telescope, by which I had found that luminary almost sixty degrees below our moral horizon. From this I proceeded to the merits of the case.

Judge Grier and Dr. Mitchell were both elders in the Presbyterian church. The Judge administered to men the eucharist oath to follow Christ, then usurped the law-making power of the United States to punish them for obeying one of the plainest precepts of the Master.

The article seemed to throw him into a furious passion. He threatened to sue Mr. Riddle for having the *Visiter* printed and sold in his office, and, as for me, I was to suffer all the pains and penalties which law and public scorn could inflict. He demanded a satisfactory retraction and apology as the least atonement he could accept for the insult. These Mr. Riddle promised in my name, and I did not hesitate to make the promise good.

My next article was headed "An Apology," and in it I stated the circumstances which had called it out, and the pleasant prospect of my being sent to Mount Airy (our county jail) in case this, my apology, was not satisfactory. I should of course do my best to satisfy his honor, but in case of failure, should take comfort in the fact that the Mount would make a good observatory. From that height I should be able to use my telescope much better than in my present valley of humiliation. Indeed, the mere prospect had so improved my glass, that I had caught a new view of our sunken star, and to-day, this dispenser of justice, this gentleman with the high sense of honor, was a criminal under sentence of death by the divine law. " He who stealeth a man and selleth him, or if he be found in his hand, he shall surely be put to death."

Judge Grier had helped a gang of thieves to steal Jerry, whose ancestors had been stolen in Africa. The original thief sold all he could sell—the title of a thief—and as the stream cannot rise above the fountain, Jerry's master held the same title to him that any man would to Judge Grier's horse, provided he had stolen it. The purchaser of a stolen horse acquired no title in him, and the purchaser of a stolen man acquired no title in him. The man who helped another steal a horse, was a horse thief, and the man who helped another steal a man, was a man thief, condemned to death by divine law. Jerry, after having been once stolen, had recovered possession of himself, and his master and other thieves had re-stolen him! Judge Grier, with full knowledge of this fact, had prostituted law for the benefit of the thieves.

Nothing more was heard of a libel suit. Two years after, James McMasters was sued for harboring a fugitive; was to be tried before Grier, and spoke to his lawyer about summoning the editor of the *Visiter*. The attorney exclaimed :

"Oh bring her, by all means! No matter what she knows, or whether she knows anything; bring her into court, and I'll win the case for you. Grier is more afraid of her than of the devil."

The editor was summoned, gave testimony, and found Judge Grier a most courteous and considerate gentleman, with no signs of fear. The case hung on the question of notice. The Judge reversed his former decision, and those who were apt to feed beggars, breathed more freely.

A case was tried for the remanding of a slave, and lawyer Snowden appeared for the master. The *Visiter* sketched the lawyer as his client's dog, Towser; a dog of the blood-hound breed, with a brand new brass collar, running with his nose to the ground, while his owner clapped his hands and shouted: "Seek him, seek him Towser ! "

This caught the fancy of the street boys, who called

him, "Towser, where's your collar?" "Seek him, Towser." He was the last Pittsburg lawyer who took a case against a slave, and public sentiment had so advanced that there never afterwards was a fugitive taken out of the county.

CHAPTER XXIV.

MINT, CUMMIN AND ANNIS.

WHILE the bench and bar were thus demanding the attention of the *Visiter*, the pulpit was examining its morals with a microscope, and defending the sum of all villainies as a Bible institution. The American churches, with three exceptions, not only neglected "the weightier matters of the law, judgment and mercy," but were the main defense of the grossest injustice, the most revolting cruelty; and, to maintain an appearance of sanctity, were particularly devout and searching in the investigation of small sins.

A religious contemporary discovered that the *Visiter* did actually advertise "Jayne's Expectorant," and such an expectoration of pious reprehension as this did call forth! The *Visiter* denied that the advertisement was immoral, and carried the war into Africa—that old man-stealing Africa—and there took the ground that chattel slavery never did exist among the Jews; that what we now charge upon them as such was a system of bonded servitude; that the contract was originally between master and servant; the consideration of the labor paid to the servant; that in all cases of transfer, the master sold to another that portion of the time and labor of the ser-

vant, which were still due; that there was no hint of
any man selling a free man into slavery for the benefit of the seller; that the servants bought from "the
heathen around about," were bought from themselves,
or in part at least, for their benefit, to bring them under general law and into the church; that nothing like
American slavery was ever known in the days of Moses, or any other day than that of this great Republic,
since our slavery was "the vilest that ever saw the
sun," John Wesley being witness.

The *Visiter* cited the purchase by Joseph of the people of Egypt, and Leviticus xxv, xxxix: "If thy brother
be waxen poor and sell himself unto thee." The Bible
had not then been changed to suit the exigencies of
slavery. In later editions, "sell himself" is converted
into "be sold," but as the passage then stood it was a
sledge-hammer with which one might beat the whole
pro-slavery Bible argument into atoms, and while the
Visiter used it with all the force it could command, it
took the ground that if the Bible did sanction slavery,
the Bible must be wrong, since nothing could make
slavery right.

CHAPTER XXV.

FREE SOIL PARTY.

THE Free Soil or Barnburner party was organized
in '48, and nominated Martin Van Buren for President.
The *Visiter* dropped its Birney flag and raised the Van
Buren standard. In supporting him the editor of the
Visiter was charged with being false to the cause of

the slave, and of playing into the hands of the Whigs.
All the editor had ever said about that pro-slavery
ex-President was cast into its teeth by Democratic,
Liberty Party and Garrisonian papers, which, one and
all, held that Van Buren was a cunning old fox, as pro-
slavery as in those days when, as President of the U.
S. Senate, he gave his casting vote for the bill which
authorized every Southern post-master to open all the
mail which came to his office, search for and destroy
any matter that he might think dangerous to Southern
institutions. In his present hostility to slavery, he
was actuated by personal hatred of Louis Cass, the
Democratic candidate, and sought to draw off enough
Democratic votes to defeat him.

The object of the *Visiter* in supporting Van Buren was to smash one of the great pro-slavery parties of the nation, or gain an anti-slavery balance of
power to counteract the slavery vote for which both
contended. A few thousand reliable votes would compel one party to take anti-slavery ground. The Van
Buren movement was almost certain to defeat the Democrats, and force the Whigs to seek our alliance. True,
the Free Soil platform did not suit Liberty Party men,
who said it simply proposed to confine slavery to its
present limits, and not destroy it where it already ex-
isted.

To all of which, and much more, the little *Visiter*
replied, that with Van Buren's motives it had
nothing to do. His present attitude was one of hostility to the spread of slavery, and this being a long
step in advance of other parties, was a position desirable to gain and hold. To decline aiding those who

proposed to circumscribe slavery because they did not propose its destruction, was as if a soldier should refuse to storm an outpost on the ground that it was not the citadel.

Checking the advance of an enemy was one step toward driving him off the field, and a rusty cannon might be worth several bright-barreled muskets in holding him at bay. The Lord punished Israel by the hand of Jehu and Hazael, both wicked men. Slavery was bursting her bounds, coming over on us like the sea on Holland. One very dirty shovel might be worth a hundred silver teaspoons in keeping back the waters, and this Free Soil party could do more to check its advance than a hundred of the little Liberty Party with that pure patriot, Gerrit Smith, at its head. In doing right, take all the help you can get, even from Satan. Let him assist to carry your burden as long as he will travel your road, and only be careful not to turn off with him when he takes his own.

The *Visiter* had thousands of readers scattered over every State and Territory in the nation, in England and the Canadas. It was quoted more perhaps than any other paper in the country, and whether for blame or praise, its sentiments were circulated, and men of good judgment thought it made thousands of votes for the Free Soil party.

CHAPTER XXVI.

WHEN slavery thought to reap the fruits of the war into which she had plunged the nation with Mexico, lo! there was a lion in her path, and not a Bunyan lion either, for this kingly beast wore no collar, no chain held him. The roused North had laid her great labor paw on the California gold fields and stood showing her teeth while the serpent with raised crest was coiled to strike, and the world waited and wondered.

Henry Clay, the synonym for compromise, was still in the United States Senate, and, with his cat-like tread, stepped in between the belligerents with a cunning device—a device similar to that by which the boys disposed of the knife they found jointly—one was to own, the other to carry and use it. So by this plan the lion was to own California, and the snake was to occupy it as a hunting-ground; nay, not it alone, but every State and Territory in the Union must be given up to its slimy purposes. In other words, California was to be admitted as a free State, upon condition of the passage of the Fugitive Slave Bill, which authorized the slave-hunter to follow the fugitive into every home, every spot of this broad land; to tear him from any altar, and demand the services of every " good citizen " in his hellish work. Men by thousands, once counted friends of freedom, bowed abjectly to this infamous decision.

Daniel Webster, the leading Whig statesman, made

a set speech in favor of thus giving up the whole country to the dominion of the slave power. It was another great bid for the next presidential nomination, which must be controlled by the South. The danger was imminent, the crisis alarming, and the excitement very great. I longed to be in Washington, so I wrote to Horace Greeley, who answered that he would pay me five dollars a column for letters. It was said that this was the first time a woman had been engaged in that capacity.

I went to Washington in the early part of '50, going by canal to the western foot of the Alleghenies, and then by rail to the foot of the inclined plane, where our cars were wound up and let down by huge windlasses. I was in a whirl of wonder and excitement by this, my first acquaintance with the iron-horse, but had to stay all night in Baltimore because the daily train for Washington had left before ours came.

I had letters to the proprietor of the Irving House, where I took board. Had others to Col. Benton, Henry Clay, and other great men, but he who most interested me was Dr. Gamaliel Bailey, editor of the *National Era*. The great want of an anti-slavery paper at the capitol had been supplied by five-dollar subscriptions to a publication fund, and Dr. Bailey called from Cincinnati to take charge of it, and few men have kept a charge with more care and skill. He and the *Era* had just passed the ordeal of a frightful mob, in which he was conciliatory, unyielding and victorious; and he was just then gravely anxious about the great crisis, but most of all anxious that the *Era* should do yeoman service to the cause which had called it into life.

The *Era* had a large circulation, and high literary standing, but Dr. Bailey was troubled about the difficulty or impossibility of procuring anti-slavery tales. Mrs. Southworth was writing serials for it, and he had hoped that she, a Southern woman with Northern principles, could weave into her stories pictures of slavery which would call damaging attention to it, but in this she had failed.

Anti-slavery tales, anti-slavery tales, was what the good Doctor wanted. Temperance had its story writer in Arthur. If only abolition had a good writer of fiction, one who could interest and educate the young. He knew of but one pen able to write what he wanted, and alas, the finances of the *Era* could not command it. If only he could engage Mrs. Stowe. I had not heard of her, and he explained that she was a daughter of Lyman Beecher. I was surprised and exclaimed:

"A daughter of Lyman Beecher write abolition stories! Saul among the prophets!"

I reminded the Doctor that President Beecher and Prof. Stowe had broken up the theological department of Lane Seminary by suppressing the anti-slavery agitation raised by Theodore Weld, a Kentucky student, and threw their influence against disturbing the Congregational churches with the new fanaticism; that Edward Beecher invented the "organic sin," devil, behind which churches and individuals took refuge when called upon to "come up to the help of the Lord against the mighty." But Dr. Bailey said he knew them personally, and that despite their public record, they were at heart anti-slavery, and that prudence alone dictated their course. Mrs. Stowe was a graphic story-teller, had been in Kentucky, taken in the situation and could describe the peculiar institution as no one else could. If he could only enlist her, the whole family would most likely follow into the abolition ranks; but the bounty money, alas, where could he raise it?

Where there is the will there is a way, and it was but a few months after that conversation when Dr. Bailey forwarded one hundred dollars to Mrs. Stowe as a retaining fee for her services in the cause of the slave, and lo! the result, "Uncle Tom's Cabin." As it progressed he sent her another, and then another hundred dollars. Was ever money so well expended?

That grand old lion, Joshua R. Giddings, had also passed through the mob, and as I went with him to be presented to President Taylor, a woman in the crowd stepped back, drew away her skirts, and with a snarl exclaimed,

"A pair of abolitionists!"

The whole air of Freedom's capital thrilled and palpitated with hatred of her and her cause. On the question of the pending Fugitive Slave Bill, the feeling was intense and bitterly partisan, although not a party measure. Mr. Taylor, the Whig President, had pronounced the bill an insult to the North, and stated his determination to veto it. Fillmore, the Vice-President, was in favor of it. So, Freedom looked to a man owning three hundred slaves, while slavery relied on "a Northern man with Southern principles." President Taylor was hated by the South, was denounced as a traitor to his section, while Southern men and women fawned upon and flattered Fillmore. Webster, the great Whig statesman of the North, had bowed the knee to Baal, while Col. Benton, of Missouri, was on the side of Freedom.

The third, or anti-slavery party, represented by Chase and Hale in the Senate, was beginning to make itself felt, and must be crushed and stamped out at all hazards—the infant must be strangled in its cradle.

While abolition was scoffed at by hypocritical priests as opening a door to amalgamation, here, in the nation's capital, lived some of our most prominent statesmen in open concubinage with negresses, adding to their income by the sale of their own children, while one could neither go out nor stay in without meeting indisputable testimony of the truth of Thomas Jefferson's statement: "The best blood of Virginia runs in the veins of her slaves." But the case which interested me most was a family of eight mulattoes, bearing the image and superscription of the great New England statesman, who paid the rent and grocery bills of their mother as regularly as he did those of his wife.

Pigs were the scavengers, mud and garbage the rule, while men literally wallowed in the mire of licentiousness and strong drink. In Congress they sat and loafed with the soles of their boots turned up for the inspection of the ladies in the galleries. Their [language and gestures as they expectorated hither and thither were often as coarse as their positions, while they ranted about the "laws and Constitution," and cracked their slave-whips over the heads of the doughfaces sent from the Northern States.

Washington was a great slave mart, and her slave-

pen was one of the most infamous in the whole land.
One woman, who had escaped from it, was pursued in
her flight across the long bridge, and was gaining on
the four men who followed her, when they shouted to
some on the Virginia shore, who ran and intercepted her. Seeing her way blocked, and all hope of
escape gone, with one wild cry she clasped her hands
above her head, sprang into the Potomac, and was
swept into that land beyond the River Death, where
alone was hope for the American slave. Another woman with her two children was captured on the steps
of the capitol building, whither she had fled for protection, and this, too, while the stars and stripes floated over it.

One of President Tyler's daughters ran away with
the man she loved, in order that they might be married, but for this they must reach foreign soil. A
young lady of the White House could not marry the
man of her choice in the United States. The lovers
were captured, and she was brought to His Excellency,
her father, who sold her to a slave-trader. From that
Washington slave-pen she was taken to New Orleans
by a man who expected to get twenty-five hundred
dollars for her on account of her great beauty.

My letters to the New York *Tribune*, soon attracted
so much attention that is was unpleasant for me to
live in a hotel, and I became the guest of my friend
Mrs. Emma D. E. N. Southworth. It was pleasant to
look into her great, dreamy grey eyes, with their heavy
lashes, at the broad forehead and the clustering brown
curls, and have her sit and look into the fire and talk

9

as she wrote of the strange fancies which peopled her busy brain.

Among the legislative absurdities which early attracted my attention was that of bringing every claim against the government before Congress. If a man thought government owed him ten dollars, the only way was to have the bill pass both houses. In my *Tribune* letters, I ventilated that thoroughly, and suggested a court, in which Brother Jonathan could appear by attorney. Mr. Greeley seconded the suggestion warmly, and this, I think, was the origin of the Court of Claims.

There was yet one innovation I wanted to make, although my stay in Washington would necessarily be short. No woman had ever had a place in the Congressional reporter's gallery. This door I wanted to open to them, called on Vice-President Fillmore and asked him to assign me a seat in the Senate gallery. He was much surprised and tried to dissuade me. The place would be very unpleasant for a lady, would attract attention, I would not like it; but he gave me the seat. I occupied it one day, greatly to the surprise of the Senators, the reporters, and others on the floor and in the galleries; but felt that the novelty would soon wear off, and that women would work there and win bread without annoyance.

But the Senate had another sensation that day, for Foot, in a speech alluded to " the gentleman from Missouri." Benton sprang to his feet, and started toward him, but a dozen members rushed up to hold him, and he roared:

" Stand off, gentlemen! Unhand me! Let me reach the scoundrel!"

Every one stamped, and ran, and shouted "Order!" The speaker pounded with his mallet, and Foot ran down the aisle to the chair, drawing out a great horse-pistol and cocking it, cried:

"Let him come on, gentlemen! let him come on!" while he increased the distance between them as fast as time and space would permit. After the hubbub had subsided, Foot explained:

"Mr. Speaker, I saw the gentleman coming, and I advanced toward the chair."

I have never seen a well-whipped rooster run from his foe, without thinking of Foot's advance.

CHAPTER XXVII.

DANIEL WEBSTER.

DARKEST of the dark omens for the slave, in that dark day, was the defalcation of Daniel Webster. He whose eloquence had secured in name the great North-west to freedom, and who had so long been dreaded by the slave-power, had laid his crown in the dust; had counseled the people of the North to conquer their prejudices against catching slaves, and by his vote would open every sanctuary to the bloodhound. The prestige of his great name and the power of his great intellect were turned over to slavery, and the friends of freedom deplored and trembled for the result.

There was some general knowledge through the country of the immorality of Southern men in our national capital. Serious charges had been made by abolition-ists against Henry Clay, but Webster was supposed to be a moral as well as an intellectual giant. Brought

up in Puritan New England, he was accredited with
all the New England virtues; and when a Southern
woman said to me, in answer to my strictures on
Southern men:

"Oh, you need not say anything! Look at your
own Daniel Webster!" I wondered and began to look
at and inquire about him, and soon discovered that his
whole panoply of moral power was a shell—that his
life was full of rottenness. Then I knew why I had
come to Washington. I gathered the principal facts
of his life at the Capitol, stated them to Dr. Snod-
grass, a prominent Washington correspondent, whose
anti-slavery paper had been suppressed in Baltimore
by a mob, to Joshua R. Giddings and Gamaliel Bailey.
They assured me of the truth of what had been told
me, but advised me to keep quiet, as other people had
done. I took the whole question into careful consideration; wrote a paragraph in a letter to the *Visiter*,
stating the facts briefly, strongly; and went to read it
to my friend, Mrs. George W. Julian.

I found her and her husband together, and read the
letter to them. They sat dumb for a moment, then he
exclaimed:

"You must not publish that!"

"Is it true?"

"Oh, yes! It is true! But none the less you must
not publish it!"

"Can I prove it?"

"No one will dare deny it. We have all known
that for years, but no one would dare to make it public. No good can come of its publication; it would
ruin you, ruin your influence, ruin your work. You

would lose your *Tribune* engagement, by which you are now doing so much good. We all feel the help you are to the good cause. Do not throw away your influence!"

"Does not the cause of the slave hang on the issue in Congress?"

"I think it does."

"Is not Mr. Webster's influence all against it?"

"Yes, of course!"

"Would not that influence be very much less if the public knew just what he is?"

"Of course it would, but you cannot afford to tell them. You have no idea what his friends would say, what they would do. They would ruin you."

I thought a moment, and said:

"I will publish it, and let God take care of the consequences."

"Good!" exclaimed Mrs. Julian, clapping her hands. "I would if I were in your place."

But when I went to post the letter, I hesitated, walked back and forth on the street, and almost concluded to leave out that paragraph. I shuddered lest Mr. Julian's prediction should prove true. I was gratified by my position on the *Tribune*—the social distinction it gave me and courtesy which had been shown me. Grave Senators went out of their way to be polite, and even pro-slavery men treated me with distinguished consideration. My Washington life had been eminently agreeable, and I dreaded changing popularity for public denunciation. But I remembered my Red Sea, and my motto—" Speak unto the children of Israel that they go forward." The duty of destroying that pro-slavery influence was plain. All the objections were for fear of the consequences to me. I had said God should take care of these, and mailed the letter, but I must leave Washington. Mr. Greeley should not discharge me. I left the capitol the day after taking my seat in the reporter's gallery, feeling that that door was open to other women.

The surprise with which the Webster statement was received was fully equalled by the storm of denunciation it drew down upon me. The New York *Tribune* regretted and condemned. Other secular papers made dignified protests. The religious press was shocked at my indelicacy, and fellows of the baser sort improved their opportunity to the utmost. I have never seen, in the history of the press, such widespread abuse of any one person as that with which I was favored; but, by a strange fatality, the paragraph was copied and copied. It was so short and pointed that in no other way could its wickedness be so well depicted as by making it a witness against itself.

I had nothing to do but keep quiet. The accusation was made. I knew where to find the proof if it should be legally called for, and until it was I should volunteer no evidence, and my witnesses could not be attacked or discredited in advance. By and by people began to ask for the contradiction of this "vile slander." It was so circumstantial as to call for a denial. It could not be set aside as unworthy of attention.

What did it mean? Mr. Webster was a prominent candidate for President. Would his friends permit this story to pass without a word of denial? Mr.

Julian was right; no one would dare deny the charge. He was, however, wrong in saying it would ruin me. My motive was too apparent, and the revelations too important, for any lasting disgrace to attach to it. On all hands it was assured that the disclosure had had a telling effect in disposing of a formidable power which had been arrayed against the slave, as Mr. Webster failed to secure the nomination.

Some one started a conundrum: " Why is Daniel Webster like Sisera? Because he was killed by a woman," and this had almost as great a run as the original accusation.

When the National Convention met in Pittsburg, in 1852, to form the Free Democratic party, there was an executive and popular branch held in separate halls. I attended the executive. Very few women were present, and I the only one near the platform. The temporary chairman left the chair, came to me to be introduced, saying :

" I want to take the hand that killed Daniel Webster."

Henry Wilson was permanent chairman of that convention, and he came, too, with similar address. Even Mr. Greeley continued to be my friend, and I wrote for the *Tribune* often after that time.

CHAPTER XXVIII.

FUGITIVE SLAVE LAW.

WHEN it became certain that the Fugitive Slave Bill could pass Congress, but could not command a two-thirds vote to carry it over the assured veto of President Taylor, he ate a plate of strawberries, just as President Harrison had done when he stood in the way of Southern policy, and like his great predecessor Taylor, died opportunely, when Mr. Fillmore became President, and signed the bill. When it was the law of the land, there was a rush of popular sentiment in favor of obedience, and a rush of slave-catchers to take advantage of its provisions. Thousands of slaves were returned to bondage. Whigs and Democrats were still bidding for the Southern vote, and now vied with each other as to who should show most willingness to aid their Southern brethren in the recovery of their lost property. The church also rushed to the front to show its Christian zeal for the wrongs of those brethren who, by the escape of their slaves, lost the means of building churches and buying communion services, and there was no end of homilies on the dishonesty of helping men to regain possession of their own bodies. All manner of charges were rung about Onesimus, and Paul became the patron saint of slave-catchers.

Among the many devices brought to bear on the consciences of Pittsburgers, was a sermon preached, as per announcement, by Rev. Riddle, pastor of the Third Presbyterian church. It was received with great favor, by his large wealthy congregation, was printed in pamphlet form, distributed by thousands and made a profound impression, for Pittsburg is a Presbyterian city, and a sermon by its leading pastor was convincing. The sermon was an out and out plea for the bill and obedience to its requirements. Did not Paul return Onesimus to his master? Were not servants told to obey their masters? Running away was gross disobedience, etc., etc.

Robt. M. Riddle, in a careful leader in *The Journal*, deprecated the existence of the law; but since it did exist, counseled obedience. He was a polished and forcible writer and his arguments had great weight.

The *Visiter* published an article on "The Two Riddles," in which was drawn a picture of a scantily clad woman, with bruised and bleeding feet, clasping an infant to her bosom, panting before her pursuers up Third street. The master called on all good citizens for help. The cry reached the ears of the tall editor of the *Journal* seated at his desk. He dropped his pen, hastily donned his new brass collar and started in hot pursuit of this wicked woman, who was feloniously appropriating the property of her master.

The other Riddle—the Presbyterian pastor—planted himself by the lamp post on the corner of Third and Market streets, and with spectacles on nose and raised hands, loudly implored divine blessing on the labors of his tall namesake. The *Visiter* concluded by advising masters who had slaves to catch, to apply to these gentlemen, who would attend to business from purely pious and patriotic motives.

I did not see Mr. Riddle for two weeks after the publication of the sketch, and then we met on the street. He had never before been angry or vexed with me, but now he was both, and said:

"How could you do me such an injustice?"

"Why is it an injustice?"

"Oh you know it is! You know I would cut off my right hand, before I would aid in capturing a fugitive."

"Then why do you counsel others to do it?"

"Oh you know better! and Rev. Riddle, he and his friends are distressed about it. You do not know what you have done! I have already had three letters from the South, asking me to aid in returning fugitives, and he, too, has had similar applications. Oh it is too humiliating, too bad. You must set it right!"

I agreed to do so, and the *Visiter* explained that it had been mistaken in saying that both or either of the two Riddles would aid in returning fugitives. They both scorned the business, and Robt. M., would cut off his right hand, rather than engage in it. He only meant that other people should do what would degrade him. He was not a good citizen, and did not intend to be. As for his Reverence, he would shirk his Christian duties; would not pray by that lamp-post, or any other lamp-post, for the success of slave-catchers. He had turned his back upon Paul, and had fallen from grace since preaching his famous sermon. The gentlemen had been accredited with a patriotism and piety of which they were incapable, and a retraction was necessary; but if any other more patriotic politician or divine, further advanced in sanctification would send their names to the *Visiter*, it would notify the South.

In answering Bible arguments, as to the righteousness of the Fugitive Slave Bill, the main dependence of the *Visiter* was Deuteronomy xxiii: 15 and 16:

"Thou shalt not deliver unto his master, the servant which is escaped from his master unto thee.

"He shall dwell with thee, even among you, in that place where he shall choose, in one of thy gates, where it liketh him best, thou shalt not oppress him."

That old Bible, in spite of pro-slavery interpreters, proved to be the great bulwark of human liberty.

In 1852, Slavery and Democracy formed that alliance to which we owe the Great Rebellion. The South became solid, and Whigs had no longer any motive for catching slaves.

CHAPTER XXIX.

BLOOMERS AND WOMAN'S RIGHTS CONVENTIONS.

THE appearance of *The Visiter* was the signal for an outbreak, for which I was wholly unprepared, and one which proved the existence of an eating cancer of discontent in the body politic. Under the smooth surface of society lay a mass of moral disease, which suddenly broke out into an eruption of complaints, from those who felt themselves oppressed by the old Saxon and ecclesiastical laws under which one-half the people of the republic still lived.

In the laws governing the interests peculiar to men, and those affecting their interests in common with woman, great advance had been made during the past six centuries, but those regarding the exclusive interests of women, had remained in *statu quo*, since King Alfred the Great and the knights of his Round Table fell asleep. The anti-negro slavery object of my paper seemed to be lost sight of, both by friends and foes of human progress, in the surprise at the innovation of a woman entering the political arena, to argue publicly on great questions of national policy, and while men were defending their pantaloons, they created and spread the idea, that masculine supremacy lay in the form of their garments, and that a woman dressed like a man would be as potent as he.

Strange as it may now seem, they succeeded in giving such efficacy to the idea, that no less a person than Mrs. Elizabeth Cady Stanton was led astray by it, so that she set her cool, wise head to work and invented a costume, which she believed would emancipate woman from thraldom. Her invention was adopted by her friend Mrs. Bloomer, editor and proprietor of the *Lily*, a small paper then in infancy in Syracuse, N. Y., and from her, the dress took its name—"the bloomer." Both women believed in their dress, and staunchly advocated it as the sovereignest remedy for all the ills that woman's flesh is heir to.

I made a suit and wore it at home parts of two days, long enough to feel assured that it must be a failure; and so opposed it earnestly, but nothing I could say or do could make it apparent that pantaloons were not the real objective point, at which all discontented woman aimed. I had once been tried on a charge of purloining pantaloons, and been acquitted for lack of evidence; but now, here was the proof! The women themselves, leaders of the malcontents, promulgated and pressed their claim to bifurcated garments, and the whole tide of popular discussion was turned into that ridiculous channel.

The *Visiter* had a large list of subscribers in Salem, Ohio, and in the summer of '49 a letter from a lady came to me saying, that the *Visiter* had stirred up so much interest in women's rights that a meeting had been held and a committee appointed to get up a woman's rights convention, and she, as chairman of that committee, invited me to preside. I felt on reading this as if I had had a douche bath; then, as a lawyer might have felt who had carried a case for a corporation through the lower court, and when expecting it up before the supreme bench, had learned that all his clients were coming in to address the court on the merits of the case.

By the pecks of letters I had been receiving, I had learned that there were thousands of women with grievances, and no power to state them or to discriminate between those which could be reached by law and those purely personal; and that the love of privacy with which the whole sex was accredited was a mistake, since most of my correspondents literally agonized to get before the public. Publicity! publicity! was the persistent demand. To meet the demand, small papers, owned and edited by women, sprang up all over the land, and like Jonah's gourd, perished in a night. Ruskin says to be noble is to be known, and at that period there was a great demand on the part of women for their full allowance of nobility; but not one in a hundred thought of merit as a means of reaching it. No use waiting to learn to put two consecutive sentences together in any connected form, or for an idea or the power of expressing it. One woman was printing her productions, and why should not all the rest do likewise? They had so long followed some leader like a flock of sheep, that now they would rush through the first gap into newspaperdom.

I declined the presidential honors tendered me, on the ground of inability to fill the place; and earnestly entreated the movers to reconsider and give up the convention, saying:

"It will open a door through which fools and fanatics will pour in, and make the cause ridiculous."

The answer was that it was too late to recede. The convention was held, and justified my worst fears. When I criticised it, the reply was:

"If you had come and presided, as we wished you to do, the result would have been different. You started the movement and now refuse to lead it, but cannot stop it."

The next summer a convention was held in Akron, Ohio, and I attended, hoping to modify the madness, but failed utterly, by all protests I could make, to prevent the introduction by the committee on resolutions of this:

"*Resolved*, that the difference in sex is one of education."

A man stood behind the president to prompt her, but she could not catch his meaning, and when confusion came, she rose and made a little speech, in which she stated that she knew nothing of parliamentary rules, and when consenting to preside had resolved, if there were trouble, to say to the convention as she did to her boys at home:

"Quit behaving yourselves!"

This brought down the house, but brought no order, and she sat down, smiling, a perfect picture of self-complaisance.

People thought the press unmerciful in its ridicule of that convention, but I felt in it all there was much forbearance.   No words could have done justice to the occasion.   It was so much more ridiculous than ridicule, so much more absurd than absurdity.   The women on whom that ridicule was heaped were utterly incapable of self-defense, or unconscious of its need. The mass of nobility seekers seemed content to get before the public by any means, and to wear its most stinging sarcasms as they would a new dress cap.

In those days I reserved all my hard words for men, and in my notice of the convention mildly suggested that it would have been better had Mrs. Oliver Johnson been made president, as she had great executive ability and a good knowledge of parliamentary rules. This suggestion was received by the president as an insult never to be forgiven, and in the *Visiter* defended herself against it.   I replied, and in the discussion which followed she argued that the affairs of each family should be so arranged that the husband and wife would be breadwinner and housekeeper by turns, day or even half day about.   He should go to business in the forenoon, then in the afternoon take care of baby and permit her to go to the office, shop or warehouse from which came the family supplies.

I took the ground that baby would be apt to object, and that in our family the rule would not work, since I could not put a log on the mill-carriage, and the water would be running to waste all my day or half-day as bread-winner.

About the same time, Mrs. Stanton published a series of articles in Mrs. Bloomer's paper, the *Lily*, in which she taught that it was right for a mother to make baby comfortable, lay him in his crib, come out, lock the door, and leave him to develop his lungs by crying or cooing, as he might decide, while mamma improved her mind and attended to her public and social duties.

Against such head winds, it was hard for my poor little craft to make progress in asserting the right of women to influence great public questions.

For something over twenty years after that Akron meeting, I did not see a woman's rights convention, and in all have seen but five. Up to 1876 there had been no material improvement in them, if those I saw were a fair specimen. Their holders have always seemed to me like a woman who should undertake at a state fair to run a sewing machine, under pretense of advertising it, while she had never spent an hour in learning its use.

However, those conventions have probably saved the republic. From the readiness with which Pennsylvania legislators responded to the petition of three of four women, acting without concert, in the matter of property rights, it is probable that in a fit of generosity the men of the United States would have enfranchised its women *en masse;* and the government now staggering under the ballots of ignorant, irresponsible men, must have gone down under the additional burden of the votes which would have been thrown upon it, by millions of ignorant, irresponsible women. Before that time, the unanswerable argument of Judge Hurlbut had been published, and had made a deep impression on the minds of thinking men. Had this been followed by the earnest, thrilling appeals of Susan B. Anthony, free from all alliance with cant and vanity, we should no doubt have had a voting population to-day, under which no government could exist ten years; but those conventions raised the danger signal, and men took heed to the warning.

CHAPTER XXX.

MANY MATTERS.

THE period of the *Visiter* was one of great mental activity—a period of hobbies—and it, having assumed the reform roll, was expected to assume all the reforms. Turkish trowsers, Fourierism, Spiritualism, Vegetarianism, Phonetics, Pneumonics, the Eight Hour Law, Criminal Caudling, Magdalenism, and other devices for teaching pyramids to stand on their apex were pressed upon the *Visiter*, and it was held by the disciples of each as "false to all its professions," when declining to devote itself to its advocacy. There were a thousand men and women, who knew exactly what it ought to do; but seldom two of them agreed, and none ever thought of furnishing funds for the doing of it. Reformers insisted that it should advocate their plan of hurrying up the millenium, furnish the white paper and pay the printers. Fond parents came with their young geniuses to have them baptized in type

10

from the *Visiter* font. Male editors were far away folks, but the *Visiter* would sympathize with family hopes.

Ah, the crop of Miltons, Shakespeares, and Dry-dens which was growing up in this land, full forty years ago. What has ever become of them? Here conscience gives a twinge, for that wicked *Visiter* did advise that parents should treat young genius as sci-entists do wood, which they wish to convert into pure carbon, *i. e.*, cover it up with neglect and discourage-ment, and pat these down with wholesome discipline, solid study and useful work, and so let the fire smoul-der out of sight.

The policy of the *Visiter* in regard to Woman's Rights, was to " go easy," except in the case of those slave-women, who had no rights. For others, gain an advance when you could. Educate girls with boys, develop their brains, and take away legal disabilities little by little, as experience should show was wise; but never dream of their doing the world's hard work, either mental or physical; and Heaven defend them from going into all the trades.

The human teeth proved that we should eat flesh, and the human form proved that men should take the ore out of the mines, subdue the inertia of matter and the ferocity of animals; that they should raise the grain, build the houses, roads and heavy machinery; and that women should do the lighter work. As this work was as important as the heavier, and as it fell principally on wives and mothers, they in these rela-tions should receive equal compensation with the hus-band and father. By this plan, the estate acquired by a matrimonial firm, would belong equally to both parties, and each could devise his or her share, so that a woman would know that her accumulations would go to her heirs, not to her successor. Consequently, every wife would have an incentive to industry and economy, instead of being stimulated to idleness and extravagance as by existing laws.

Women should not weaken their cause by impracticable demands. Make no claim which could not be won in a reasonable time. Take one step at a time, get a good foothold in it and advance carefully. Suffrage in municipal elections for property holders who could read, and had never been connected with crime, was the place to strike for the ballot. Say nothing about suffrage elsewhere until it proved successful here.

Intemperance was then under treatment by Washingtonianism. By this philosophy it was held that each man consists of about thirty pounds of solid matter, wet up with several buckets of water; that in youth his mother and sweetheart, kneads, rolls, pats and keeps him in shape, until his wife takes charge of him and makes him into large loaves or little cakes, according to family requirements; but must not stop kneading, rolling, patting, on pain of having him all flatten out.

The diagnosis of drunkenness was that it was a disease for which the patient was in no way responsible, that it was created by existing saloons, and non-existing bright hearths, smiling wives, pretty caps and aprons. The cure was the patent nostrum of pledge-signing, a lying-made-easy invention, which like calomel, seldom had any permanent effect on the desease for which it was given, and never failed to produce another and a worse. Here the cure created an epidemic of forgery, falsehood and perjury.

Napoleon selected his generals for their large noses. Dr. Washingtonian chose his leaders for their great vices. The honors bestowed upon his followers were measured by their crimes, and that man who could boast the largest accumulation was the hero of the hour. A decent, sober man was a mean-spirited fellow; while he who had brought the grey hair of parents in sorrow to the grave, wasted his patrimony and murdered his wife and children, was "King o' men for a' that." The heroines were those women who had smilingly endured every wrong, every indignity that brutality could inflict; had endured them not alone for themselves but for their children; and she who had caressed the father of her child while he dashed its brains out, headed the list in saintship; for love was the kneading trough, and obedience the rolling pin, in and with which that precious mess called a man was to be made into an angel.

The *Visiter* held that the law-giver of Mount Sinai knew what was in man, and had not given any such account of him; that the commands, " Thou shalt," and " Thou shalt not," were addressed to each individual; that the disease of opening one's mouth and pouring whisky into it was under the control of the mouth-opener; that drunkenness was a crime for which the criminal should be punished by such terms of imprisonment as would effectually protect society and prevent its confirmation. It told women that that dough ought to be baked in the furnace of affliction; that the coil of an anaconda was preferable to the embraces of a drunken man; that it is a crime for a woman to become the mother of a drunkard's child; that she who fails to protect her child from the drunken fury of any man, even to the extent of taking his life on the spot, if possible, is a coward and a traitor to the highest impulses of humanity.

These sentiments made a stir in temperance ranks, and there was much defense of the dear fellows. The organization seemed to be principally occupied in teaching, that among men, only rumsellers are free moral agents, and that they and the women are to bear the iniquity of us all. One Philadelphia woman, engaged in scattering rose-leaf remedies over the great cancer of the land, concluded that the editor of the *Visiter* horsewhipped the unfortunate man she called husband, once a day, with great regularity. Much sympathy was expressed for that much-abused man; and this was amusing to those who knew he could have tied four such tyrants in a sheaf, and carried them off like a bundle of sticks. But people had found a monster, a giantess, with flaming black eyes, square jaws and big fists, who lived at the top of a very high bean-pole, and ate nothing but the uncooked flesh of men.

However, the man-eating idea came to be useful, and proved that a bad name is better than none.

In '49, the *Visiter* began a weekly series of "Letters to Country Girls," which were seized upon as a new feature in journalism, were very extensively copied, and won golden opinions from all sorts of men. In

'54 they were collected in book form, and "mine ancient enemy," George D. Prentiss, gave them kindly notice.

CHAPTER XXXI.

THE MOTHER CHURCH.

WHEN the *Visiter* entered life, it was still doubtful which side of the slavery question the Roman church would take. O'Connell was in the zenith of his power and popularity, was decidedly anti-slavery, and members of Catholic churches chose sides according to personal feeling, as did those of other churches. It was not until 1852, that abolitionists began to feel the alliance between Romanism and slavery; but from that time, to be a member of the Roman church was to be a friend of "Southern interests."

In Pittsburg there was great harmony between Catholics and Protestants, for the Protestant-Irish, by which Western Pennsylvania was so largely settled, were generally refugees driven from Ireland for their connection with the Union, or Robert Emmet rebellion. Our pastor, Rev. John Black, escaped in the night, and he and the only Catholic priest in Pittsburg, Father McGuire, were intimate friends.

The Bishop of the diocese, R. R. O'Conner, was, I think, a priest of the Capponsacchi order, one of those men by whose existence the Creator renders a reason for the continuance of the race. After the days of which I write, there was an excitement in Pittsburg about Miss Tiernan, a beautiful, accomplished girl, who became a nun, and was said to have mysteriously disappeared. When the Bishop resigned his office and became a member of an austere order of monks, there were not lacking those who charged the act to remorse for his connection with her unexplained death; but I doubt not, that whatever that connection was, it did honor to his manhood, however it may have affected his priesthood.

In the days of his Episcopal honors, he was a favorite with all sorts and conditions of men, and when he published a letter condemning our infant-system of public schools, and demanding a division of the school fund, he produced a profound sensation. I think this letter appeared in '49. It was the morning of one of the days of the week I spent regularly at the office. I found Mr. Riddle waiting to ask what I proposed to do about it. I stated, without hesitation, that I would oppose it to the best of my ability, when he replied:

"I took it for granted that you would, have consulted Mr. White (conductor of the *Gazette*), and we feel that we cannot afford to lose our Catholic patronage by taking issue with the Bishop, and that it will not be necessary. You, as a pupil of Dr. Black, ought to be able to answer Bishop O'Conner's arguments, and we will leave him to you. The religious press will, of course, be a unit against him, and the secular press need not fear to leave the case in your hands."

The two papers for which he spoke, were the two great Whig dailies of the western part of the State. The other daily was the *Democratic Post*, conducted by a Catholic, and virtually the Bishop's organ; and to meet this attack on the very foundations of civil liberty, the *Visiter*, a weekly, was the only representative of the secular press.

The Whig papers might have taken a different course, had it been known at first that Bishop O'Conner's letter was only a part of a concerted attack, and that all over the Union the Bishops had published similar letters. But this was before the days of telegraphy, and we were weeks learning the length and breadth of the movement.

Bishop O'Conner replied very courteously to my strictures on his letter, and we maintained the controversy for some length of time. Having all the right on my side, I must have been a dolt not to make it apparent; and the friends of the Bishop must have felt that he gained nothing, else they would not have been so angry; but he was courteous until he dropped the subject.

My Catholic patrons gradually withdrew their advertisements and subscriptions. Thousands of Protestants were rejoiced at what they called my triumph, and borrowed the *Visiter* to read my articles. Very many bought copies, but I think I did not gain one subscriber or advertiser by that labor in defense of a common cause. Nay, I lost Protestant as well as Catholic support, for business men did not care to be known to Catholic customers as a patron of a paper which had strenuously opposed the policy of the church. That experience and a close observation for many years have taught me that the secular papers of the United States, with a few exceptions, are almost as much under the control of the Pontiff as the press of Austria. Nor is it the secular press alone which is thus con-

trolled. There are religious papers who throw "sops
to Cerebus," as an offset to teachings demanded by
Protestant readers. These "sops" are paid for indi-
rectly by patronage, which would be withdrawn whenever the Bishop took alarm at an article in that same
paper.

Protestants do not carry their religion either into
political or business relations, and so there is no offset
to the religious, political and business concentration
of Romanism.

There was no other outbreak between me and my
Catholic neighbors until the dedication of the Pittsburg cathedral, when my report gave serious offense,
and caused Bishop O'Conner to make a very bitter
personal attack on me. He did not know how truly
the offensive features of my report were the result of
ignorance; but thought me irreverent, blasphemous. I
had never before been inside a Catholic church; never
seen a Catholic ceremonial; did not know the name of
a single vestment; was overwhelmed with astonishment, and thought my readers as ignorant as I; so
tried to give a description which would enable them
to see what I had seen, hear what I had heard.

Every bishop and priest and member of any religious brotherhood in this country and Canada was said
to be present. Some of the things they wore looked
like long night-gowns, some short ones; some like cradle quilts, some like larger quilts. There were many
kinds of patch-work and embroidery; some of the men
wore skirts and looked very funny. Quite a number
wore something on their heads which looked like two
pieces of pasteboard, the shape of a large flat-iron, and
fastened together at the right angles and points.

They formed into procession and started around the outside of the building. I thought of going "around and about" Jerusalem, and the movement had a meaning; but they walked into a fence corner, swung a censor, turned and walked into another corner, and then back into the house, without compassing the building. I said there was nothing to prevent bad spirits coming in at that side.

I copied the Bishop's angry reply, plead my ignorance and that of Protestants in general for all that seemed irreverent, and called upon him for explanations. What did it all mean? What was the spiritual significance of those externals? I ignored his evident anger; had no reason to be other than personally respectful to him, yet mv second article irritated him more than the first.

I had stated that the men in the procession were the most villainous-looking set I had ever seen; that every head and face save those of the Bishops of Orleans and Pittsburg, were more or less stamped by sensuality and low cunning. In Bishop O'Conner's reply, he said I had gone to look for handsome men. I answered that I had, and that it was right to do so. The Church, in her works of art, had labored to represent Christ and his apostles as perfectly-formed men—men with spiritual faces. She had never represented any of her saints as a winebibber, a gross beef-eater, or a narrow-headed, crafty, cringing creature. These living men could not be the rightful successors of those whose statues and pictures adorned that cathedral. Archbishop Hughes, in his sermon on that occasion, had argued that all the forms

of the church had a holy significance. What was that
significance? Moreover, in the days of John there were
seven churches. Whatever had the Church of Rome
done with the other six owned on the Isle of Patmos
by him who stood in the midst of the seven golden
candlesticks?

For two months every issue of the *Visiter* copied
and replied to one of the Bishop's articles, but never
could bring him to the point of explaining any portion
of that great mystery. But the discussion marked
me as the subject of a hatred I had not deemed possible, and I have seldom, if ever, met a Catholic so
obscure that he did not recognize my name as that of
an enemy. So bitter was the feeling, that when my
only baby came great fears were felt lest she should
be abducted; but this I knew never could be done with
Bishop O'Conner's consent.

CHAPTER XXXII.

POLITICS AND PRINTERS.

When the Pittsburg National Convention, which
formed the Free Democratic party, had finished its
labors, a committee waited on the *Visiter*, to bespeak
that support which had already been resolved upon,
and soon after a State Convention in Harrisburg in-
dorsed it by formal resolution as a party organ. It
did its best to spread the principles of the party, and
its services called out commendations, as well as the
higher compliments of stalwart opposition from the
foes of those principles.

Allegheny county was overwhelmingly Whig. The *Visiter* worked against the party, and the cry from the Whig press became:

"Why attack our party? It is better than the Democratic. If you were honest, you would devote yourself to its destruction, not to that of the Whig."

To this, the answer was:

"The Whig party is a gold-bearing quartz rock, and we mean to pound it into the smallest possible pieces, in order to get out the gold. The Democratic party is an old red sandstone, and there is plenty of sand lying all around about."

In the summer of 1852 the editor visited the World's Fair, held in New York, and on her return found the office machinery at a stand-still. She had a contract with two printers, who, in making it, had given no notice that they were the irresponsible agents of a union, and therefore had no right to dispose of their own labor. They professed to be entirely satisfied with their work and wages, and loath to leave them; but Mars' Union had cracked his whip, and disobedience was ruin, if not death. For these poor Pennsylvania self-made slaves the *Visiter* had no pity, although they plead for it. It advertised for women to take their places, stating that its editor was in its composing-room. Other, if not all other city papers, did likewise, and there was a rush of women to the printing offices; but ninety out of a hundred had not passed that stage of development in which women live by wheedling men. Those who wheedled most winningly got the places, and the result in less than two months was such a mess of scandal, as drove them, like whipped curs, back to their kennels; but the editor of the *Vis-iter* took a good look at each of the hundred appli-cants, and from them selected three, who had heads, not hat pins, on their shoulders.

Mr. Riddle was a partner in the *Visiter*, and en-gaged a woman. The editor refused to give her a case, when he indignantly said:

"Women have no mercy on each other. There is that poor woman who has been trying to make a living at her trade making vests, and is now on the point of starvation. I have mercy on her, but you have none."

The answer was:

"A woman who cannot make a living at one good trade already learned, will not mend matters by learn-ing another. I do not propose to turn this office into an eelemosynary establishment. I want the women whom the work wants, not those who want the work. How long could that weak woman maintain her re-spectability among all these men? Would it be any kindness to put her in a place she is incapable of fill-ing, and where she must inflict incalculable injury on herself, and the general cause of woman's right to la-bor? Do not let your generosity run away with your judgment."

My three typos came to be the main stay of the *Journal*, as well as the only typos of the *Visiter*, for they were the nucleus of an efficient corps of female type-setters, who held their places until Mr. Riddle's last illness broke down his establishment.

Soon after the opening of the Pa. C. R. R., there was a bad accident, one train running into another in a deep cut, at night; commenting on it the *Visiter* suggested a red light on the rear of every train. The suggestion was accepted immediately, and this is the origin of the red light signal.

CHAPTER XXXIII.

SUMNER, BURLINGAME AND CASSIUS M. CLAY.

THE Republican party was organized in Pittsburg, and when it became national through the Philadelphia convention in the summer of '56, and nominated Fremont, it seemed that it might injure rather than aid the party to have a woman take a prominent place in it. The nurseling—political abolition—was out of its cradle, had grown to man's estate, and with bearded lip had gone forth to battle, a man among men. There were honors and emoluments to be won in the cause of the slave, and no doubt of its final triumph.

The *Visiter* had been sold to Mr. Riddle and united with his weekly, thus extending its circulation, and cutting off the ruinous expense of its publication. The *Journal* was thoroughly Republican, and would be ably conducted. No further need of a page devoted to freedom, when every page was consecrated to the overthrow of slavery.

Before taking action, it was best to consult an old subscriber, Charles Sumner, then on the Allegheny Mountains, recovering from the Brook's assault. I took baby and went to see him.

He was domiciled in the family of Dr. Jackson, Pennsylvania State Geologist, and seemed to be one of it. In the sitting-room were his desk and lounge, where he wrote or lay and talked, principally with Dr. Furness, of Philadelphia, who was with him, devoting an ever-growing store of information to the amusement of his friend. Dr. Jackson was full of instruction, and no man more ready than Sumner to learn. He held that all knowledge was useful in adding to one's resources—inquired minutely about the shoeing of the horse he rode; and over a watermelon at dessert the doctor gave a lecture on amputation, which became a large capital to one at least of his hearers, and was of intense interest to Sumner.

The children loved him, loved to be near him, and never seemed to be in his way. Once when a toddling wee thing crept to his side while he was absorbed in writing, took hold of his clothes, drew herself to his feet and laid her head against his knee, he placed a weight to hold his paper, laid his hand on her head and went on with his work. When some one would have removed her, he looked up and said:

" Oh, let the little one alone!"

He spoke with profound admiration of Mrs. Purviance, wife of the member of Congress from Butler, Pa. Said he was sorry never to have met her. Her influence in Washington society had been so ennobling that the friends of freedom owed her a lasting debt of gratitude. She boarded with her husband at the National where her wealth, independence and sparkling social qualities made her a recognized leader, while all her influence was cast upon the right side. He thought the success of the North in the famous struggle which elected Banks Speaker of the House, was largely due to Mrs. Purviance.

He was oppressed with anxiety about Burlingame, who had gone to Canada to fight a duel, and there was great rejoicing, when he suddenly appeared one evening after the sun had hidden behind the pine trees.

He and Sumner met and greeted each other with the abandon of boys. No duel had been fought, since Brooks, the challenger, had refused to pass through Pennsylvania to Clifton, the place of meeting, for fear of mob violence. Even the offer of a safe conduct of troops by the governor, failed to reassure him, and Burlingame had hurried on to set his friend's mind at rest. After the general rejoicing, the two sat facing each other, when Sumner leaned forward, placed a hand on each of Burlingame's shoulders, and said:

"Tell me, Anson, you did not mean to shoot that man, did you?"

Burlingame's head dropped an instant, then raising it, he said, slowly:

"I intended to take the best aim I could." Here he drew back his right arm, and took the position of holding a gun, "at the broadest part of him, his breast; wait for the word, and then—fire!"

Sumner dropped back in his chair, let his hands fall on his knees and exclaimed, sorrowfully:

"Oh, Anson! I did not believe it."

Burlingame's eyes filled with tears, and he said:

"Charles, I saw you lying bleeding and insensible on the Senate floor, when I did not expect ever again to hear you speak; and I intended then to kill him. I tell you, Charles, we have got to meet those fellows with guns, some day, and the sooner we begin, the better."

On being consulted, both these champions of the right said the *Visiter* must not desert the cause. Sumner added solemnly:

"The slave never had more need of it; never had more need of you."

So that editor went on with her work, feeling such an opinion as almost a divine call.

In talking with Mr. Sumner during that visit, I learned that the same doctor attended both President Harrison and President Taylor in their last illness, and used his professional authority to prevent their friends seeing them until the fatal termination of their illness was certain. Also, that it was that same doctor who was within call when Brooks made his assault on Sumner, took charge of the case, and made an official statement that the injury was very slight, gave it a superficial dressing, and sought to exclude every one from the room of his patient. Said Sumner:

"I shuddered when I recovered consciousness, and found this man beside me."

He dismissed him promptly, and did not hesitate to say that he believed he would not have recovered under his treatment. When the South seceded, this useful man left Washington and joined the Confederacy.

The campaign of 1856 was very spirited. A large mass meeting was held in Pittsburg, and Cassius M. Clay was the orator of the occasion. He was at the heighth of a great national popularity, and seemed as if any honor might be open to him. He dined that evening with Robert Palmer, of Allegheny, and a small party of friends. The house was brilliantly

11

lighted, and at the table, while Clay was talking, and every one in gala day spirits, the light suddenly went out, and what a strange sensation fell on one guest—a feeling of coming evil.

There was no re-lighting. The gas had failed, prophetic of the going out of that brilliant career, and its slow ending in the glimmer of a single candle.

CHAPTER XXXIV.

FINANCE AND DESERTION.

THE *Pittsburg Saturday Visiter* began life with two subscribers, and in the second year reached six thousand, but was always a heavy drain on my income. My domestic duties made it impossible I could give any attention to the business department, and I was glad, at the close of the first year, to transfer a half interest to Mr. Riddle, who became equal partner and co-editor. At the end of the second year he proposed to buy my interest, unite the *Visiter* with his weekly, and pay me a salary for editing a page.

Had the proposal been made directly to me, I should have accepted at once, but it was made through my brother-in-law, William Swisshelm, who had been clerk and business manager of the *Visiter* for eighteen months. He advised me not to accept; said the paper was netting fifteen hundred a year, and that if I would retain my interest he would purchase Mr. Riddle's, get type, have all the work done in a separate establishment, and make it a decided success.

I was afraid of this arrangement, but was anxious

to keep up the paper as a separate publication, and agreed on condition that he would assume the entire financial responsibility, keep my interest at Mr. Riddle's valuation, and leave me no further risk than my services. If there were profits, we would share them; if none, I got no pay, as usual, but sunk no money. To make the changes he desired, I loaned him money until I had most of my small estate invested, and supposed the paper was prospering until suddenly informed that the sheriff was about to sell it. We transferred it to Mr. Riddle, with my services two years in advance, to pay the debts, and I wrote for the New York *Tribune*, at five dollars a column, to meet my personal expenses, as my income from my property was gone.

I forget at what time the *Visiter* was united to the weekly *Journal;* but very soon after the presidential campaign of '52, I learned that my late partner had endorsed several notes which were not likely to be paid by the persons who gave them, and that one of these was already entered as a lien against his interest in the family estate. We had had no settlement, so I went to my lawyer, William M. Shinn, who said that the entire interest of my debtor in his father's will was worth less than my claim since his death, without heirs, before his mother, transferred his share to the other heirs. He advised me, if possible, to get a deed of that share as the only security for which I could hope. I directed him to prepare it, went immediately to the office, saw my late partner, and told him that if he did not execute that deed, I would sue him for a settlement before I left the city. He did, and I took it home early in the afternoon.

In March '57, I resigned my place on the *Family Journal and Visiter*, feeling that my public work was over, and that no life save one of absolute solitude was possible for me.

I had lived over twenty years without the legal right to be alone one hour—to have the exclusive use of one foot of space—to receive an unopened letter, or to preserve a line of manuscript

"From sharp and sly inspection."

In the latter half of the nineteenth century, a Pennsylvania court decided that a husband had a right to open and read any communication addressed to his wife. Living as I did, under this law I had burned the private journal kept in girlhood, and the letters received from my brother, mother, sister and other friends, to preserve their contents from the comments of the farm laborers and female help, who, by common custom, must eat at our table and take part in our conversation. At the office I had received, read and burned, without answer, letters from some of the most prominent men and women of the era; letters which would be valuable history to-day; have, therefore, no private papers, and write this history, except a few public dates, entirely from memory.

Into the mists some rays of light penetrated, and by them I saw that the marriage contract by which I was bound, was that one which I had made and which secured my liberty of conscience and voice in choosing a home.

The fraud by which church and state substituted that bond made for Saxon swine-herds, who ate boar's heads, lived in unchinked houses and wore brass collars, in the days when Alfred the Great was king, was such as would vitiate any other contract, and must annul even that of marriage; but, granting that it was binding, it must bind both parties, and had been broken by the party of the other part through failure to comply with its requirements.

Our marriage had been a mistake, productive of mutual injury; but for one, it was not too late to repair the wrong. He, a man in the prime of life, with unspotted reputation, living without labor, on the income of a patrimonial estate, to which he had made large additions, could easily find a help-mate for him; one who could pad matrimonial fetters with those devices by which husbands are managed. My desertion would leave him free to make a new choice, and I could more easily earn a living alone.

The much-coveted and long-delayed birth of a living child appeared to have barred my appeal to this last resort, but the mother's right to the custody of her infant is one I would defend to the taking of life.

My husband would consent to no separation, and we had a struggle for my separate, personal property or its equivalent; a struggle in which Wm. M. Shinn was my lawyer, and Judge Mellon his, and in which I secured my piano by replevin, Dr. John Scott being my bondsman, and learned that I might not call a porter into the house to remove my trunk. I therefore got my clothing, some books, china and bedding by stealth, and the assistance of half a dozen families of neighbors.

A test suit as to my right to support was decided in 1859, and in it a judge in my native city, charged the jury that:

" If a wife have no dress and her husband refuse to provide one, she may purchase one—a plain dress—not silk, or lace, or any extravagance; if she have no shoes, she may get a pair; if she be sick and he refuse to employ a physician, she may send for one, and get the medicine he may prescribe; and for these necessaries the husband is liable, but here his liability ceases."

The suit was about goods I had purchased by my lawyer's advice—two black silk dresses, a thirty dollar shawl, a dozen pairs black kid gloves, stockings, flannel, linen, half dozen yards white Brussels lace, any one of which would have outlawed the bill, even if I had gone in an Eden costume to make the purchase; but being clothed when I made my appearance at the counter, the merchant could not plead that I " had no dress," and lost his case.

In a subsequent suit carried up to the Supreme Court and decided in '68, it was proved that my husband had forbidden our merchant to credit me on his account, and the merchant's books presented in court showed that for twelve years he had kept two separate accounts, one against my husband and one against me. On his were charged clothing for himself, mother, brothers and employes, common groceries, etc.; while on mine were entered all my clothing, all high-priced tea, white sugar, etc., all table-ware, fine cutlery, table linen, bedding, curtains and towels; on his were, credits for farm products; on mine, only cash; and he was credited with butter and eggs on the same day that I was charged with bed-ticking and towels. My personal expenses from Nov. 18, '36, the date of our marriage, until Nov. 18, '56, twenty years, averaged less than fifty dollars a year. All my husband's labor for all his life, and mine for twenty years, with a large part of my separate property, had gone to swell his mother's estate, on the proceeds of which she kept her carriage and servants until she died, aged ninety-four, while I earned a living for myself and his only child.

I left Pittsburg with my baby about the 20th of May, '57, and went by boat to St. Paul. Before leaving, I went to settle with Mr. Riddle and say good-bye, and found him much troubled. He said:

"Why is it I have known nothing of all this? I did not dream there was anything wrong in your domestic relations, and may have been selfish and inconsiderate."

My husband, mine no more, came upon the boat while she lay at the wharf, held baby on his knee and wept over her; when the last bell rang, he bade me good-bye; carried her to the gangway, held her to the last moment, then placed her in my arms, sprang ashore and hurried up the wharf. He would, I think, have carried her off, but that he knew she would break his heart crying for mother before I could get to her.

He had once taken her away in a fit of anger and walked the floor with her most of the night, seriously alarmed for her life, and could not venture on that experiment again. He loved her most tenderly, and his love was as tenderly returned. Since, as a duty to her, I was careful to teach her to "honor thy father" on earth as well as in heaven.

Had he and I gone into the pine woods, as he proposed, upon marriage; had we been married under an

equitable law or had he emigrated to Minnesota, as he
proposed, before I thought of going, there would have
been no separation; but after fifteen years in his
mother's house I must run away or die, and leave my
child to a step-mother. So I ran away. He thought
I would return; enlarged and improved the house,
wrote and waited for us; could make no deed without
my signature; I would sign none, and after three years
he got a divorce for desertion. In '70 he married
again, and I having, voluntarily, assumed the legal
guilt of breaking my marriage contract, do cheerfully
accept the legal penalty—a life of celibacy—bringing no
charge against him who was my husband, save that he
was not much better than the average man. Knew his
rights, and knowing sought to maintain them against
me; while, in some respects, he was to me incalcul-
ably more than just. Years after I left him, he said
to our neighbor, Miss Hawkins, when speaking of me:

"I believe she is the best woman God ever made,
and we would have had no trouble but for her friends."

My sister had removed with her husband to St.
Cloud, Minnesota, and through him I had secured
forty acres of land on the shore of one of a nest of
lovely lakes, lying on the east side of the Mississippi,
twelve miles from St. Cloud. On this little farm I
would build a cabin of tamarac logs, with the bark on
and the ends sticking out at the corners criss-cross.
My cabin would have one room and a loft, each with
a floor of broad rough boards well jointed, and a lad-
der to go from one to the other. It would have an
open fire-place, a rough flag hearth, and a rustic porch,
draped with hop vines and wild roses. I would have

a boat, catch fish and raise poultry. No sound of strife should ever come into my cabin but those of waves, winds, birds and insects. Ah, what a paradise it would be!

I had not yet learned that every human soul is a Shunamite, "a company of two armies," and wherever there is one, there is strife.

> To live is to contend,
> And life is finished when contentions end.

At St. Paul I took a stage, and night came on when we were still twenty miles from St. Cloud. The wolves stood and looked at the stage, and I knew they were between me and my hermitage; but they were only prairie wolves, and all day my cabin had been growing more and more beautiful. The lakes, the flowers, the level prairies and distant knolls, but most of all the oak openings were enchanting, and in one of these my cabin would stand.

The passengers talked politics and I talked too, and one man said to me:

"Did you say you were going to St. Cloud?

"Yes."

"Well, I tell you, madam, them sentiments of yours won't go down there. Gen. Lowrie don't allow no abolition in these parts and he lives in St. Cloud."

I had had many surprises, but few to equal this; had heard of Gen. Lowrie as a man of immense wealth and influence, but no one had hinted at this view of his character. I had thought of him as the friend of my friends; but as the other passengers were confirming this account and I watching the wolves, there flashed across my mind the thought:

"This is a broad country; but if this be true, there is not room in it for Gen. Lowrie and me."

CHAPTER XXXV.

MY HERMITAGE.

IT was midnight before we reached East St. Cloud, and the ferry-boat had stopped running, so that it was a bright morning the 7th of June when I found myself in half a dozen pairs of loving arms. In a few days we made an excursion to the site of my cabin. It was more beautiful than I had thought. On the opposite side of the lake lived Captain Briggs, with a head full of sea-stories, and a New England wife. My hermitage would be greatly improved by such neighbors only one mile distant, and as the captain had lately killed two large bears between his house and the site of mine, there would soon be no more bears. But I must have the loft of my cabin large enough for several beds, as the children insisted on spending their summers with me. Brother Harry bespoke a second room, for he would want a place to stay all night when out hunting with his friends, and my hermitage began to grow into a hotel.

I had commenced arrangements with workmen, when Harry said to me:

"Sis, Elizabeth and I have talked this matter over, and if you persist, we will take out a writ of lunacy. There is not a man in this territory who would not say on oath, that you are insane to think of going where the bears would eat you if the Indians did not kill you.

The troops are ordered away from the forts; you'll get frontier life enough with us, for we are going to have music with the Indians."

Next day the troops from Fort Ripley marched past, on their way to Kansas, to put down the Free State party. Bleeding Kansas was called on for more blood, and United States soldiers were to sacrifice the friends of freedom on the altar of slavery. The people of Minnesota were left without protection from savages, that the people of Kansas might be given over to the tender mercies of men no less barbarous than the Sioux.

I had run away from the irrepressible conflict, feeling that my work was done; had fled to the great Northwest—forever consecrated to freedom by solemn act and deed of the nation—thinking I should see no more of our national curse, when here it confronted me as it had never done before.

My cabin perished in a night, like Jonah's gourd— perished that liberty might be crushed in Kansas; for without a garrison at Fort Ripley, my project was utterly insane.

CHAPTER XXXVI.

THE MINNESOTA DICTATOR.

EVERY day, from my arrival in St. Cloud, evidence had been accumulating of the truth of that stage-whisper about Gen. Lowrie, who lived in a semi-barbaric splendor, in an imposing house on the bank of the Mississippi, where he kept slaves, bringing them from and

returning them to his Tennessee estate, at his convenience, and no man saying him nay.

He owned immense tracts of land; had and disposed
of all the government contracts he pleased; traveled
over Europe with his salaried physician; said to this
man "go," and he went, to that "come," and he came,
and to a third "do this," and it was done.   But of all
his commands "go" was most potent; for, as president of a claim club, his orders to pre-emptors were
enforced by Judge Lynch.   He never condescended
to go to Congress, but sent an agent; furnished all the
Democratic votes that could possibly be wanted in any
emergency, and nobody wondered when a good list
came from a precinct in which no one lived.

Republicans on their arrival in his dominion, were
converted to the Democratic faith, fast as sinners to
Christianity in a Maffitt meeting, and those on whom
the spirit fell not, kept very quiet.   People had gone
there to make homes, not to fight the Southern tiger,
and any attempt against such overwhelming odds
seemed madness, for Lowrie's dominion was largely
legitimate.   He was one of those who are born to command—of splendid physique and dignified bearing,
superior intellect and mesmeric fascination.   His natural advantages had been increased by a liberal education; he had been brought up among slaves, lived
among Indians as agent and interpreter, felt his own
superiority, and asserted it with the full force of honest conviction.

On all hands he was spoken of as Dictator, and there
was both love and respect mingled with the fear by
which he governed.   His father was a Presbyterian

minister, who taught that slavery was divine, and both were generous and lenient masters. He was the embodiment of the slave power. All its brute force, pious pretenses, plausibility, chivalry, all the good and bad of the Southern character; all the weapons of the army of despotism were concentrated in this man, the friend of my friends, the man who stood ready to set me on the pinnacle of social distinction by his recognition. Across the body of the prostrate slave lay the road to wealth, and many good men had shut their eyes and stepped over.

The territorial government under Buchanan was a mere tool of slavery. Every federal officer was a Southerner, or a Northern man with Southern principles. Government gold flowed freely in that channel, and to the eagles Gen. Lowrie had but to say, as to his other servants, " come," and they flew into his exchequer.

So thoroughly was Minnesota under the feet of slavery, that in September, '60—after we thought the State redeemed—the house of William D. Babbitt, in Minneapolis, was surrounded from midnight until morning by a howling mob, stoning it, firing guns and pistols, attempting to force doors and windows, and only prevented gaining entrance by the solidity of the building and the bravery of its defense. It was thus besieged because its owner and occupant had dared interfere to execute the common law in favor of freedom.

Minneapolis and its twin-city St. Anthony each had a large first-class hotel, to which Southern people resorted in summer, bringing their slaves, holding them often for months, and taking them back to the

South, no one daring to make objection; until one
woman, Eliza Winston, appealed to Mr. Babbitt, who
took her into court, where Judge Vanderbilt decreed her
freedom, on the ground that her claimant had forfeited
his title by bringing her into a free State.

At the rendering of this decree, Rev. Knickerbocker,
rector of the only Protestant Episcopal Church in the
city, arose in open court, and charged the judge with
giving an unrighteous judgment.   He condemned the
law as at war with Scripture and the rights of the master, and its enforcement as injurious to the best interests of the community.   It was the old story of Deme-
trius; and the people, already keenly alive to the profit
of boarding Southern families with their servants, were
glad to have a mantle of piety thrown over their love
of gain.   The court room was packed, and under the
eloquent appeal of the reverend gentleman, it soon
became evident the populace would make a rush, take
the woman out of the hands of the law, and deliver
her to the master.

She and her friends had about lost hope, when an
unlooked for diversion called attention from them.
The red head of " Bill King," afterwards post-master
of the U. S. House of Representatives, arose, like the
burning bush at the foot of Mount Horeb, and his
stentorian voice poured forth such a torrent of denunciation on priest-craft, such a flood of solid swearing
against the insolence and tyranny of ecclesiasticism,
that people were surprised into inactivity, until Mr.
Babbitt got the woman in his carriage and drove off
with her.

There could no longer be a question of her legal

right to her own body and soul; but her friends knew that the law of freedom had lain too long dormant to be enforced now without further serious opposition, and Mr. Babbitt brought into use his old training on the underground railroad to throw the blood-hounds off the scent, so secreted the woman in the house of Prof. Stone, and prepared his own strong residence to bear a siege. For that siege preparations were made by the clerical party during the afternoon and evening, without any effort at concealment, and to brute force the besieging party added brute cunning.

It was known that in my lecturing tours, I was often Mr. Babbitt's guest, and might arrive at any hour. So, shortly after midnight, the door-bell was rung, when Mr. Babbitt inquired:

" Who is there?"

" Mrs. Swisshelm.'

" It is not Mrs. Swisshelm's voice?"

" William Griffin (a colored porter) is with her."

" It is not William Griffin's voice."

Then, for the first time, there were signs of a multitude on the porch, and with an oath the speaker replied :

" We want that slave."

" You cannot have her."

A rush was made to burst in the door, but it was of solid walnut and would not yield, when the assailants brought fence-posts to batter it in, and were driven back by a shot from a revolver in the hall. The mob retired to a safer distance, and the leader—mine host of a first-class hotel—mounted the carriage-block and harangued his followers on the sacred duty of securing the financial prosperity of the two cities by restoring Eliza Winston to her owners, and made this distinct declaration of principles :

"I came to this State with five thousand dollars; have but five hundred left, but will spend the last cent to see 'Bill' Babbitt's heart's blood."

After which heroic utterance a fresh volley of stones and shots were fired, and fresh rush made for doors and windows. The side-lights of the front door had been shattered, and one burly ruffian thrust himself half-way in, but stuck, when a defender leveled a revolver at his head, and said to Mrs. Babbitt, who was then in command of the hall, while her husband defended the parlor windows:

" Shall I shoot him ? "

" Yes, shoot him like a dog."

But Mrs. Edward Messer, her sister, who knew Mr. Babbitt's dread of taking life, knocked the pistol up and struck the ruffian's head with a stick, when it was withdrawn, and again the mob fell back and resorted to stones and sticks and oaths and howlings and gunshots, and threats of firing the house.

Mrs. Babbitt thought that personal appeals might bring citizens to the rescue, and in an interval of black darkness between lightning flashes, escaped through a back cellar way, and had almost reached the shelter of a cornfield adjoining the garden, when the lightning revealed her and three men started in pursuit. It was two months before the birth of one of her children, and Mr. Elliott, a neighbor who was hastening to the rescue, saw her danger and ran to engage her pursuers. Stumbling through the corn, he encoun-

tered one and cudgeled him, but all were separated by
the darkness. Mrs. Babbitt, however, succeeded in
reaching the more thickly settled portion of the city,
and the first man she called upon for help, replied:

"You have made your bed—lie in it!"

The sheriff came, with two or three men, and talked
to the mob, which dispersed before daylight, with open
threats to "have Babbitt's heart's blood," and for
months his family lived in momentary apprehension
of his murder. For months he was hooted at in the
streets of Minneapolis as "nigger thief," and called
"Eliza." No arrests were made, and he has always
felt it fortunate that Mrs. Messer prevented the shooting of the man in the side-light, as he thinks to this
day that in the state of public sentiment, the man
firing the shot would have been hanged for murder by
any Hennepin county jury, and his home razed to the
ground or burned.

Eliza Winston was sent by underground railroad to
Canada, because Minnesota, in the year of grace, 1860,
could not or would not defend the freedom of one declared free by decision of her own courts.

When such events were actual facts in '60, near the
center of the State, under a Republican administration,
what was the condition of public sentiment in the
northern portion of the territory in '57, when there
was scarce a pretense of law or order, and the Southern democracy held absolute sway? I soon understood the situation; had known for years that the
Southern threats, which Northern men laughed at as
"tin kettle thunder," were the desperate utterances of
lawless men, in firm alliance with the "Hierarchy of
Rome for the overthrow of this Republic.

12

CHAPTER XXXVII.

ANOTHER VISITER.

GEORGE BROTT was proprietor of lower St. Cloud and had started a paper, *The Advertiser*, to invite immigration. There were two practical printers in town, both property-owners, both interested in its growth, and when the resources of *The Advertiser* had been consumed and they had had union rates for work done on it, they fell back on their dignity and did nothing. They had enlisted in the wrong army, did not belong with this band of pioneers, making its way against savage beasts and men. They were soldiers of a union whose interests were all opposed to those of St. Cloud, so they were looking on, waiting to see if the great need of a paper would not compel their neighbors to pay tribute to their union.

Mr. Brott asked me if I would take charge of a paper and take town lots for a salary. I told him I was an abolitionist. He laughed, and said:

"A lady has a right to be of whatever politics she pleases," and went on to say, that if I could recommend Minnesota to emigrants, and St. Cloud as a town site, he cared nothing for my opinions on other points. He thought we might unite all the town proprietors, and so raise money to pay the printers, so I wrote to each one, asking his support to the St. Cloud *Visiter*, as an advertising medium. All, save Gen. Lowrie, were prompt in making favorable response; but from him I had not heard, when there had been three issues of the paper. Mr. Brott was in the office, and I said:

"There is one thing more. I feel that some day I will attack Gen. Lowrie, who is your friend. He will set Shepley on me; I will make short work of him. Then we will have a general melee, and I will clear out that clique. Shepley is your lawyer, and I do not want to use your press in that way without your consent."

While I spoke, his jaw dropped and he sat staring at me in literal open-mouthed wonder, then threw back his head, laughed heartily and said:

"Oh, go ahead! I bake no bread in any of their ovens!"

Very soon I had a letter from Gen. Lowrie, saying:

"I myself will give the St. Cloud *Visiter* a support second to that of no paper in the territory, if it will support Buchanan's administration. Otherwise I can do nothing."

I had not finished reading, when the thought came: "Now I have you." Yet still I knew it looked like, ah, very like a man catching a whale with a fish hook secured to his own person, when there were a hundred chances to one that the whale had caught him. I replied that the St. Cloud *Visiter* would support Mr. Buchanan's administration, since it could not live without Gen. Lowrie's assistance, and such was his ultimatum.

On the second day after that contract was made, brother Harry came, all trembling with rage, and said:

"Lowrie is telling all over town that he has bought you, and that the *Visiter* is to support Buchanan!"

"It is true," was the astounding answer, when he said bad words, rushed from the room and slammed the door.

Then followed ten days, the only ones since he became my brother when he would not call me "Sis." Elizabeth said:

"I would have seen Lowrie and his money in the bottom of the sea, first! What would mother say?"

The next issue of the *Visiter* made no allusion to its change of base, and there was plenty of time to discuss the question. Those who knew my record refused to believe I had sold out, and took bets on it. However, the next number contained an editorial which relieved the minds of friends, but which created the gravest apprehension. It stated that the *Visiter* would, in future, support Buchanan's administration, and went on to state the objects of that administration as being the entire subversion of Freedom and the planting of Slavery in every State and Territory, so that Toombs could realize his boast, and call the roll of his slaves at the foot of Bunker Hill. It reminded its readers that John Randolph had said in the United States Senate when speaking to Northern men:

"We have driven you to the wall, and will drive you there again, and next time we will keep you there and nail you to the counter like base money."

Mr. Buchanan, a Northern man, had fulfilled the prediction. Henry Clay had said that Northern workingmen were "mudsills, greasy mechanics and small-fisted farmers." These mudsills had been talking of voting themselves farms; but it would be much more appropriate if they would vote themselves masters. Southern laborers were blessed with kind masters, and Mr. Buchanan and the St. Cloud *Visiter* were most anxious that Northern laborers should be equally well provided for.

When the paper was read, there was a cry of " Sold! Sold! Lowrie had sold himself instead of buying the *Visiter*." At first there was a laugh, then a dead stillness of dread, and men looked at me as one doomed.

CHAPTER XXXVIII.

BORDER RUFFIANISM.

In Lowrie's first ebulition of wrath, he vowed vengeance, but an intimate friend of his, who had been a Democrat in Pittsburg, begged him to do nothing and said:

"Let her alone, for God's sake! Let her alone, or she will kill you. I know her, and you do not. She has killed every man she ever touched. Let her alone!"

But Lowrie knew it was too late for letting alone, and sent me a verbal message, by one he knew I would believe, that I must stop or the consequences would be fatal. Stopping was no part of my plan, and so I told his messenger.

The second number of Buchanan's organ explained how it was that I became a supporter of a policy I had so long opposed. Gen. Lowrie owned Northern Minnesota, land and inhabitants, bought folks up as fast as they came to it, and had bought me. He was going to support the *Visiter* in great power and glory, if it gave satisfaction as a democratic organ. I would work hard for the money, and it would be odd if any

one gave Mr. Buchanan a more enthusiastic support
than I. Indeed, I was his only honest supporter. All
the others pretended he was going to do something
quite foreign to his purpose, while I was in his confidence. The one sole object of his administration was
the perpetuation and spread of slavery, and this object
the *Visiter* would support with the best arguments in
its power.

This was vitriol dressing on a raw wound, and the
suppression of the *Visiter* was expected by Judge
Lynch. Brave men held their breath to see me beard
the lion in his den, not knowing my armor as I did.

Then came an announcement with a great flourish
of trumpets of a lecture on " Woman," by the Hon.
Shepley, the great legal light and democratic orator of
Minnesota. The lecture was delivered in due time to
a densely packed house, and was as insulting as possible. The lecture divided women into four classes—
coquettes, flirts, totally depraved, and strong-minded.
He painted each class and found some redeeming
trait in all save the last.

The speaker might as well have named me as the
object of his attack, and his charges thus publicly made
were not to be misunderstood. At every point there
were rounds and shouts of applause by clacquers, and
brother Harry once rose in a towering rage, but I
dragged him down and begged him to keep quiet.

In my review of the lecture, I praised it, commend-
ed its eloquence and points, but suggested that the
learned gentleman had not included all women in his
classification. For instance, he had left out the frontier belle who sat up all night playing cards with gen-

tlemen; could beat any man at a game of poker, and laugh loud enough to be heard above the roaring of a river. In this I struck at gambling as a social amusement, which was then rapidly coming into fashion in our little city, and which to me was new and alarming.

Mr. Shepley pretended to think that the picture resembled his wife, and this idea was seized upon as drowning men catch at straws. Behind this they sought to conceal the whole significance of the quarrel. Gen. Lowrie cared not for my attacks on himself. Oh, no, indeed! He was suddenly seized by a fit of chivalry, and would defend to the death a lady whom he had never seen.

An effort was made to dispose of me by mob, as a means of clearing the moral atmosphere of the city. It was being discussed in a grocery while "Tom" Alden lay on the counter. He rose, brought down his big fist, and with a preface of oaths, said:

"Now, boys, I tell you what it is. We're Democrats. This is a fight between her and Lowrie, and we're going to see fair play. If she licks him, let him take it. No woman is going to be mobbed in this city! So there!"

Gen. Lowrie had an uncle who lived with him, a very eccentric, single-minded man, who was greatly distressed about the affair, and who became a messenger bent on making peace. He begged me to desist for Lowrie's sake, that I might not drive him to cover himself with shame, and bring lasting regret. He insisted that I knew nothing of the dangers which environed me; I would be secretly murdered, with personal indignities; would be tied to a log and set afloat on the Mississippi. I had no wish to court danger—shrank from the thought of brute force; but if I let this man escape, his power, now tottering, would be re-established; slavery triumphant in the great Northwest; Minnesota confirmed a democratic strong-hold, sending delegates of dough-faces to Congress to aid in the great conspiracy against the nation's life. So I told the messenger that I would continue to support Buchanan's administration, that I would pile my support upon it until it broke down under the weight and sunk into everlasting infamy.

The night after I had sent this, as my final answer to the offer of leniency, the *Visiter* was visited by three men in the "wee sma' hours, anent the twal," the press broken, some of the type thrown into the river, some scattered on the road, and this note left on the table:

"If you ever again attempt to publish a paper in St. Cloud, you yourself will be as summarily dealt with as your office has been.   VIGILANCE."

The morning brought intense excitement and the hush of a great fear. Men walked down to the bank of the great Mississippi, looked at the little wrecked office standing amid the old primeval forest, as if it were a great battle-ground, and the poor little type were the bodies of the valiant dead. They only spoke in whispers, and stood as if in expectation of some great event, until Judge Gregory arrived, and said, calmly:

"Gentlemen, this is an outrage which must be resented. The freedom of the press must be established if we do not want our city to become the center of a gang of rowdies who will drive all decent people away and cut off immigration. I move that we call a public meeting at the Stearns House this evening, to express the sentiments of the people at St. Cloud."

This motion was carried unanimously, but very quietly, and I said:

"Gentlemen, I will attend that meeting and give a history of this affair."

CHAPTER XXXIX.

SPEAK IN PUBLIC.

AT length the time had come when I could no longer skulk behind a printing press. That bulwark had been torn down, and now I must literally open my mouth for the dumb, or be one of those dogs spoken of in Scripture who would not bark. The resolve to speak at that meeting had come in an instant as a command not to be questioned, and I began to prepare. James McKelvey, a lawyer, and nephew of my husband, drew my will and I executed it, settled my business and wrote a statement of the *Visiter* trouble that it might live if I ceased to do so, then went to bed, sent for Miles Brown to come to my room, and saw him alone.

He was a Pennsylvanian, who had the reputation of being a dead shot, and had a pair of fine revolvers. He pledged himself solemnly to go with me and keep near me, and shoot me square through the brain, if there was no other way of preventing me falling alive into the hands of the mob. My mind was then at ease, and

I slept until my mail was brought. In it was a letter from William M. Shinn, saying that without his knowledge, my husband had succeeded in having my one-third interest in the Swissvale estate sold at sheriff's sale, and had become the purchaser. Mr. Shinn added his opinion that the sale was fraudulent, and proposed entering suit to have it set aside; but I could attend to no suit and lost all hope of saving anything from my separate estate. Surely the hand of the Lord lay heavily upon me that day, but I never doubted that it was His hand. The Good Shepherd would lead me and feed me and I should know no want.

When it was time to go to the meeting, I was dressed by other hands than my own. I knew Harry and my brother-in-law, Henry Swisshelm, had organized for defense, and asked no questions, but went with them. Elizabeth carried her camphor bottle as coolly as if mobs and public meetings were things of every day life, while Mrs. Hyke, a New England woman, held my arm, saying:

"We'll have a nice time in the river together, for I am going in with you. They can't separate us."

As we approached the Stearns House, the crowd thickened and pressed upon us. Harry stopped and said:

"Gentlemen, stand back, if you please!"

The guard closed around me, every man with his hand on his revolver. There were oaths and growls, but the mob gave way, and made no further opposition to our entrance.

The meeting was called to order by Thomas Stearns, the owner of the house and for whom the county had been named, who with his brave wife had made every possible arrangement for the meeting. The large parlors were packed with women, and every other foot of space downstairs and even up, were filled with men, while around the house was a crowd. It was a wonder where all the people could have come from. A rostrum had been erected at the end of the parlor next the hall, but I had no sooner taken it than there was an omnious murmur outside, and it was discovered that my head made a tempting target for a shot through the front door, so the rostrum was moved out of range.

There was not much excitement until I named Gen. Lowrie and two other men as the persons who had de-destroyed the *Visiter* office. Then there was a perfect howl of oaths and cat-calls. Gen. Lowrie was on the ground himself, leading his forces outside. A rush was made, stones hurled against the house, pistols fired, and every woman sprang to her feet, but it was to hear and see, not shriek. Harry held the door-way into the hall; Henry that into the dining room. Brown had joined Harry, and I said in a low, concentrated voice :

"Brown."

He turned and pressed up to the rostrum.

"Don't fail me! Don't leave me! Remember!"

"I remember! Don't be afraid! I'll do it! But I'm going to do some other shooting first."

"Save two bullets for me!" I plead, "and shoot so that I can see you."

"I will, I will," but all the time he was looking to the door; Mrs. Hyke was clinging to me sobbing:

"We'll go together; no one can part us."

The mob were pressed back and comparative quiet restored, and when I finished the reading of my address I began to extemporize. What I said seemed to be the right words at the right time. A hushed attention fell upon the audience, inside and out. Then there was applause inside, which called forth howls from the outside, and when I stepped from the platform, I was overwhelmed with congratulations, and more astonished than any one, to learn that I could speak in public.

T. H. Barrett, a young civil engineer, was chairman of the committee on resolutions, and brought in a set which thrilled the audience. They were a most indignant denunciation of the destruction of the office, an enthusiastic endorsement of the course of the *Visiter*, and a determination to re-establish it, under the sole control of its editor. They were passed singly by acclamation until the last, when I protested that they should take time to think—should consider if it were not better to get another editor. There could be no peace with me in the editorial chair, for I was an abolitionist and would fight slavery and woman-whippers to the death, and after it. There was a universal response of "Good! Good! give it to 'em, and we'll stand by you."

This was the beginning of the final triumph of free speech, but the end was yet in the dim distance, and this I knew then as well as afterwards. T. H. Barrett, who carried that meeting, is the man who fought the last battle of the Rebellion at the head of his negro troops away down in Texas, ten days after Lee's surrender, and before that news had reached him, Brown was charged with cowardice, in having kept back among the women, and I had to explain on his account.

CHAPTER XL.

A FAMOUS VICTORY.

THE day after the Stearns House meeting, I was thought to be dying. All that medical skill and loving hands could do was done to draw me from the dark valley into which I seemed to have passed; while those men who had planted themselves and their rifles between me and death by violence, came on tip-toe to know if I yet lived. When I was able to be out it was not thought safe for me to do so—not even to cross the street and sit on the high green bank which overlooked the river. Harry was constantly armed and on guard, and a pistol shot from his house, night or day, would have brought a score of armed men in a very short time.

A printing company had been formed to re-establish the *Visiter*. In it were forty good men and true, and they sent an agent to Chicago to buy press and type. The St. Cloud *Visiter* was to begin a new life as the mouth-piece of the Republican party, and I was no longer a scout, conducting a war on the only rational plan of Indian warfare. I begged my friends to stand aside and leave Lowrie and me to settle the trouble, saying to them:

"I cannot fight behind ramparts of friends. I must take the risks myself, must have an open field. Protect me from brute force and give me moral aid, but stand aside."

But they were full of enthusiasm, and would bear the brunt of battle. There were open threats of the destruction of the new press, and it was no time to quit the field. Of the first number of the resurrected *Visiter*, the St. Cloud Printing Co. was publisher, and I sole editor. I prepared the contents very carefully, that they might not give unnecessary offense, dropped the role of supporting Buchanan, and tried to make a strong Republican paper of the abolition type, and in the leader gave a history of the destruction of my office.

The paper gave great satisfaction to the publishers, who had not thought I could be so calm; but Lowrie threatened a libel suit for my history of that outrage, and I said to the printing company:

"You must get out of my way or I will withdraw."

At once they gave me a bill of sale for the press and material, and of the second number I was sole editor and proprietor, but it was too late. The libel suit was brought, damages laid at $10,000, and every lawyer in that upper country retained for the prosecution.

This was in the spring of '58. The two years previous the country had been devastated by grasshoppers, and no green thing had escaped. There was no old grain, the mass of people had been speculating in town lots, and such had been the demand for city charters, that a wag moved in legislature to reserve one-tenth of the land of Minnesota for agricultural purposes. The territorial had just been exchanged for a state government, which was not yet in working order. The capital of every man in the printing company was buried in corner lots, or lots which were not on a corner. The wolves and bears cared nothing for sur-

veyor's stakes, and held possession of most of the
cities, howling defiance at the march of civilization.
The troops were still in Kansas establishing slavery,
and we lived in a constant state of alarm. The men
were organized for defense against Indians, and must
do picket duty. All the money was in the hands of
the enemy. Citizens had everything to buy and nothing to buy it with. Provisions were brought up from
St. Paul by wagon, except when a boat could come
from St. Anthony. Those men of the company who
were especially marked, were men of families, and it
is hard to starve children for the freedom of the press.
The nearest court was St. Anthony. Any defense of
that suit must be ruinous to those men, and I advised
them to compromise.

A committee was appointed to meet six lawyers,
and were in despair when they learned the ultimatum
of the great Dictator. With the terms demanded,
they had no inclination to comply, but sent J. Fowler to me with the contract they were required to
sign.

This bound the company in a bond of $10,000 act-
ual payment, that the *St. Cloud Visiter* should publish in its columns a card from Mr. Shepley, of which
a copy was appended, and which stated that the destruction of the office was not for any political cause,
but was solely on account of an attack made by its
editor on the reputation of a lady. Also, that said
Visiter should never again discuss or refer to the destruction of its office.

Fowler burned with indignation, and was much
surprised when I returned the paper, saying that I

would comply with these demands. He protested that
I should not—that they had set out to defend the freedom of the press.

"Which you cannot do," I remarked. "You sign
that paper just as you would hand your money to a
robber who held a pistol to your head and demanded
it. There is a point at which the bravest must yield,
where resistance is madness, and you have reached
this point. The press is mine, leave its freedom to
me. Defend me from brute force and do your duty
to your families."

He returned to the consultation room, where every
one was surprised at my compliance. They had all
given me credit for more pluck, but since I surren-
dered, the case was lost. The contract was signed,
the bond executed, and everything made tight and fast
as law could make it. The friends of free press were
indignant, but bided their time. Stephen Miller, a
nephew of my mother-in-law, and afterwards governor
of Minnesota, was on a visit to Harrisburg during all
this trouble, and when he returned, he flew into a
towering rage over what he termed the cowardly back-
down of the printing company, and published a card
in the St. Paul papers, washing his hands of it.

But to the victors belong the spoils and glory, and
now they made much of them. Ladies got out their
silks, their jewels and their laces. There were sounds
of revelry by night, where fair women and gallant
men drew around the social board, on which sparkled
the wine-cup and glimmered the yellow gold, to be
taken up by the winner. Champagne was drunk in
honor of the famous victory, hands were shaken over

it, stray sheep were brought back into the true Democratic fold, and late opinions about presses and types were forgotten.

Though, among all the rejoicings, the Bar had the best of it. For once its members had not been like the blades of a pair of scissors; had not even seemed to cut each other, while only cutting that which came between. For once its members were a band of brothers, concentrated into one sharp, keen dagger, with which they had stabbed Freedom to the heart. That triumphant Bar stroked its bearded chin, and parted its silky mustache; hem'd its wisest hem; haw'd its most impressive haw.

" If Gen. Lowrie had ah, but ah, taken legal advice ah, in the first instance ah, all would have been well ah!"

They were the generals who had won this famous victory, and wore their laurels with a jaunty air, while a learned and distinguished divine from the center of the State, in a sermon, congratulated the Lord on having succeeded in "restoring peace to this community, lately torn by dissensions,"—and all was quiet on the Mississippi.

On its bank sat poor little I, looking out on its solemn march to the sea, thinking of Minnesota; sending a wail upon its bosom to meet and mingle with that borne by the Missouri from Kansas; thinking of a sad-faced slave, who landed with her babe in her arms here, just in front of my unfinished loft, performed the labor of a slave in this free Northern land, and embarked from this same landing to go to a Tennessee auction block, nobody saying to the master, " Why do ye this?"

13

Against the power which thus trampled constitutional guarantees, congressional enactments and State rights in the dust, I seemed to stand alone, with my hands tied—stood in a body weighing just one hundred pounds, and kept in it by the most assiduous care. I was learning to set type, and as I picked the bits of lead from the labeled boxes, there ran the old tune of St. Thomas, carrying through my brain these words:

> "Yea, though I walk in death's dark vale,
> Yet will I fear none ill."

Why did the heathen rage and kings vex themselves? God, even our God, should dash them together like potsherds. What an uneven fight it was—God and I against that little clique—against a world!

I rented the office to the boys, who at once gave me notice that I was no longer wanted in it. They issued a half-sheet *Visiter*, with "the Devil" as editor and proprietor. His salutatory informed his readers, that he was in full possession and was going to have a good time; had taught the *Visiter* to lie, and was going to tunnel the Mississippi. Those were bright boys, and they had a jolly week. Mr. Shepley's card appeared, as per agreement, and thus far the terms of release for the printing company complied with, and the contract with the *Dictator* filled. But what next? Had I actually given up the publication? Of course I had. Its finances were desperate, and what else could I do? What motive could I have for attempting to go on with it? Oh, what a famous victory. The next publication day passed and no *Visiter*. There was a dress parade of triumphant troops, and that most famous victory was bearing fruit.

Next day the *St. Cloud Democrat* made its appearance, and I was sole editor and proprietor. Into the first editorial column I copied verbatim, with a prominent heading, the article from the *Visiter* on which the libel suit was founded, and gave notice that I alone was pecuniarily responsible for all the injury that could possibly be done to the characters of all the men who might feel themselves aggrieved thereby. Of the late *Visiter* I had an obituary; gave a short sketch of its stormy life; how it was insulted, overborne, enslaved; that it could not live a slave, and died in its new chains.

It seems strange that those lawyers should have been so stupid, or should have accredited me with such amazing stupidity when they drew up that bond; but so it was, and the tables were completely turned. To sue me for libel was folly, for in St. Paul or St. Anthony I should have had the gratuitous services of the best legal talent in the state, and they and their case would have been ground into very small and dirty dust. No famous victory was ever before turned into a more total rout by a more simple ambush, and by it I won the clear field necessary to the continuance of my work.

I still had protection from physical violence, but had no fear of legal molestation, and after the next fall election, border ruffianism fell into such disrepute in St. Cloud that loaded guns seemed no longer necessary to sustain the freedom of the press.

CHAPTER XLI.

STATE AND NATIONAL POLITICS.

WHEN *The St. Cloud Democrat* began its career as the organ of the Republican party in Northern Minnesota, the central and southern portions of the S.ate were fairly supplied with republican papers, the conductors all being more or less skillful in the art of plowing and sowing the political field; but with no very bright prospect of harvesting a victory. Under the Lowrie dictatorship of the North, it is difficult to see how the success of a Republican could have been made possible, any more than giving the electoral vote of Southern Republican States to the Republican candidate in 1880.

To overthrow that dictatorship was the work I had volunteered to do, and in doing it, my plan was to "plow deep," subsoil to the beam. Preachers held men accountable to God for their Sunday services, but it was my aim to urge the divine claim to obedience, all the rest of the week. I held that election day was of all others, the Lord's day. He instituted the first republic. All the training which Moses gave the Jews was to fit them for self-government, and at his death the choice of their rulers was left with them and they were commanded to

"Choose men, fearing God and hating coveteousness, and set them to rule over you."

For no creed, no form of worship, no act of his life, is a man more directly responsible to God, than for casting his vote or the non-fulfillment of that duty.

When the nominations were made for the second State election in 1859, Gen. Lowrie had lost ground so fast that he needed the indorsement of his party. This was given in his nomination for Lieut. Governor. The Republicans nominated Ignatius Donnelly, a fiery young orator, who took the stump, and was not deterred by any super-refinement from making the most of his opponent's reputation as the stealthy destroyer of a printing office, because he had made a bad bargain in buying its editor. He and the party which had made his methods its own by nominating him, were held up to the most unmerciful ridicule. The canvass seemed to turn on the indorsement or repudiation of border-ruffianism, press-breaking, woman-mobbing. My *personnel* had then become familiar to the people of the State, and the large man who instituted a mob to suppess a woman of my size, and then failed, was not a suitable leader for American men, even if they were Democrats.

The death-knell of Democratic rule in Minnesota was rung in that election. The whole Republican State ticket was elected, with Gov. Ramsey at its head, and he was the first Governor to tender troops to President Lincoln for the suppression of the Rebellion. The result was gratifying, although our own county, Stearns, was overwhelmingly Democratic, and must remain so, since the great mass of the people were Catholics.

However, the election of the State ticket was largely due to the personal popularity of Gov. Ramsey, and this could not be depended upon for a lasting arrangement, so I spent the winter following lecturing through

the State, sowing seed for the coming presidential
campaign. I never spoke in public during an election
excitement, never advocated on the platform the claims
of any particular man, but urged general principles.

Stephen Miller was our St. Cloud delegate to the
Chicago Convention which nominated Mr. Lincoln,
led the canvass in the State, as the most efficient
speaker and was chairman of the Electoral College.
His prominent position in the Border Ruffian war
added largely to his popularity in the State, and once
more that little printing office under the grand old
trees was plunged into politics; this time into an election on which hung the destinies of the nation. How
that election was carried on in other States I know
not, but in Minnesota the banner of Republicanism
and human freedom was borne aloft over a well fought
field. There was not much surface work. Men struggled for the Right against the old despotism of Might,
and planted their cause on foundations more enduring
than Minnesota granite itself.

Yet, even then, the opposition of the Garrisonians
was most persistent. There was a large anti-slavery
element among the original settlers of Minnesota, but
it was mostly of the Garrisonian or non-voting type,
and had lain dormant under pro-slavery rule. To
utilize this element at the polls was my special desire.
The ground occupied by them was the one I had
abandoned, *i. e.*, the ground made by the Covenanters
when the Constitution first appeared. They pronounced it "a covenant with death and an agreement
with hell," and would not vote or hold office under it;
would not take an oath to support it. So firmly had

Garrison planted himself on the old Covenanter platform, that it is doubtful whether he labored harder for the overthrow of slavery or political anti-slavery; whether he more fiercely denounced slave-holders or men who voted against slave-holding. Once after a "flaming" denunciation of political abolitionists, some one said to him:

"Mr. Garrison, I am surprised at the ground you take! Do you not think James G. Birney and Gerrit Smith are anti-slavery?"

He hesitated, and replied:

"They have anti-slavery tendencies, I admit."

Now, James G. Birney, when a young man, fell heir to the third of an Alabama estate, and arranged with the other heirs to take the slaves as his portion. He took them all into a free State, emancipated them, and left himself without a dollar, but went to work and became the leader of political abolitionists, while Gerrit Smith devoted his splendid talents and immense wealth to the cause of the slave. When their mode of action was so reprehensible to Mr. Garrison, we may judge the strength of his opposition to that plan of action which resulted in the overthrow of slavery. His non-resistance covered ballots as well as bullets, and slavery, the creation of brute force and ballots, must not be attacked by any weapon, save moral suasion. So it was, that Garrisonianism, off the line of the underground railroad, was a rather harmless foe to slavery, and was often used by it to prevent the casting of votes which would endanger its power.

From the action of the slave power, it must by that time have been apparent to all, that adverse votes was what it most dreaded; but old-side Covenanters, Quakers, and Garrisonians could not cast these without soiling their hands by touching that bad Constitution. But that moral *dilettanteism*, which thinks first of its own hands, was not confined to non-voting abolitionists; for the "thorough goers" of the old Liberty Party, could not come down from their perch on platforms which embraced all the moralties, to work on one which only said to slavery "not another foot of territory."

Both these parties attacked me. The one argued that I, of necessity, endorsed slavery everywhere by recognizing the Constitution; the other that I must favor its existence where it then was, by working with the Republican party, which was only pledged to prevent its extension. To me, these positions seemed utterly untenable, their arguments preposterous, and I did my best to make this appear. I claimed the Constitution as anti-slavery, and taught the duty of overthrowing slavery by and through it, but no argument which I used did half the service of an illustration which came to me:

I had a little garden in which the weeds did grow, and little Bobbie Miller had a little broken hoe. When I went into my garden to cut the weeds away, I took up Bobbie's little hoe to help me in the fray. If that little hoe were wanting, I'd take a spoon or fork, or any other implement, but always keep at work. If any one would send me a broader, sharper hoe, I'd use it on those ugly weeds and cut more with one blow; but till I got a better hoe, I'd work away with Bobbie's. I'd ride one steady-going nag, and not a dozen hobbies; help any man or boy, or fiend to do what needed doing, and only stop when work came up which done would call for rueing.

This conceit struck popular fancy as plain argument could not have done, and the Republican party came to be called "Robbie Miller's Hoe"—an imperfect means of reaching a great end, and one that any one might use without becoming responsible for its imperfections.

During the heat of that Lincoln campaign, Galusha A. Grow, then Speaker of the U. S. House of Representatives, came to St. Cloud to speak, and found me ill with quinsy; but I went to the meeting. It was held in Wilson's Hall, which was on the second floor of a frame building, and was so packed that before he began fears were felt lest the floors should give way. But the speaker told the audience that the floor would "hold still" if they did; and any one who felt uneasy had better leave now. No one left, and for two hours and a half he held that packed assembly in close and silent attention. He was very popular on the frontier on account of his homestead bill, yet the hall was surrounded all the time he spoke by a howling Democratic mob, who hurled stones against the house, fired guns, shouted and yelled, trying to drown his voice. To make it more interesting and try to draw out the audience, they made a huge bonfire and burned me in effigy as—

"The mother of the Republican party."

The result of that campaign is known, for in it Minnesota was made so thoroughly Republican that the party must needs split, in order to get rid of its supremacy.

CHAPTER LXII.

RELIGIOUS CONTROVERSIES.

THE *St. Cloud Democrat* found in orthodoxy a foe almost as powerful and persistent as slavery itself. In a local controversy about dancing, I recommended that amusement as the only substitute for lascivious plays, and this was eagerly seized upon by those who saw nothing wrong in wholesale concubinage of the South. A fierce attack was made on *The Democrat* by a zealous Baptist minister; to which I replied, when it was announced and proclaimed that on a certain Sabbath, at 10 A. M., this minister would answer *The Democrat.* At the appointed hour the house overflowed, and people crowded around the doors and windows, while Gen. Lowrie occupied a prominent seat in the audience.

It surely was an odd sight to see that preacher mount the stand, carrying an open copy of *The Democrat,* lay it down beside the Bible, and read verse about from the two documents. The sermon was as odd as the text. It disposed of me by the summary mode of denunciation, but also disposed of David, Solomon and Miriam at the same time. When I gave the discourse a careful Scriptural criticism, I carried the community, and was strengthened by the controversy. But another, more serious and general dispute was at hand.

When Theodore Parker died, the orthodox press from Maine to Georgia, handed him over to Satan to be tormented; and then my reputation for heresy reached its flood-tide.

Rev. John Renwick, one of our Covenanter martyrs, was my ideal of a Christian, and when he lay in the Edinburg prison under sentence of death, his weeping friends begged him to conform and save his life. They said to him:

"Dinna ye think that we, who ha' conformit may be saved?"

"Aye, aye. God forbid that I should limit his grace."

"An' dinna ye think, ye too could be saved and conform?"

"Oh, aye aye. The blood of Christ cleanseth fra all sin."

"Weel, what mair do ye want, than the salvation o' yer saul?"

"Mair, mickle mair! I want to honor my Master, and bear witness to the truth."

To satisfy this want, he died a felon's death. The central idea of that old hero-making Westminster theology was, that man's chief end is to glorify God first, and enjoy him forever when that is done. In all the religious training of my youth, I had never heard the term "seek salvation." We were to seek the privilege of serving God; yet I was willing to be dead-headed into heaven, with the rest of the Presbyterians.

A Protestant Episcopal convention had pointedly refused to advise members of that church to respect the marriage relation among their slaves, and so had dimmed the Elizabethian glory of a church which once stood for freedom so nobly that the winds and waves became her allies, and crowned her with victory. The General Assembly had laid the honor of its martyrs in the dust by endorsing human slavery; and I must be false to every conviction if I did not protest against calling that Christianity which held out crowns of glory to man-thieves and their abettors, and everlasting torments to those who had spent their lives glorifying God and bearing witness to the truth. My defense of Parker and unwillingness to have all Unitarians sent to the other side of the Great Gulf, won for me a prominent place among those whom the churches pronounced " Infidels."

But there came a time when "Providence" seemed to be on the side of the slave.

Rev. J. Calhoun was a highly-cultured gentleman, a Presbyterian clergyman, and one of those urbane men who add force and dignity to any opinion. His wife was Gen. Lowrie's only sister. He preached gratuitously in St. Cloud, and Border Ruffianism and Slavery gained respectability through their connection, when he and his wife made that fatal plunge off the bridge in St. Cloud—a plunge which sent a thrill of horror through the land. I accompanied my sympathetic, respectful obituary notice, with the statement that the costly cutter wrecked, and the valuable horse instantly killed, were both purchased with money obtained by the sale of a woman and her child, who had been held as slaves in Minnesota, in defiance of her law, and been taken by this popular divine to a Tennessee auction block.

The accident was entirely owing to the unprecedented and unaccountable behavior of that horse, and people shuddered with a new horror on being reminded of the price which had been paid for him—bodies and souls of two citizens and the honor of that free State.

CHAPTER XLIII.

FRONTIER LIFE.

The culture which the pale faces introduced into that land of the Dakotas was sometimes curious. The first sermon I heard there was preached in Rockville —a town-site on the Sauk, twelve miles from its confluence with the Mississippi—in a store-room of which the roof was not yet shingled. The only table in the town served as a pulpit; the red blankets from one wagon were converted into cushions for the front pews, which consisted of rough boards laid on trussles. There was only one hymn book, and after reading the hymn, the preacher tendered the book to any one who would lead the singing, but no one volunteered. My scruples about psalms seemed to vanish, so I went forward, took the book, lined out the hymn, and started a tune, which was readily taken up and sung by all present. We were well satisfied with what the day brought us, as we rode home past those wonderful granite rocks which spring up out of the prairie, looking like old hay-ricks in a meadow.

There were people in our frontier town who would have graced any society, and with the elasticity of true culture adapted themselves to all circumstances. At my residence, which adjoined the *Democrat* office, I held fortnightly receptions, at which dancing was the amusement, and coffee and sandwiches the refreshments. At one of these, I had the honor to entertain Gov. Ramsey, Lieut.-Gov. Donnelly, State Treas. Shaeffer, and a large delegation from St. Paul; but not having plates for seventy people, I substituted squares of white printing paper. When Gov. Ramsey received his, he turned it over, and said:

"What am I to do with this?"

"That is the ticket you are to vote," was the answer.

In our social life there was often a weird mingling of civilization and barbarism. Upon one occasion, a concert was given, in which the audience were in full dress, and all evening in the principal streets of St. Cloud a lot of Chippewas played foot-ball with the heads of some Sioux, with whom they had been at war that day.

In those days, brains and culture were found in shanties. The leaders of progress did not shrink from association with the rude forces of savages and mother nature.

St. Cloud was the advance post of that march of civilization by which the Northern Pacific railroad has since sought to reach the Sascatchewan, a territory yet to be made into five wheat-growing States as large as Illinois. All the Hudson Bay goods from Europe passed our doors, in wagons or on sleds, under the care of the Burbanks, the great mail carriers and express men of Minnesota, and once they brought a young lady who had come by express from Glasgow, Scotland, and been placed under the charge of their agent at New York, and whom they handed over to the officer she had come to marry on the shores of Hudson Bay. But their teams usually came east with little freight, as the furs sent to Europe came down in carts, not one of which had so much iron as a nail in them, and which came in long, creaking trains, drawn by oxen or Indian ponies.

In each train there was generally one gorgeous equipage—a cart painted blue, with a canvas cover, drawn by one large white ox in raw-hide harness In this coach of state rode the lady of the train—who was generally a half-breed—on her way to do her shopping in St. Paul.   Once the lady was a full-blooded Indian, and had her baby with her, neatly dressed and strapped to a board.   A bandage across the forehead held the head in place, and every portion of the body was as secure as board and bandages could make them, except the arms from the elbow down, but no danger of the little fellow sucking his thumb.   His lady mamma did not have to hold him, for he was stood up in a corner like a cane or umbrella, and seemed quite comfortable as well as content.   She had traveled seven weeks, had come seventeen hundred miles to purchase some dresses and trinkets, and would no doubt be a profitable customer to St. Paul merchants, for the lady of the train was a person of wealth and authority, always the wife of the commander-in-chief, and her sentence of death might have been fatal to any man in it.

In these trains were always found Indians filling positions as useful laborers, for the English government never gave premiums for idleness and vagabondism among Indians, by feeding and clothing them without effort on their own part.   Their dexterity in turning griddle cakes, by shaking the pan and giving it a jerk which sent the cake up into the air and brought it down square into the pan other side up, would have made Biddy's head whirl to see.

The "Gov. Ramsey" was the first steamboat which ran above the falls of St. Anthony, and in the spring of '59 she was steamed and hawsered up the Sauk Rapids, and ran two hundred miles, until the falls of Pokegamy offered insurmountable barriers to further progress. It was thought impossible to get her down again, there was no business for her, and she lay useless until, the next winter, Anson Northup took out her machinery and drew it across on sleds to the Red River of the North, where it was built into the first steamboat which ever ran on that river.

Before starting on his expedition, Mr. Northup came to the *Democrat* office to leave an advertisement and ask me to appeal to the public for aid in provisions and feed to be furnished along the route. He was in a Buffalo suit, from his ears to his feet, and looked like a bale of furs. On his head he wore a fox skin cap with the nose lying on the two paws of the animal just between his eyes, the tail hanging down between his shoulders. He was a brave, strong man, and carried out his project, which to most people was wild.

Nothing seemed more important than the cultivation of health for the people, and to this I gave much earnest attention, often expressed in the form of badinage. There were so many young houskeepers that there was much need of teachers. I tried to get the New England women to stop feeding their families on dough—especially hot soda dough—and to substitute well-baked bread as a steady article of diet. In trying to wean them from cake, I told of a time when chaos reigned on earth, long before the days of the

mastodons, but even then, New England women were
up making cake, and would certainly be found at that
business when the last trump sounded. But they bore
with my "crotchets" very patiently, and even seemed
to enjoy them.

CHAPTER XLIV.

PRINTERS.

THE printer's case used to be one of the highways to
editorial and congressional honors; but the little fellows of the craft invented a machine which goes over
it like a "header" over a wheat-field and leaves a dead
level of stalks, all minus the heads, so that no tall fellows are left to shame them by passing on from
the "stick" to the tripod or speaker's mallet. Their
great Union rolling-pin flattens them all out like pie-
crust, and tramps are not overshadowed by the superiority of industrious men. But the leveling process
makes impassable mountains and gorges in other walks
of life—makes it necessary that a publisher with one
hundred readers must pay as much for type-setting as
he with a hundred thousand. The salary of editors
and contributors may vary from nothing to ten thousand a year; but through all mutations of this life, the
printer's wages must remain in *statu quo*. So the
Union kills small papers, prevents competition in the
newspaper business, builds up monster establishments,
and keeps typos at the case forever and a day.

I knew when the *Visiter* started that it could not
live and pay for type-setting the same price as paid by
14

the New York *Tribune*, and the day the office became mine, I stated that fact to the printers, who took their hats and left. In '52, I had spent some part of every day for two weeks in a composing room, and with the knowledge then acquired, I, in '58 started the business of practical printer. I took a proof of my first stick, and lo, it read from right to left. I distributed that, but had to mark the stick that I might remember.

The first day I took two boys as apprentices. First, Wesley Miller, who had spent two months in a Harrisburg office, and knew something of the art, but did not like anything about it except working the press. Second, my nephew, William B. Mitchell, who was thirteen, knew nothing of types, but was a model of patient industry.

Our magnanimous printers hung around hotels, laughing at the absurdity of this amateur office. We might set type, but when it came to making and locking up a form, ha, ha, would n't there be sport? That handsome new type would all be a mess of pi, then somebody would be obliged to come to their terms or St. Cloud would be without a paper. It was their great opportunity to display their interest in the general welfare, and they embraced it to the full; but of the little I had learned in that short apprenticeship six years ago, I retained a clear conception of the principles of justification by works. I brought these to bear on those forms, made them up, locked them, and sent for Stephen Miller to carry them to the press, when each one lifted like a paving stone; but alas, alas, the columns read from right to left. I unlocked them, put the matter back in the galleys, made them up new, and we had the paper off on time.

From that time until the first of January, '63, I carried on the business of practical printer, issued a paper every week, did a large amount of job work, was city and county printer for half a dozen counties, did all the legal advertising, published the tax lists, and issued extras during the Indian massacres.

CHAPTER XLV.

THE REBELLION.

WHEN, after Mr. Lincoln's election, the South made the North understand that her threats of disunion meant something more than "tin kettle thunder," there was little spirit of compromise among the Republicans and Douglas Democrats of Minnesota, who generally looked with impatience on the abject servility with which Northern men in Congress begged their Southern masters not to leave them, with no slaves to catch, no peculiar institution to guard.

I was in favor of not only permitting the Southern States to leave the Union, but of driving them out of it as we would drive tramps out of a drawing room. *Put* them out! and open every avenue for the escape of their slaves. But from that spirit of conciliation with which the North first met secession, the change was sudden. The fire on Sumter lit an actual flame of freedom, and the people were ready then to wipe slavery from the whole face of the land. When Gen. Fremont issued his famous order confiscating the slaves of rebels in arms, I was in receipt of a large exchange list, and have never seen such unanimity on any sub-

ject. I think there were but two papers which offered
an objection; but this land was not worthy to do a
generous deed. So, President Lincoln rescinded that
order, and the great rushing stream of popular enthusiasm was dammed, turned back to flow into the dismal
swamp of constitutional quibbles and statutory inven-
tions. There it lay, and bred reptiles and miasmas
to sting and poison the guilty inhabitants of this great
land; and never since have we been permitted to reach
an enthusiasm in favor of any great principle; for
history has no record of a great act so thoroughly di-
vested of all greatness by the meanness of the motive,
as is our "Act of Emancipation."

Long after the war was in progress, the old habit
of yielding precedence to the South manifested itself
so strongly as to sour and disgust the staunchest Republicans. The only two important military appoint-
ments given by Mr. Lincoln's administration to St.
Cloud were given to two Southern Democrats, office-
holders under Buchanan and supporters of Breckin-
ridge, the Southern candidate for President in '60. In
the autumn of '61, I asked a farmer to take out and
post bills for a meeting to send delegates to the county convention. He had been an active worker in the
campaign of '60, had never sought an office, and I was
surprised when he declined so small a service, but his
explanation was this:

"If the Democrats win the election, the Democrats
will get the offices. If the Republicans win the election, the Democrats will get the offices, and I don't
see but we may as well let them win the election."

When I explained that the more false others were

to a party or principle, the more need there was for him to be true, he took the bills and managed the meeting; but running a Republican ticket under a Republican administration was not so easy as running the same ticket under Buchanan. Then men had hope and enthusiasm, but this was killed by a victory through which the enemy was made to triumph.

As Gov. Ramsey was the first to tender troops to President Lincoln for the suppression of the Rebellion, so the men of Minnesota were among the first to organize and drill. Stephen Miller raised a company in St. Cloud, with it joined the first regiment at Ft. Snelling, and was appointed Lieut. Col.

We went to Ft. Snelling to see our first regiment embark. It was a grand sight to see the men in red shirts and white Havelocks march down that rocky, winding way, going to their Southern graves, for very few of them ever returned.

More troops were called for, and two companies formed in St. Cloud. While they waited under marching orders, they and the citizens were aroused at two o'clock one morning by the cry from the east side of the river of, "Indians, Indians." A boat was sent over and brought a white-lipped messenger, with the news of the Sioux massacre at Ft. Ridgley.

CHAPTER XLVI.

MY first public speech was the revelation of a talent hidden in a napkin, and I set about putting it to usury. I wrote a lecture—"Women and Politics"—as a reason for my anomalous position and a justification of those men who had endorsed my right to be a political leader, and gave sketches of women in sacred and profane history who had been so endorsed by brave and wise men.

The lecture gave an account of the wrongs heaped upon women by slavery, as a reason why women were then called upon for special activity, and I never failed to "bring down the house" by describing the scene in which the tall Kentuckian proposed to the tall Pennsylvanian that he should horsewhip an old woman one hundred and two times, to compel her to earn two hundred dollars with which his mightiness might purchase Havana cigars, gold chains, etc., or to elicit signs of shame by relating the fact of the United States government proposing to withdraw diplomatic relations with Austria for whipping Hungarian women for political offenses, while woman-whipping was the principal industry of our American chivalry.

I stated that men had sought to divide this world into two fields—religion and politics. In the first, they were content that their mothers and wives should dwell with them, but in the second, no kid slipper was ever to be set. Horace Mann had warned women to stand back, saying: "Politics is a stygian pool." I insisted that politics had reached this condition through the permit given to Satan to turn all the waste water of his mills into that pool; that this grant must be rescinded and the pool drained at all hazards. Indeed the emergency was such that even women might handle shovels.

Chicago had once been in a swamp, but the City Fathers had lifted it six feet. Politicians must "raise the grade," must lift their politics the height of a man, and make them a habitation for men, not reptiles. At this an audience would burst into uproarous applause.

As for the grand division, no surveyor could find the line; for no line was possible between religion and politics. The attempt to divide them is an assumption that there is some part of the universe in which the Lord is not law-giver. The Fathers of the Republic had explored and found a country they thought was outside the Divine jurisdiction, and called it Politics. Because old world government had bowed to popes and prelates, they would ignore Deity, and say to Omnipotence what Canute did to the sea: " Thus far shalt thou go but no further, and here shall thy proud waves be stayed." But God laughed them to scorn, and would certainly dash them to pieces. The government which they had set up like the golden image of Nebuchadnezzer, and demanded that all should bow before it, this same government was bound to sustain men in scourging women for chastity. Every man who voted a democratic ticket voted to put down as insurrection any attempt to stand between the cradle and its robber.

I never spoke of the St. Cloud trouble—there was too much else to talk about. I was seldom interrupted by anything but applause; but in Stillwater I was hissed for denouncing Buchanan's administration. I waited a moment, then lowered my voice, and said I had raised a good many goslings, and thought I had left them all in Pennsylvania, but found some had followed me, and was sorry to have no corn for them. There was no further interruption.

I was at that time the guest of a son of my Pittsburg friend, Judge McMillan, who led the singing in our church, and with whom I expect to sing "St. Thomas" in heaven. My host of that evening afterwards became U. S. Senator from Minnesota.

A considerable portion of three winters I traveled in Minnesota and lectured, one day riding thirty miles in an open cutter when the mercury was frozen and the wind blew almost a gale. Have crossed houseless prairies between midnight and morning, with only a stage driver, and I never encountered a neglect or a rudeness; but found gentlemen in red flannel shirts and their trowsers stuffed into the tops of their boots, who had no knowledge of grammar, and who would, I think, have sold their lives dearly in my defense.

Late in '60 or early in '61, I lectured in Mantorville, and was the guest of Mr. Bancroft, editor of the *Express*, when he handed me a copy of the New York *Tribune*, pointed to an item, and turned away. It was a four line announcement that he who had been my husband had obtained a divorce on the ground of desertion. I laid down the paper, looked at my hands, and thought:

"Once more you are mine. True, the proceeds of your twenty years of brick-making are back there in

Egypt with your lost patrimony, but we are over the Red Sea, out in the free desert; no pursuit is possible, and if bread fails, God will send manna."

While I sat, Mrs. Bancroft came to me, caressed me, and said:

" Old things have passed away, and all things have become new."

CHAPTER XLVII.

OUT INTO THE WORLD AND HOME AGAIN.

IN my first lecturing winter I spoke in the Hall of Representatives, St. Paul, to a large audience, and succeeded past all my hopes. I spoke there again in the winter of '61 and '62, on the anti-slavery question, and in a public hall on " Woman's Legal Disabilities." Both were very successful, and I was invited to give the latter lecture before the Senate, which I did. The hall was packed and the lecture received with profound attention, interrupted by hearty applause.

The Senate was in session, and Gen. Lowrie occupied his seat as a member. It was a great fall for him to tumble from his dictatorship to so small an honor. He sat and looked at me like one in a dream, and I could not but see that he was breaking. I hoped he would come up with others when they began to crowd around me, but he did not.

I had come to be the looked-at of all lookers ; the talked-of of all talkers; was the guest of Geo. A. Nurse, the U. S. Attorney, dined with the Governor, and was praised by the press. I was dubbed the "Fanny Kemble of America," and reminded critics of the then greatest Shylock of the stage. A judge from Ohio said there was "not a man in the State who could have presented that case (Woman's Legal Disabilities) so well." Indeed, I was almost as popular as if I were about to be hanged!

A responsible Eastern lecture-agent offered me one hundred dollars each for three lectures, one in Milwaukee, one in Chicago and one in Cleveland. I wanted to accept, but was overruled by friends, who thought me too feeble to travel alone, and that I would make more by employing an agent. They selected a pious gentleman, whose name I have forgotten, and we left St. Paul at four o'clock one winter morning, in a prairie schooner on bob-sleds, to ride to La Crosse.

One of the passengers was a pompous Southerner, who kept boasting of the "buck niggers" he had sold and the "niggers" he had caught, and his delight in that sort of work. His talk was aimed at me, but he did not address me, and for hours I took no notice; then, after an unusual explosion, I said quietly:

"Can you remember, sir, just exactly how many niggers you have killed and eaten in your day?"

He looked out on the river and seemed to begin a calculation, but must have found the lists of his exploits too long for utterance, for he had spoken not another word when we reached La Crosse, where we took cars for Madison, Wisconsin.

We reached that beautiful city of lakes in time to meet news of the Ft. Donelson fatal victory; that victory made so much worse than a hundred defeats by the return to their masters of the slaves who remained in the fort and claimed the protection of our flag— the victory which converted the great loyal army of the North into a gang of slave-catchers. Alas, my native land! All hope for the preservation of the government died out in my heart. What could a just God want with such a people? What could he do but destroy them?

That victory was celebrated in Madison with appropriate ceremonies. Men got drunk and cursed "niggers and abolitionists," sat up all night in noisy orgies drinking health and success to him who was the synonym of American glory.

The excitement and sudden revulsion against abolitionists with the total incompetence of my agent, caused a financial failure of my lecture, but I made pleasant friendships with Gov. Harvey, Prof. Carr and their wives.

I started along the route we had come, and everywhere, in cars, hotels, men were hurrahing for Grant and cursing "niggers and abolitionists."

The hero had healed the breach between the loving brothers of the North and South, who were to rush into each others arms across the prostrate form of Liberty. Thank God for the madness of the South; for that sublime universal government which maketh "the wrath of man to praise him." Even in that hour of triumph for despotism, I did not doubt but Freedom would march on until no slave contaminated the earth; but before that march this degraded government must share the fate of that other Babylon, which once dealt "in slaves and souls of men."

My first small town lecture was another financial failure, and in the hall I paid and dismissed that highly respectable incubus—my agent.

That night I slept in a hotel, and going to a bed which had not been properly ventilated, wondered if it could be my duty to breast that storm of popular frenzy. Could I at any time be required to drink tea out of a coarse delf cup and sleep in such a bed? Luxuries I wanted none; but a china cup, silver spoon and soft blankets were necessaries of life. As I lay, uncertain always whether I slept, I seemed to sit on a projecting rock on the side of a precipice draped with poisonous vines. There was no spot on which I could place my feet, while out of holes, snakes hissed at me, and on ledges panthers glared at me with their green fiery eyes, and the tips of their tails wagging. Far below lay a lovely green valley, walled on both sides by these haunted precipitous banks, but stretching up and down until lost in vista. I knew that to the right was north—the direction of home; and to the left, south—the way out into the great unknown. If I could only reach that lovely valley and the clear stream which ran through it; but this was a vain longing, until there appeared in it a young man in a grey suit and soft broad-brimmed black felt hat. He came up the precipice toward me, and a way made itself before him, until he held up his hand, and said:

"Come down!"

I saw his face, and knew it was Christ. After seeing that face, all the conceptions of all the artists are an offense. Moreover, the Christ of to-day, in the person of his follower, has often come to me in the garb of a working man, but never in priestly robes. He led me down the precipice without a word, pointed northward and said:

" Walk in the valley and you will be safe."

He was gone, and I became conscious that I had been seeking popularity, money, and these were not for me; I must go home, but first I would try to repair the loss incurred by that agent. I lectured in a small town, a nucleus of a Seven Day Baptist settlement, and was the guest of the proprietor, who had built a great many concrete walls. Coming out into a heavy wind, I took acute inflammation of the lungs. My hostess gave me every attention; but I must go go home for my symptoms were alarming, so took the train the next morning, with my chest in wet compresses, a viol of aconite in my pocket, and was better when by rail and schooner I reached the house of the good Samaritan, Judge Wilson, of Winona.

Here I was made whole, lectured in Winona and other towns, and got back to St. Paul with more money than when I left. I started for home one morning in a schooner. At one the next morning our craft settled down and refused to go farther. The snow was three feet deep; it had been raining steadily for twelve hours, and when the men got out to pry out the runners, they went down, down, far over their knees. The driver and express agent were booted for such occasions, but the two Germans were not. Myself, " these four and no more, " were down in the book of fate for a struggle with inertia. It was muscle and mind against matter. To the muscle I contributed nothing, but might add something to the common stock of mind.

The agent and driver concluded that he should take a horse and go to the nearest house, two miles back, to get shovels to dig us out. I asked if there were fresh horses and men at the house.

"No."

"How far is it to St. Cloud?"

"Six miles."

"Are there fresh horses and men there?"

"Oh, plenty."

"If you dig us out here, how long will it be before we go in again?" This they did not know.

"Then had not the driver better go to St. Cloud with both horses? The horse left here would be ruined standing in that slush."

"But, madam," said the agent, "if we do that we will have to leave you here all night."

"Well," I said, "I do not see how you are going to get rid of me."

So the driver started with the two horses on that dreadful journey; had I known how dreadful, I should have tried to keep him till morning. As he left, I made the Germans draw off their boots and pour out the water, rub their chilled feet and roll them up in a buffalo robe. The agent lay on his box, I cuddled in a corner, and we all went to sleep to the music of the patter of the soft rain on our canvas cover. At sunrise we were waked by a little army of men and horses and another schooner, into which we passed by bridge. We reached St. Cloud in time for breakfast, and were greeted by the news that General Lowrie had been sent home insane. He was confined in his own house, and his much envied young wife, with her two babies, had become an object of pity.

CHAPTER XLVIII.

THE ARISTOCRACY OF THE WEST.

BEFORE going to Minnesota, I had the common Cooper idea of the dignity and glory of the noble red man of the forest; and was especially impressed by his unexampled faithfulness to those pale-faces who had ever been so fortunate as to eat salt with him. In planning my hermitage, I had pictured the most amicable relations with those unsophisticated children of nature, who should never want for salt while there was a spoonful in my barrel. I should win them to friendships as I had done railroad laborers, by caring for their sick children, and aiding their wives. Indeed, I think the Indians formed a large part of the attractions of my cabin by the lakes; and it required considerable time and experience to bring me to any true knowledge of the situation, which was, and is, this:

Between the Indian and white settler, rages the world-old, world-wide war of hereditary land-ownership against those who beg their brother man for leave to live and toil. William Penn disclaimed the right of conquest as a land title, while he himself held an English estate based on that title, and while every acre of land on the globe was held by it. He could not recognize that title in English hands, but did in the hands of Indians, and while pretending to purchase of them a conquest title, perpetrated one of the greatest swindles on record since that by which Jacob won the birthright of his starving brother.

This Penn swindle has been so carefully cloaked

that it has become the basis of our whole Indian policy, the legitimate parent of a system never equalled
on earth for crime committed with the best intentions.
It intends to be especially just, by holding that the
Creator made North America for the exclusive use of
savages, and that civilization can only exist here by
sufferance of the proprietors. This sufferance it tries
to purchase by engaging to support these proprietors
in absolute idleness, fro m the proceeds of the toil they
license, even as kings and other landed aristocrats are
supported by the labor of their subjects and tenants.

As the successors of the tent-maker of Tarsus have
for thirteen centuries been found on the side of aristocrats in every contest with plebians, so the piety of
the East, controlled by men who live without labor,
was and is on the side of the royal red man, who has
a most royal contempt for plows, hoes and all other
degrading implements.

The same community of interests which arrayed the
mass of the clergy on the side of Southern slaveholders,
arrayed that same clergy on the side of the Western slave
holder, and against the men who seek, with plows and
hoes, to get a living out of the ground. Under this ar-
rangment we have the spectacle of a Christian people
arrayed in open hostility to those who plant Christian
churches, schools and libraries on the lair of the wolf;
and in alliance with the savage who coolly unjoints the
feet and hands of little children, puts them in his hunting pouch as evidence of his valor, and leaves the victim to die at leisure; of those who thrust Christian
babies into ovens, and deliberately roast them to death;

of those who bind infants, two by two, by one wrist, and throw them across a fence to die; of those who collect little children in groups and lock them up in a room, to wail out their little lives; of those who commit outrages on innocent men and women which the pen must forever refuse to record. The apology with which piety converts the crimes of its pets into virtues, is that its own agents have failed to carry out its own contract with its own friends.

The men and women who take their lives in their hands to lead the westward march of civilization, are held as foes by the main body of the army, who conspire with the enemy, and hand them over as scapegoats whose tortures and death are to appease divine wrath for the crimes which this same main body say it has itself committed against Indians.

No one pretends that Western settlers have injured Indians, but Eastern philanthropists, through the government they control, have, according to their own showing, been guilty of no end of frauds; and as they do not, and cannot, stop the stealing, they pay their debts to the noble red man by licensing him to outrage women, torture infants and burn homes. When gold is scarce in the East, they substitute scalps and furnish Indians with scalping-knives by the thousand, that they may collect their dues at their own convenience.

This may seem to-day a bitter partisan accusation, but it must be the calm verdict of history when this comes to be written by impartial pens.

Under the pretense that America belonged, in fee simple, and by special divine right, to that particular

15

hoard of savages, who, by killing off some other hoard
of savages, were in possession when Columbus first
saw the Great West, the Eastern States, which had already secured their land by conquest, have become
more implacable foes to civilization than the savages
themselves.

The Quaker would form no alliance with Southern
slave-holders. He recoiled from the sale of women and
children in South Carolina, but covered with his gray
mantle of charity the slave trade in Minnesota.
When a settler refused to exchange his wife or daughter with an Indian for a pony, and that Indian massa-
cered the whole family to repair his wrongs, his Quaker lawyer justified the act on the score of extreme
provocation, and won triumphal acquittal from the jury
of the world.

When the Sioux, after the Bull Run disaster, arose
as the allies of the South, and butchered one thousand
men, women and children in Minnesota, the Quakers
and other good people flew to arms in their defense,
and carried public sentiment in their favor. The
agents of the Eastern people had delayed the payment
of annuity three weeks, and then insulted Mr. Lo by
tendering him one-half his money in government
bonds, and for this great wrong the peaceable Quaker,
the humanitarian Unitarian, the orthodox Congrega-
tionalist and Presbyterian, the enthusiastic Methodist
and staid Baptist, felt it but right Mr. Lo should have
his revenge.

Most Eastern Christians are opposed to polygamy
in Utah, and Fourierism in France, but in Minnesota
among Indians these institutions are sacred. They

demanded that England should by law prohibit wid-
ow-burning and other heathen customs in India, but
nothing so rude as statutes must interfere with the
royal privileges of these Western landlords. If by
gentle means Mr. Lo can be persuaded to stop taking all the wives he can get, extorting their labor
by the cudgel, and selling them and their children at
will, all well and good! Millions are expended on the
persuading business, and prayer poured out like the
rains in Noah's flood, without any perceptible effect; but still they keep on paying and praying, and
carefully abstain from all means at all likely to accomplish the desired result. All the property of
every tribe must be held in common, so that there
can possibly be no incentive to industry and economy; but if the Indian refuse to be civilized on that
plan, he must go on taking scalps and being excused,
until extermination solve the problem.

Long before I saw an Indian on his native soil, the
U. S. Government had spent millions in carrying out
this Penn policy. For long years, Indians had sat
like crows, watching the white farmers and artisans
sent to teach them industry, and had grunted their honest contempt. They watched the potato planting, that
they might pick out the seed for present use. They
pulled down fences, and turned their ponies into the
growing crops, used the rails for fire wood, burned
mills and houses built for them, rolled barrels of
flour up steep acclivities, started them down and
shouted to see them leap and the flour spurt through
the staves; knocked the heads out of other barrels,
and let the ponies eat the flour; poured bags of corn

on the ground when they wanted the bag, and in every way showed their contempt for the government, whose policy they believed to be the result of cowardice. Thousands of dollars' worth of agricultural machinery lay "rotting in the sun" while the noble red aristocrat played poker in the shade; his original contempt for labor intensified by his power to extract a living from laborers, through their fear of his scalping knife.

Hole-in-the-day, the Chippewa chief, had been educated by Baptist missionaries, and was a good English scholar, but would not condescend to speak to the government except through an interpreter. For him six hundred acres of land had been fenced, and a large frame cottage built and painted white. In this he lived with six wives, and a United States salary of two thousand a year and his traveling expenses. He dressed like a white man, dined with State officers in St. Paul, went to church with a lady on his arm, sat in a front pew, and was a highly distinguished gentleman of the scalping school.

CHAPTER XLIX.

THE INDIAN MASSACRE OF '62.

The Indians had been ugly from the first outbreak of the Rebellion, and Commissioner Dole, with Senator Wilkinson, had come out to pacify them. The party passed through St. Cloud, and had camped several miles west, when in the night there came up one of those sudden storms peculiar to this land. Their tents were whisked away like autumn leaves, and they left clinging to such productions of mother nature as were at hand, well rooted in her bosom, to avoid a witches' dance in the air.   But it grew worse when the rain had covered the level ground six inches deep in water, and they must keep their heads above the surface.

They returned to St. Cloud in the morning in sorry plight, and the delay was one of the injuries to the poor Indians, and counted as sufficient justification for the subsequent massacre.· The delay, however, saved their lives.   The messenger who aroused the people of St. Cloud in the small hours was traveling post after this Dole commission, for whose safety there was much anxiety, but none for St. Cloud, since the Indians would not attack us while there were two companies of soldiers in town.   True, they were unarmed, but surely arms would be sent and their marching orders rescinded.   The outbreak was mysterious.   It was of course in the interests of the South, and meant to prevent the troops leaving the State; but why had not the tribes struck together?

The answer was that after the massacre had been arranged in council, two Sioux visited a white family in which they had often been entertained, were drunk, and could not resist the impulse to butcher their entertainers.   This precipitated the attack, for so soon as the news reached the tribe, they went to work to execute their bloody purpose.

Johnson, a converted Chippewa, hurried to inform us that his tribe with Hole-in-the-day in council had resolved to join the Sioux and were to have made St. Cloud their base of operations, but the Sioux had broken out before the arms and ammunition came, and these they were hourly expecting. On the same day a formal message came from Hole-in-the-day that Commissioner Dole must come to the reservation to confer with his young braves, who would await his arrival ten days, after which time their great chief declined to be responsible for them.

A runner arrived from Ft. Abercrombie, who'had escaped by crawling through the grass, and reported the Fort besieged by a thousand savages, and quite unprepared for defense. There were several St. Cloud people in the Fort, and so far from expecting aid from it it must be relieved. The garrison at Ft. Ripley had not a man to spare for outside defense. People began to pour into St. Cloud with tales of horror to freeze the blood, and the worst reports were more than confirmed. The victorious Sioux had undisputed possession of the whole country west, southwest and northwest of us, up to within twelve miles of the city, and had left few people to tell tales. Our troops spent their time teaching women and children the use of fire-arms, and hoping for arms and orders to go to the relief of Abercrombie. There was no telegraph, and the last mail left no alternative but to start for Fort Snelling, with such short time to get there that every available man and horse must go to hurry them forward. They left in the afternoon, and that was a dreadful night. Many of the more timid women had gone east, but of those that remained some paced the streets, wringing their hands and sobbing out their fear and despair and sorrow for the husbands and brothers and sons taken from them at such a crisis.

When the troops left, we thought there were no more

men in St. Cloud, but next morning found a dozen, counting the boys, who were organized to go out west to the rescue of settlers, and still there were some guards and pickets, and some who did nothing but find fault with everything any one else did.

Men and women spoke with stiffened lips and blanched faces. Families in the outskirts gathered to more central places, and there were forty-two women and children in my house the night after the troops left, and for every night for weeks. We kept large kettles of boiling water as one means of defense. I always had the watchword, and often at midnight I would go out to see that the pickets were on duty, and report to the women that all was well. Brother Harry was appointed General of State troops, succeeding Gen. Lowrie, and arms were sent to him for distribution, while women kept muskets by them and practiced daily. The office of my democratic contemporary was closed, and he fled to New England, while his assistant went with my only male assistant to rescue settlers. I had two young ladies in the office, one a graduate of a New York high school, and through all the excitement they kept at work as coolly as at any other time. We got out the paper regularly, and published many extras.

The history of the horrors and heroisms which reached us during the six weeks in which Ft. Abercrombie held out until relief came, would make a volume, and cannot be written here. The unimaginable tortures and indecencies inflicted on brave men and good women, are something for which the Christian supporters and excusers of the Sioux must yet account

at the bar where sentimental sympathy with crimi-
nals is itself a crime; and where the wail of tortured
infants will not be hushed by reckoning of bad beef
and a deficiency in beans.

While the Sioux sat in council to determine that
butchery, some objected, on the ground that such crimes
would be punished, but Little Crow, leader of the war
party, quieted their fears by saying:

"White man no like Indian! Indian catch white
man, roast him, kill-him! White man catch Indian,
feed him, give him blankets," and on this assurance
they acted.

One thing was clearly proven by that outbreak, viz.:
that services to, and friendship for, Indians, are the
best means of incurring their revenge. Those families who had been on most intimate terms with them,
were those who were massacred first and with the
greatest atrocities. The more frequently they had
eaten salt with a pale-face, the more insatiable was
their desire for vengeance. The missionaries were
generally spared, as the source through which they expected pardon and supplies. The Indian was much
too cunning to kill the goose that laid the golden egg.
The tribe do not object to the conversion of individuals. Saying prayers does not interfere with their
ideas of their own importance. Preachers do not
labor with their hands, and Indians can join the clerical order or get religion, without losing caste, for labor to them is pollution.

Two wagon loads of arms and ammunition *en route* for
Hole-in-the-day, were intercepted during the massacre,
and for want of them he was induced to keep quiet.

For being such a good Indian, he had a triumphal trip to Washington at government expense, got ten thousand dollars, and a seventh wife.

CHAPTER L.

A MISSIVE AND A MISSION.

SOON after the people had returned to such homes as were left them, I received a letter from General Lowrie, who was then in an insane asylum in Cincinnati. I caught his humor and answered as carefully as if he had been a sick brother, gave an extract in the *Democrat*, accompanied by a notice, and sent him a copy; after which he wrote frequently, and I tried earnestly to soothe him. In one of his letters was this passage:

"Your quarrel and mine was all wrong. There was no one in that upper country capable of understanding you but me, no one capable of understanding me, but you. We should have been friends, and would have been, if we had not each had a self which we were all too anxious to defend."

After the Sioux had finished their work of horror, Minnesota men, aided by volunteers from Iowa and Wisconsin, pursued and captured the murderers of one thousand men, women and children; tried them, found them guilty, and proposed to hang them just as if they had been white murderers. But when the general government interfered and took the prisoners out of the hands of the State authorities, and when it became evident that Eastern people endorsed the massacre and condemmed the victims as sinners who deserved their fate, one of the State officers proposed that I should go East, try to counteract the vicious public sentiment, and aid our Congressional delegation in their effort to induce the Administration either to hang the Sioux murderers, or hold them as hostages during the war.

To me this was a providential call, for I had been planning to make a home in the East, that our daughter, then old enough to live without me, might spend a portion of her time with her father.

With letters from all our State officers, I left my Minnesota home at four o'clock A. M., January 2nd, '63, leaving the *Democrat* in charge of my first apprentice, William B. Mitchell.

In Washington, the Minnesota delegation secured the use of Dr. Sutherland's church, and a packed audience for my lecture on Indians. It was enthusiastically applauded, and for a time I did hope for some security for women and children on the frontier; but the Secretary of the Interior assured me it was not worth while to see the President, for "Mr. Lincoln will hang nobody!" and our Minnesota delegation agreed with him. Indeed, there was such a *furor* of pious pity for the poor injured Sioux, such admiration for their long suffering patience under wrong, and final heroic resistance, that I might about as well have tried to row myself from the head of Goat Island up the rapids of Niagara, as stem that current. The ring which makes money by caudling Indians, had the ear of both President and people, and the Bureau had a paying contract in proving Little Crow's sagacity. The Sioux never were so well supplied with blankets and butcher-knives, as when they received their reward for that massacre; never had so many prayers said and hymns sung over them, and their steamboat ride down the Minnesota and Mississippi and up the Missouri, to a point within two days' walk of the scene of their exploits, furnished them an excursion of about two thousand miles, and left them well prepared for future operations.   They appreciated their good fortune, have been a terror to United States troops and Western settlers ever since, and have enjoyed their triumph to the full.

One morning Senator Wilkinson and I went to see the President, and in the vestibule of the White House met two gentlemen whom he introduced as Sec. Stanton and Gen. Fremont.   The first said he needed no introduction, and I said I had asked Senator Wilkinson to see him on my account.   He replied:

"Do not ask any one to see me!   If you want anything from me, come yourself.   No one can have more influence."

Gen. Fremont inquired where I was staying, and said he would call on me.   This frightened me, and I felt like running away.   But they were so kind and cordial that our short chat is a pleasant memory; but Mr. Wilkinson and I failed to see Mr. Lincoln.   Next day Sec. Stanton gave me an appointment in the Quarter Master General's office, but there was no place for me to go to work.

Gen. Fremont called at the houses of two friends where I was visiting, but both times I was absent. In 1850 I had also missed the calls of his wife and sister, and so I seemed destined never to meet the people I admired above all others.

My friends wished me to attend a Presidential reception; but it was useless to see Mr. Lincoln on the business which brought me to Washington, and I did not care to see him on any other. He had proved an obstructionist instead of an abolitionist, and I felt no respect for him; while his wife was every where spoken of as a Southern woman with Southern sympathies—a conspirator against the Union. I wanted nothing to do with the occupants of the White House, but was told I could go and see the spectacle without being presented. So I went in my broadcloth traveling dress, and lest there should be trouble about my early leave-taking, would not trust my cloak to the servants, but walked through the hall with it over my arm. I watched the President and Mrs. Lincoln receive. His sad, earnest, honest face was irresistible in its plea for confidence, and Mrs. Lincoln's manner was so simple and motherly, so unlike that of all Southern women I had seen, that I doubted the tales I had heard. Her head was not that of a conspirator. She would be incapable of a successful deceit, and whatever her purposes were, they must be known to all who knew her.

Mr. Lincoln stood going through one of those, dreadful ordeals of hand-shaking, working like a man pumping for life on a sinking vessel, and I was filled with indignation for the selfish people who made this useless drain on his nervous force. I wanted to stand between him and them, and say, "stand back, and let him live and do his work." But I could not resist going to him with the rest of the crowd, and when he took my hand I said:

"May the Lord have mercy on you, poor man, for the people have none."

He laughed heartily, and the men around him, joined in his merriment. When I came to Mrs. Lincoln, she did not catch the name at first, and asked to hear it again, then repeated it, and a sudden glow of pleasure lit her face, as she held out her hand and said how very glad she was to see me. I objected to giving her my hand because my black glove would soil her white one; but she said:

"Then I shall preserve the glove to remember a great pleasure, for I have long wished to see you."

My escort was more surprised than I by her unusual cordiality, and said afterwards:

"It was no polite affectation. I cannot understand it from her."

I understood at once that I had met one with whom I was in sympathy. No politeness could have summoned that sudden flash of pleasure. Her manner was too simple and natural to have any art in it; and why should she have pretended a friendship she did not feel? Abolitionists were at a discount. They had gone like the front ranks of the French cavalry at Waterloo, into the sunken way, to make a bridge, over which moderate men were rushing to honors and emoluments. Gideon's army had done its work, and given place to the camp followers, who gathered up the spoils of victory. None were so poor that they need do them reverence, and I recognized Mrs. Lincoln as a loyal, liberty-loving woman, more staunch even than her husband in opposition to the Rebellion and its cause, and as my very dear friend for life.

CHAPTER LI.

NO USE FOR ME AMONG THE WOUNDED.

I HAD not thought, even after deciding to remain in Washington, of doing any hospital work—knew nothing about it; and in strength was more like a patient than a nurse; but while I waited for a summons to go to the duties of my clerkship, I met some ladies interested in hospitals.

One of these, Mrs. Thayer, had an ambulance at her command, and took me for a day's visiting among the forts, on a day when it was known that our armies in Virginia were engaged with the enemy. The roads were almost impassable, and as a skillful driver and two good horses used their best efforts to take us from place to place, I felt like a thief; that ambulance ought to be at the front, and us with it, or on our knees pleading for the men whose breasts were a living wall between us and danger, between Liberty and her deadly foes.

The men in the forts had no special need of us, and sometimes their thanks for the tracts we brought them, gave an impulse to strike them square in the face, but Mrs. Thayer was happy in her work, and thought me uncivil to her friends.

We reached the last fort on our round before I saw anything interesting; and here a sorrowful woman drew me aside to tell me of the two weeks she had spent with her husband, now in the last stage of camp-fever, and of her fruitless efforts to get sufficient straw for his bed, while the bones were cutting through the

skin as he lay on the slats of his cot. She wrung her
hands in a strange, suppressed agony, and exclaimed
" Oh! If they had only let me take him home when I
came first; but say nothing here, or they will not let
me stay."

I verified her statement of her husband's condition,
so that I could speak from observation without com-
promising her, and spoke to the surgeon, who politely
regretted the scarcity of straw, and hoped to get some
soon.

I returned to the sufferer, who was from New Hamp-
shire, and a very intelligent man; and after talking
with him and his wife, concluded to look up the commander of that fort, and put some powder and a lighted match into his ear; but first consulted Mrs. Thayer,
who begged me to take no notice, else she would no
longer be permitted to visit the fort. She had introduced me to two fashionably dressed ladies, officers'
wifes, resident there; and when I must say or do
nothing about this man, lest I should destroy Mrs.
Thayer's opportunity for doing good, I concluded we
had discovered a new variety of savage, and came away
thinking I could do something in the city.

Next morning I stated the case to Miss Dix, who
was neither shocked nor surprised. I had never before
seen her, but her tall, angular person, very red face,
and totally unsympathetic manner, chilled me. The
best ambulance in the service was exclusively devoted
to her use, and I thought she would surely go or send
a bed to that man before noon; but she proposed to
do nothing of the kind, had engagements for the day,
which seemed to me of small import compared to that

of placing that man on a comfortable bed; but she could do nothing that day, by reason of these engagements, and nothing next day, it being Sunday, on which day she attended to no business. We spoke of the great battle then in progress, and I tendered my services, could take no regular appointment, would want no pay, could not work long; but might be of use in an emergency! Emergencies were things of which she had no conception. Everything in her world moved by rule, and her arrangements were complete. She had sent eight nurses to the front, and more could only be in the way,

I inquired about hospital supplies, and she grew almost enthusiastic in explaining the uselessness, nay, absurdity, of sending any. Government furnished everything that could possibly be wanted. The Sanitary and Christian Commissions were all a mistake; Soldiers' Aid Societies a delusion and a snare. She was burdened with stores sent to her for which there was no use; and she hoped I would use my influence to stop the business of sending supplies.

From her I went direct to the Sanitary Commission, and found a large house full of salaried clerks and porters, and boxes, and bales, although this was not their storehouse.

Here again I stated the case of the man without a bed, and found listeners neither surprised nor shocked. Every one seemed quite familiar with trifles of that nature, and by and by, I, too, would look upon them with indifference.

I do not remember whether it was Saturday engagements, or Sunday sanctity, or lack of jurisdiction, which barred the Commission from interference; but think they must wait until the fort surgeon sent a requisition.

I inquired here about hospital stores, and found there was great demand for everything, especially money. They declined my services in every capacity save that of inducing the public to hurry forward funds and supplies. I told them of Miss Dix's opinion on that subject, and they agreed that it was quite useless to send anything to her, since she used nothing she received, and would not permit any one else to use stores.

Late in the next week Mrs. Thayer came, in great tribulation, to know how I ever could have done so foolish and useless a thing as report that case to Miss Dix! Oh dear! Oh dear! It was so unwise!

Miss Dix had gone to the fort on Monday, taken the surgeon to task about that bed, gave me as her authority, and for me Mrs. Thayer was responsible, and would be excluded from that fort on account of my indiscretion. There was another standing quarrel between the directress of nurses and the surgeons. The bitterness engendered would all be visited upon the patients, and it was so deplorable to think I had been so imprudent.

Her distress was so real, and she was so real in her desire to do good, that I felt myself quite a culprit, especially as the man got no bed, and died on his slats.

I was so lectured and warned about the sin of this, my first offense, in telling that which " folk wad secret keep" in hospital management, that I was afraid to

16

go to another, lest I should get some one into trouble; so stayed at home while the Washington hospitals were being filled with wounded from the battle of Chancellorville. I think it was the afternoon of the second Sabbath that I went with Mrs. Kelsey to visit Campbell, to get material for a letter, and tendered my services, but their arrangements were complete. Passing through the wards it did indeed seem as if nothing was wanting.

As a matter of form, I asked James Bride, of Wisconsin, if there was anything I could do for him, was surprised to see him hesitate, and astounded to have him answer:

" Well, nothing particular, unless—" he stopped and picked at the coverlid—" unless you could get us something to quench thirst."

"Something to quench thirst? Why, I have been told you have everything you can possibly require!"

" Well, they are very good to us, and do all they can; but it gets very hot in here in the afternoons, we cannot go out into the shade, and get so thirsty. Drinking so much water makes us sick, and if we had something a little sour!"

" But, would they let me bring you anything?"

" O yes! I see ladies bring things every day."

"Then I shall be glad to bring you something tomorrow."

CHAPTER LII.

FIND WORK.

THAT evening I wrote to the New York *Tribune*, relating the incident of the man asking for cooling drinks, and saying that if people furnished the material, I would devote my time to distributing their gifts. Next morning I got two dozen lemons, pressed the juice into a jar, put in sugar, took a glass and spoon and, so soon as visitors were admitted, began giving lemonade to those men who seemed to have most need. Going to the water tank for every glass of water made it slow work, but I improved my walks by talking to the men, hearing their wants and adding to their stock of hope and cheerfulness, and was glad to see that the nurses did not seem to object to my presence, even though Campbell was the one only hospital in the city from which female nurses were rigorously excluded.

So noted had it become for the masculine pride of its management, that I had been warned not to stay past the length of an ordinary visit, lest I should be roughly told to go away; and my surprise was equal to my pleasure, when a man came and said:

"Would it not be easier for you if you had a pitcher?"

I said it would, but that I lived too far away to bring one.

"Oh! I will bring you a pitcher! Why did you not ask for one?"

"I did not want to trouble you, for they told me you did not like to have women here."

He laughed, and said: "I guess we'll all be glad enough to have you! Not many of your sort. First thing they all do is to begin to make trouble, and it always takes two men to wait on one of them."

He brought the pitcher, and I felt that I was getting on in the world. Still I was very humble and careful to win the favor of " the King's Chamberlain "—those potencies, the nurses, who might report me to that Royal woman-hater, Dr. Baxter, surgeon in charge, whose name was a terror to women who intruded themselves into military hospitals.

As I passed, with my pitcher, I saw one man delerious, and expectorating, profusely, a matter green as grass could be—knew this was hospital gangrene, and remembered all Dr. Palmer had told me years before, of his experience in Paris hospitals, and the antidotes to that and scurvey poison. Indeed, the results of many conversations with first-class physicians, and of some reading on the subject of camp diseases, came to me; and I knew just what was wanted here, but saw no sign that the want was likely to be supplied. For this man it was too late, but I could not see that anything was being done to prevent the spread of this fearful scourge.

Passing from that ward into the one adjoining, I came suddenly upon two nurses dressing a thigh stump, while the patient filled the air with half-suppressed shrieks and groans. I had never before seen a stump, but remembered Dr. Jackson's lecture over the watermellon at desert, on amputation, for the benefit of Charles Sumner; and electricity never brought light quicker than there came to me the memory of all he had said about the proper arrangement of the muscles over the end of the bone; and added to this, came a perfect knowledge of the relations of those mangled muscles to the general form of the body. I saw that the nurse who held the stump tortured the man by disregarding natural law, and setting down pitcher and glass on the floor, I stepped up, knelt, slipped my hands under the remains of that strong thigh, and said to the man who held it:

"Now, slip out your hands! easy! easy! there!"

The instant it rested on my hands the groans ceased, and I said:

"Is that better?"

"Oh, my God! yes!"

"Well, then, I will always hold it when it is dressed!"

"But you will not be here!"

"I will come!"

"That would be too much trouble!"

"I have nothing else to do, and will think it no trouble!"

The nurse, who did the dressing, was very gentle, and there was no more pain; but I saw that the other leg was amputated below the knee, and this was a double reason why he should be tenderly cared for. So I took the nurse aside, and asked when the wounds were to be dressed again. He said in the morning, and promised to wait until I came to help. Next morning I was so much afraid of being late that I would not wait for the street cars to begin running, but walked. The guard objected to admitting me, as it was not time for visitors, but I explained and he let me pass.

I must not go through the wards at that hour, so went around and came in by the door near which he lay. What was my surprise to find that not only were his wounds dressed, but that all his clothing and bed had been changed, and everything about him made as white and neat and square as if he were a corpse, which he more resembled than a living man. Oh, what a tribute of agony he had paid to the demon of appearance! We all pay heavy taxes to other people's eyes; but on none is the levy quite so onerous as on the patients of a model hospital! I saw that he breathed and slept, and knew his time was short; but sought the head nurse, and asked why he had not waited for me; he hesitated, stammered, blushed and said:

"Why, the fact is, sister, he has another wound that it would not be pleasant for you to see."

"Do you mean that that man has a groin wound in addition to all else?"

"Yes, sister! yes! and I thought—"

"No matter what you thought, you have tortured him to save your mock-modesty and mine. You could have dressed that other wound, covered him, and let me hold the stump. You saw what relief it gave him yesterday. How could you—how dare you torture him?"

"Well, sister, I have been in hospitals with sisters a great deal, and they never help to dress wounds. I thought you would not get leave to come. Would not like to."

"I am not a sister, I am a mother; and that man had suffered enough. Oh, how dared you? how dared you to do such a thing?"

I wrung my hands, and he trembled like a leaf, and said.

"It was wrong, but I did not know. I never saw a sister before—"

"I tell you I am no sister, and I cannot think whatever your sisters are good for."

He promised to let me help him whenever it would save pain, and I returned to the dying man. The sun shone and birds sang. He stirred, opened his eyes, smiled to see me, and said.

"It is a lovely morning, and I will soon be gone."

I said, "Yes; the winter of your life is past; for you the reign of sorrow is over and gone; the spring time appears on the earth, and the time for the singing of birds has come; your immortal summer is close at hand; Christ, who loveth us, and has suffered for us, has prepared mansions of rest, for those who love him, and you are going soon."

"Oh, yes; I know he will take me home, and provide for my wife and children when I am gone."

"Then all is well with you!" He told me his name and residence, in Pittsburg, and I remembered that his parents lived our near neighbors when I was a child. So, more than ever, I regretted that I could not have made his passage through the dark valley one of less pain; but it was a comfort to his wife to know I had been with him.

When he slept again, I got a slightly wounded man to sit by him and keep away the flies, while I went to distribute some delicacies brought to him by visitors, and which he would never need.

At the door of Ward Three, a large man stood, and

seemed to be an officer. I asked him if there were
any patients in that ward who would need wine penado.
He looked down at me, pleasantly, and said:

"I think it very likely, madam, for it is a very bad
ward."

It was indeed a very bad ward, for a settled gloom
lay upon the faces of the occupants, who suffered because the ward-master and entire set of nurses had re-
cently been discharged, and new, incompetent men
appointed in their places.

As I passed down, turning from right to left, to give
to such men as needed it the mild stimulant I had
brought, I saw how sad and hopeless they were; only
one man seemed inclined to talk, and he sat near the
centre of the ward, while some one dressed his shoulder from which the arm had been carried away by a
cannon ball. A group of men stood around him, talking of that strange amputation, and he was full of
chat and cheerfulness.

They called him Charlie; but my attention was
quickly drawn to a young man, on a cot, close by,
who was suffering torture from the awkwardness of a
nurse who was dressing a large, flesh-wound on the
outside of his right thigh.

I set my bowl on the floor, caught the nurse's wrist,
lifted his hand away, and said:

"Oh, stop! you are hurting that man! Let me do
that!"

He replied, pleasantly,

"I'll be very glad to, for I'm a green hand!"

I took his place; saw the wounded flesh creep at the
touch of cold water, and said:

"Cold water hurts you!"

"Yes ma'am, a little!"

"Then we must have some warm!" But nurse said there was none.

"No warm water?" I exclaimed, as I drew back and looked at him, in blank astonishment.

"No, ma'am! there's no warm water!"

"How many wounded men have you in this hospital?"

"Well, about seven hundred, I believe."

"About seven hundred wounded men, and no warm water! So none of them get anything to eat!"

"Oh, yes! they get plenty to eat."

"And how do you cook without warm water?"

"Why, there's plenty of hot water in the kitchen, but we're not allowed to go there, and we have none in the wards."

"Where is the kitchen?"

He directed me. I covered the wound—told the patient to wait and I would get warm water. In the kitchen a dozen cooks stopped to stare at me, but one gave me what I came for, and on returning to the ward I said to Charlie:

"Now you can have some warm water, if you want it."

"But I do not want it! I like cold water best!"

"Then it is best for you, but it is not best for this man!"

I had never before seen any such wound as the one I was dressing, but I could think of but one way— clean it thoroughly, put on clean lint and rags and bandages, without hurting the patient, and this was very easy to do; but while I did this, I wanted to do something more, viz.: dispel the gloom which hung over that ward. I knew that sick folks should have their minds occupied by pleasant thoughts, and never addressed an audience with more care than I talked to that one man, in appearance, while really talking to all those who lay before me and some to whom my back was turned.

I could modulate my voice so as to be heard at quite a distance, and yet cause no jar to very sensitive nerves close at hand; and when I told my patient that I proposed to punish him now, while he was in my power, all heard and wondered; then every one was stimulated to learn that it was to keep him humble, because, having received such a wound in the charge on Marie's Hill, he would be so proud by and by that common folks would be afraid to speak to him. I should be quite thrown into the shade by his laurels, and should probably take my revenge in advance by sticking pins in him now, when he could not help himself.

This idea proved to be quite amusing, and before I had secured that bandage, the men seemed to have forgotten their wounds, except as a source of future pride, and were firing jokes at each other as rapidly as they had done bullets at the enemy. When, therefore, I proposed sticking pins into any one else who desired such punishment, there was quite a demand for my services, and with my basin of tepid water I started to wet the hard, dry dressings, and leave them to soften before being removed. Before night I discovered that lint is an instrument of incalculable torture, and should never be used, as either blood or pus quickly converts some portion of it into splints, as irritating as a pine shaving.

CHAPTER LIII.

HOSPITAL GANGRENE.

About nine o'clock I returned to the man I had come to help, and found that he still slept. I hoped he might rouse and have some further message for his wife, before death had finished his work, and so remained with him, although I was much needed in the "very bad ward."

I had sat by him but a few moments when I noticed a green shade on his face. It darkened, and his breathing grew labored—then ceased. I think it was not more than twenty minutes from the time I observed the green tinge until he was gone. I called the nurse, who brought the large man I had seen at the door of the bad ward, and now I knew he was a surgeon, knew also, by the sudden shadow on his face when he saw the corpse, that he was alarmed; and when he had given minute directions for the removal of the bed and its contents, the washing of the floor and sprinkling with chloride of lime, I went close to his side, and said in a low voice:

"Doctor, is not this hospital gangrene?"

He looked down at me, seemed to take my measure, and answered:

"I am very sorry to say, madam, that it is."

"Then you want lemons!"

"We would be glad to have them!"

"Glad to have them?" I repeated, in profound astonishment, "why, you *must* have them!"

He seemed surprised at my earnestness, and set about explaining:

"We sent to the Sanitary Commission last week, and got half a box."

"Sanitary Commission, and half a box of lemons? How many wounded have you?"

"Seven hundred and fifty."

"Seven hundred and fifty wounded men! Hospital gangrene, and half a box of lemons!"

"Well, that was all we could get; Government provides none; but our Chaplain is from Boston—his wife has written to friends there and expects a box next week!"

"To Boston for a box of lemons!"

I went to the head nurse whom I had scolded in the morning, who now gave me writing materials, and I wrote a short note to the *New York Tribune* :

"Hospital gangrene has broken out in Washington, and we want lemons! *lemons!* LEMONS! LEMONS! No man or woman in health, has a right to a glass of lemonade until these men have all they need; send us lemons!"

I signed my name and mailed it immediately, and it appeared next morning. That day Schuyler Colfax sent a box to my lodgings, and five dollars in a note, bidding me send to him if more were wanting; but that day lemons began to pour into Washington, and soon, I think, into every hospital in the land. Gov. Andrews sent two hundred boxes to the Surgeon General. I received so many, that at one time there were twenty ladies, several of them with ambulances, distributing those which came to my address, and if there was any more hospital gangrene that season I neither saw nor heard of it.

The officers in Campbell knew of the letter, and were glad of the supplies it brought, but some time passed before they identified the writer as the little sister in the bad ward, who had won the reputation of being the " best wound-dresser in Washington."

CHAPTER LIV.

GET PERMISSION TO WORK.

RULES required me to leave Campbell at five o'clock, but the sun was going down, and I lay on a cot, in the bad ward, feeling that going home, or anywhere else, was impossible, when that large doctor came, felt my pulse, laid his hand on my brow, and said:

" You must not work so hard or we will lose you! I have been hunting for you to ask if you would like to remain with us?"

" Like to remain with you? Well, you will have to send a file of soldiers with fixed bayonets to drive me away."

He laughed quite heartily, and said:

" We do not want you to go away. I am executive officer Surgeon Kelley; and Dr. Baxter, surgeon in charge, has commissioned me to say that if you wish to stay, he will have a room prepared for you. He hunted for you to say so in person, but is gone; now I await your decision. Shall I order you a room?"

"Surgeon Baxter! Why—what does he know about me?"

"Oh, Surgeon Baxter, two medical inspectors, and the surgeon of this ward were present this morning when you came in and took possession."

His black eyes twinkled, and he shook with laughter when I sat up, clasped my hands, and said:

"Oh, dear? Were they the men who were standing around Charlie? Why I had not dreamed of their being surgeons!"

"Did you not know by their shoulderstraps?"

"Shoulderstraps? Do surgeons have shoulderstraps? I thought only officers wore them!"

"Well, surgeons are officers, and you can know by my shoulderstraps that I am a surgeon."

"Oh, I do not mind you; but Dr. Baxter! How I did behave before him! What must he have thought? And he does not allow women to come here!"

"Well. You passed inspection; and as you propose to stay with us, I will have a room prepared for you."

He then went on to state that the reason Doctor Baxter would not have female nurses, was that he would not submit to Miss Dix's interference, did not like the women she chose, and army regulations did not permit him to employ any other.

"But," he continued, "no one can object to his entertaining a guest, and as his guest you can employ your time as you wish."

Ah! what a glorious boon it was, this privilege of work, and my little barrack-room, just twice the width of my iron cot, I would not have exchanged for any suite in Windsor palace.

CHAPTER LV.

FIND A NAME.

Nothing was more needed in the bad ward, than an antidote for homesickness, and, to furnish this, I used my talking talent to the utmost, but no subject was so interesting as myself. I was the mystery of the hour. Charlie was commissioned to make discoveries, and the second day came, with a long face, and said:

"Do you know what they say about you?"

"No indeed! and suspect I should never guess."

"Well, they say you're an old maid!"

I stopped work, rose from my knees, confronted him and exclaimed, with an injured air:

"An old maid! Why Charlie! is it possible you let them talk in that manner about me, after the nice pickles I gave you?"

The pickles had made him sick, and now there was a general laugh at his expense, but he stuck to his purpose and said:

"Well, ain't you an old maid?"

"An old maid, Charlie? Did any one ever see such a saucy boy?"

"Oh, but tell us, good earnest, ain't you an old maid?"

"Well then, good earnest, Charlie, I expect I shall be one, if I live to be old enough."

"Live to be old enough! How old do you call yourself?"

I set down my basin, counted on my fingers, thought it over and replied:

"Well, if I live two months and five days longer, I shall be sixteen."

Then there was a shout at Charlie's expense, and I resumed my work, grave as an owl. That furnished amusement until it grew stale, when Charlie came to ask me my name, and I told him it was Mrs. Snooks.

"Mrs. Snooks?" repeated a dozen men, who looked sadly disappointed, and Charlie most of all, as I added:

"Yes; Mrs. Timothy Snooks, of Snooksville, Minnesota."

This was worse and worse. It was evident no one liked the name, but all, save one, were too polite to say so, and he roared out:

"I don't believe a word of it!"

I sat at some distance with my back to him, dressing a wound ; and, without turning, said,

"Why? What is the matter with you?"

"I don't believe that such a looking woman as you are ever married a fellow by the name of Snooks:"

"That is because you are not acquainted with the Snooks' family; brother Peter's wife is a much better looking woman than I am!"

"Good lookin'!" he sneered; "call yourself good lookin', do you?"

"Well, I think you intimated as much, did he not boys?"

They all said he had, and the laugh was turned on him; but he exclaimed doggedly,

"I don't care! I'm not goin' to call you Snooks!"

"And what do you propose to call me?"

"I'll call you Mary."

"But Mary is not my name."

"I don't care! It's the name of all the nice girls I know!"

"Very good! I too shall probably be a nice girl if I live to grow up, but just now it seems as if I should die in infancy—am too good to live."

"You're the greatest torment ever any man saw."

The last pin was in that bandage; I arose, turned, and the thought flashed through my brain, "a tiger." His eyes literally blazed, and I went to him, looking straight into them, just as I had done into Tom's more than once. A minnie rifle ball had passed through his right ankle, and when I saw him first the flesh around the wound was purple and the entire limb swollen almost to bursting. The ward master told me he had been given up three days before, and was only waiting his turn to be carried to the dead house. Next morning the surgeon confirmed the account, said he had been on the amputation table and sent away in hope the foot might be saved, adding:

"I think we were influenced by the splendor of the man's form. It seemed sacrilege to mangle such a leg then, before we knew it was too late."

I thought the inflammation might be removed. He said if that were done they could amputate and save him, and the conversation ended in the surgeon giving the man to me to experiment on my theory. This seemed to be generally known, and the case was watched with great interest. No one interfered with my treatment of him, and nurses designated him to me as "your man."

He was a cross between a Hercules and Apollo—

17

grey-eyed, brown-haired, the finest specimen of physical manhood I have ever seen, and now his frail hold
on life was endangered by the rage into which I had
unwittingly thrown him.   So I sat bathing and sooth-
ing him, looking ever and anon steadily into his eyes,
and said:

"You had better call me mother."

"Mother!" he snarled, "You my mother!"

"Why not?"

"Why, you're not old enough!"

"I am twice as old as you are!

"No, you're not; and another thing, you're not big
enough!"   He raised his head, surveyed me leisurely
and contemptuously, his dark silky moustache went
up against his handsome nose as he sank back and
said slowly:

"Why, you-'re-not-much-bigger-'an-a-bean!"

"Still, I am large enough to take care of you and
send you back to your regiment if you are reasonable:
but no one can do anything for you if you fly into a
rage in this way!"

"Yes! and you know that, and you put me in a
rage going after them other fellows.   You know I've
got the best right to you.   I claimed you soon as you
come in the door, and called you afore you got half
down the ward.   You said you'd take care of me, and
now you don't do it.   The surgeon give me to you
too.   You know I can't live if you don't save me,
and you don't care if I die!"

I was penitent and conciliatory, and promised to be
good, when he said doggedly:

"Yes! and I'll call you Mary!"

"Very well, Mary is a good name—it was my mother's, and I shall no doubt come to like it."

"I guess it is a good name! It was my mother's name too, and any woman might be glad to be called Mary. But I never did see a woman 'at had any sense!"

He soon growled himself to sleep, and from that time I called him "Ursa Major;" but he only slept about half an hour, when a nurse in great fright summoned me. They had lifted him and he had fainted.

I helped to put him back into bed, and bathed him until consciousness returned, when he grasped my wrist with a vice-like hold and groaned.

"Oh God! Oh mother! Is this death?"

I heard no more of Miss Mary, or nice girls; but God and mother and death were often on his lips.

To the great surprise of every one I quelled the inflammation and fever, banished the swelling, and got him into good condition, when the foot was amputated and shown to me. The ankle joint was ground into small pieces, and these were mingled with bits of leather and woolen sock. No wonder the inflammation had been frightful; but it was some time after that before I knew the foot might have been saved by making a sufficient opening from the outside, withdrawing the loose irritating matter, and keeping an opening through which nature could have disposed of her waste. I do not know if surgery have yet discovered this plain, common-sense rule, but tens of thousands of men have died, and tens of thousands of others have lost limbs because it was not known and acted upon. All those men who died of gun-shot flesh wounds were victims to surgical stupidity.

I nursed the cross man until he went about on crutches, and his faith in me was equal in perfection to his form, for he always held that I could "stop this pain" if I would, and rated me soundly if I was "off in ward Ten" when he wanted me. One day he scolded worse than usual, and soon after an Irishman said, in an aside:

"Schure mum, an' ye mustn't be afther blamin' de rist av us fur that fellow's impidence. Schure, an' there's some av us that 'ud kick him out av the ward, if we could, for the way he talks to ye afther all that you have done for 'im an' fur all av us."

"Why! why! How can you feel so? What difference is it to me how he talks? It does him good to scold, and what is the use of a man having a mother if he cannot scold her when he is in pain? I wish you would all scold me! It would do you ever so much good. You quite break my heart with your patience. Do, please be as cross as bears, all of you, whenever you feel like it, and I will get you well in half the time."

"Schure mum, an' nobody iver saw the likes of ye!"

A man was brought from a field hospital, and laid in our ward, and one evening his stump was giving him great pain, when the cross man advised him to send for me, and exclaimed:

"There's mother, now; send for her."

"Oh!" groaned the sufferer, "what can she do?"

"I don't know what she can do; an' she don't know what she can do; but just you send for her! She'll come, and go to fussin' an' hummin' about just like an old bumble-bee, an' furst thing you know you won"' know nothin', for the pain 'll be gone an' you'll be asleep."

CHAPTER LVI.

DROP MY ALIAS.

THE second or third day of my hospital work, Mrs. Gaylord, the Chaplain's wife, came and inquired to what order I belonged, saying that the officers of the hospital were anxious to know. I laughed, and told her I belonged exclusively to myself, and did not know of any order which would care to own me. Then she very politely inquired my name, and I told her it was Mrs. Jeremiah Snooks, when she went away, apparently doubting my statement. I had been in Campbell almost a week, when Dr. Kelly came and said:

"Madam, I have been commissioned by the officers of this hospital to ascertain your name. None of us know how to address you, and it is very awkward either in speaking to you, or of you, not to be able to name you."

"Doctor, will not Mrs. Snooks do for a name, for all the time I shall be here?"

"No, madam, it will not do."

I was very unwilling to give my name, which was prominently before the public, on account of my Indian lecture and *Tribune* letters, but I seemed to have at least a month's work to do in Campbell. Hospital stores were pouring in to my city address, and being sent to me at a rate which created much wonder, and the men who had given me their confidence had a right to know who I was.

So I gave my name, and must repeat it before the Doctor could realize the astounding fact; even then he took off his cap and said:

"It is not possible you are *the* Mrs. ———, the lady who lectured in Doctor Sunderland's church!"

So I was proclaimed, with a great flourish of trumpets. For two hours my patients seemed afraid of me, and it did seem too bad to merge that giantess of the bean-pole and the press and the tall woman of the platform both in poor little insignificant me! It was like blotting out the big bear and the middle-sized bear from the old bear story, and leaving only the one poor little bear to growl over his pot of porridge.

In Ward Five was one man who had been laid on his left side, and never could be moved while he lived. His right arm suffered for lack of support, and when I knelt to give him nourishment from a spoon, and pray with him that the deliverer would soon come, he always laid that arm over my shoulders. The first time I knelt there after I was known, he said:

"Ah, you are such a great lady, and do not mind a poor soldier laying his arm over you!"

"Christ, the great Captain of our Salvation," I replied, "gathers you in his arms and pillows your head upon his bosom. Am I greater than he? Your good right arm has fought for liberty, and it is an honor to support it, when you are no longer able."

But nothing else I could ever say to him, was so much comfort as the old cry of the sufferer by the wayside, "Jesus, thou son of David, have mercy on me."

Over and over again we said that prayer in concert, while he waited in agony for the only relief possible—that of death; and from our last interview I returned to the bad ward, so sad that I felt the shadow of my face fall upon every man in it.   I could not drive away death's gloom; but I could work and talk, and both work and talk were needed.

I sat down between two young Irishmen, both with wounded heads, and began to bathe them, and comfort them, and said:

"If you are not better in the morning, I shall amputate both those heads; they shall not plague you in this manner another day."

Maybe my sad face made this funny, for their sense of the ridiculous was so touched that they clasped their sore heads and shrieked with laughter.   Every man in the ward caught the infection, and I was called upon for explanations of the art of amputating heads, and inquiries as to Surgeon Baxter's capacity of performing the operation.

This grotesque idea proved a fruitful subject of conversation, and aided in leading sufferers away from useless sorrow, toward hope and health; and bad as the ward was we lost but two men in it.

CHAPTER LVII.

HOSPITAL DRESS.

In that sad ward one superior, intelligent young man, who was thought to be doing well, suddenly burst an artery, and ropes were put up to warn visitors and others not to come in, and we who were in, moved with bated breath lest some motion should start the life-current. While his last hope was on a stillness which forbade him to move a finger, two lady visitors came to the door, were forbidden to enter, but seeing me inside, must follow the sheep instinct of the sex, and go where any other woman had gone. So, with pert words, they forced their way in, made a general flutter, and, oh horror! one of them caught her hoops on the iron cot of the dying man. He was only saved from a severe jerk by the prompt intervention of the special nurse. They were led out as quietly as possible, but the man had received a slight jerk and a serious shock. The hemorrhage would probably have returned if they had not come in, but it did return, and the young, strong life ebbed steadily away in a crimson current which spread over the floor.

From that day until the end of my hospital work, one fact forced itself upon my attention, and this is, that with all the patriotism of the American women, during that war, and all their gush of sympathy for the soldier, a vast majority were much more willing to "kiss him for his mother" than render him any solid service, and that not one in a hundred of the women who succeeded in getting into hospitals would dress so as not to be an object of terror to men whose life depended on quiet.

Women were capable of any heroism save wearing a dress suitable for hospital work. The very, very few who laid aside their hoops, those instruments of dread and torture, generally donned bloomers, and gave offense by airs of independence.

Good women would come long distances to see dying husbands, brothers and sons, and fill the wards with alarm by their hoops. When any one was hurt by them they were very sorry, but never gave up the cause of offense, while their desire to look well, and the finery and fixings they donned to improve their appearance, was a very broad and painful burlesque. Women were seldom permitted to stay in a hospital over night, even with a dying friend, and the inhabitants were generally glad when they started for home.

It was the dress nuisance which caused nuns to have the preference in so many cases; but I could not see or hear that they ever did anything but make converts to the church and take care of clothing and jellies.

One thing is certain, *i. e.*, that women never can do efficient and general service in hospitals until their dress is prescribed by laws inexorable as those of the Medes and Persians. Then, that dress should be entirely destitute of steel, starch, whale-bone, flounces, and ornaments of all descriptions; should rest on the shoulders, have a skirt from the waist to the ankle, and a waist which leaves room for breathing. I never could have done my hospital work but for the dress which led most people to mistake me for a nun.

CHAPTER LVIII.

SPECIAL WORK.

IN the wilderness of work I must choose, and began to select men who had been given up by the surgeons, and whom I thought might be saved by special care. Surgeon Kelly soon entered into my plan, and made his ward my headquarters. To it my special patients were brought, until there was no more room for them. That intuitive perception of the natural position of muscles, and the importance of keeping them in it, which came to me on first seeing a wound dressed, gave me such control over pain that I used to go through the wards between midnight and morning and put amputation cases to sleep at the rate of one in fifteen minutes.

In these morning walks I saw that the nurses were on duty and had substantial refreshments, saw those changes for the worse, sure to come, if they came at all, in those chill hours. Seeing them soon was important to meeting them successfully, and I succeeded in breaking up many a chill before it did serious damage, which must have proved fatal if left until the morning visit of the Surgeon. Also, in those walks I chose special cases; have more than once sat down by a man and calculated in this way:

"You may have twenty, forty years of useful life, if I can save you; I shall certainly die one year sooner for the labor I expend on you, but there will be a large gain in the average of life and usefulness; and when you risked all of your life for the country as much mine

as yours, it is but just that I should give a small part
of mine to save you."

Every man lived whom I elected to life, and Dr.
Kelly, who knew more than any one else about my
plans, and on whom I most counted for aid, has said
that I saved enough to the government in bounty
money, by returning men to duty who would otherwise have died, to warrant it in supporting me the
balance of my life; but his statements could not always
be relied upon, for he insisted that I never slept, had
not been asleep during the seven weeks spent in Campbell, was a witch and would float like a cork, if thrown
from the Long Bridge into the Potomac.

In selecting a man in desperate case to be saved, I
always took his temperament and previous life into
consideration. A man of pure life and sanguine temperament was hard to kill. Give him the excuse of
good nursing and he would live through injuries which
must be fatal to a bilious, suspicious man, or one who
had been guilty of any excess. A tobacco chewer or
smoker died on small provocation. A drunkard or
debauchee was killed by a scratch.

There were two ward surgeons who disapproved of
the innovation of a woman in Campbell, and especially
of one held amenable to no rules. They were both in
favor of heroic treatment, which I did not care to witness, and I spent little time in their wards. One of
them kept a man, with two bricks tied to his foot and
hanging over the foot of the bed, until he died, after
ten days of a sleepless agony such as could not well
have been excelled in an Inquisition; while his wife
tried to comfort him under a torture she begged in
vain to have remitted.

The night after she started home with his body, I was pasing through the ward, when I came upon a young Philadelphia Zouave in a perfect paroxysm of anguish. Three nurses stood around him, and to my inquiry "What *is* the matter?" replied by dumb show that coming death was the matter, and that soon all would be over; while in words they told me he had not slept for forty-eight hours.

I had one place a chair for me, sat down, and with my long, thin hands grasped the thigh stump, which was making all the trouble, drew and pressed the muscle into a natural, easy position, cooed and talked and comforted the sufferer, as I should have done a sick baby, and in ten minutes he was asleep.

Then I whispered the nurses to bring cotton and oakum, and little cushions; made them put the cotton and oakum, in small tufts, to my index fingers; and while I crooned my directions in a sing-song lullaby air, I worked in this support, gradually and imperceptibly withdrawing my hands, until I could substitute the little cushions for the force by which they held the muscle in proper position. This done, my boy-soldier slept as sweetly as ever he had done in his crib.

Next morning a nurse came running for me to hurry to him. He had slept six hours, waked, had his breakfast, and had his wound dressed, and now the pain was back bad as ever. I went, fixed the mangled muscle with reference to his change of position, made a half-mould to hold it there, and before I had finished he began an eight-hour sleep. Ten days after he was sent home to his mother, and I saw or heard of him no more.

CHAPTER LIX.

HEROIC AND ANTI-HEROIC TREATMENT.

The other ward in which I was not welcome, adjoined that one in which my room was situated, and to reach it I must go out of doors or pass through one-half the length of that ward. In these passages I had an opportunity for studying Piemia and its ordinary treatment, and could give the men lemonade when they wanted it.

In this ward lay a young German with a wounded ankle. He had a broad, square forehead, skin white as wax, large blue eyes and yellow hair, inclined to curl. His whole appearance indicated high culture, and an organization peculiarly sensitive to pleasure or pain; but no one seemed to understand that he suffered more than others from a like cause.

Surgeon and nurses scoffed at his moans, and thought it babyish for a muscular man over six feet to show so many signs of pain. I think that from some cause, the surgeon felt vindictive toward him, and that his subordinates took their cue from him. When I went to give him lemonade, he would clutch my hand or dress, look up in my face, and plead:

" Oh, mutter! mutter!"

But if I sat down to soothe and comfort him, a nurse always came to remind me of the surgeon's orders, and I used to go around on the outside, that he might not see and call me. When he was in the amputation room I heard his shrieks and groans, and carried a glass of wine to the door for him.

He heard my voice, and called "Mutter! mutter!"

I pushed past the orderly, ran to him, and his plead-ing eyes seemed to devour me as he fastened his gaze on my face. I cannot think to this day why he should have been nude for the amputation of a foot; but he was, and some one threw a towel across his loins as I approached.

Dr. Baxter said:

"No sympathy! no sympathy!"

So I stood by him, placed a hand on each side of his corrugated brow, steadied my voice and said:

"Be a man and a soldier!"

He had asked me for bread; I gave him a stone, and no wonder he dashed it back in my face. With a fierce cry he said:

"I hev been a man and a sojer long enough!"

Ah! verily had he, and much too long. Days be-fore that he should have been "a boy again;" aye, a baby, a very infant—should have been soothed and softened and comforted with all the tenderness of moth-er-love; but even now, in this cruel extremity, every sign of sympathy was denied him. Some one put a hand gently but firmly on each of my shoulders, turned my back to him, took me out of the room, and I hurried away, while the air shuddered with his shrieks and groans. After he had been brought back to his place in the ward I could often hear him as I passed to and from my room, and even while I occu-pied it.

Once he saw me through the open door, and called, "Mutter! mutter!"

I went, knelt by him, took his hands, which were

stretched appealingly to me, and spoke comforting words, while his blue eyes seemed ready to start from their sockets, as he clung to my hands with the old familiar cry:

"Oh, Mutter! Mutter!"

He was strapped down to his iron cot, about as closely as he had been to the amputation table, and the cot fastened to the floor. I had not been five minutes at his side when his special nurse hurried up and warned me to leave, saying:

"It's surgeon's orders. He's not going to have any babyin'!"

I drew my hands from the frantic grasp, took away that last hold on human sympathy, and hurried out, while his cry of "Oh, mutter! mutter!" rung in my ears as I turned and looked on his pure high brow for the last time.

Next morning I heard he had lock-jaw, and that the surgeon was to leave.

The night after that victim of some frightful, fiendish experiment had been carried to the dead-house, I was passing through the ward, when attracted by sounds of convulsive weeping, and I found a young man in an agony of grief, in one of those sobbing fits sure to come to the bravest. He was in a high fever, and while I bathed his face and hands, I asked the cause of his outbreak, and he sobbed:

"Oh, the pain in my wound! This is the third night I have not slept, and my God! I can bear it no longer!"

It was a flesh-wound in the thigh, such an one as usually proved fatal, and while I set him to talking I began patching scraps of observation into a theory. He was from Pennsylvania, and bitterly charged his State with having done nothing for her wounded, and when I asked why he had not sent for me, he said:

"Oh, I thought you were from Massachusetts, like all the rest of them; and if my own State would do nothing for me, I would not beg. People come here every day looking for Massachusetts soldiers. Since I have been frantic here, ladies have come and stood and looked at me, and said 'Poor fellow!' as if I had been a dog. I was as well raised as any of them, even if I am a common soldier."

I thought his recovery very doubtful, and talked to draw his thoughts to the better land. To his charges against his native land, I said: "I am a Pennsylvanian; and more than that, the Governor of Pennsylvania sent me to you; bade me come to-night, that you might know he had not forgotten you."

"He did? Why, how did he know anything about it?"

"He just knows all about it, and has been caring for you all this time. I do not mean Andy Curtin. He is nothing but a subaltern; but the dear Lord, our Father in Heaven, who never forgets us, though he often afflicts us. He sent me to you now, that you might know he loves you. It was he who made me love you and care to help you. All the love and care that come to you are a part of his love."

"He wept afresh but less bitterly, and said:

"Oh you will think I am a baby!"

"Well! That is just what you ought to be. Your past life is sufficient certificate of manhood; and now has come your time to be a baby, while I am mother. You have been lying here like an engine, under a high pressure of steam, and the safety-valve fastened down with a billet of wood, until there has been almost an explosion. Now just take away that stick of wood— your manhood and pride, and let out all the groans and tears you have pent in your heart. Cry all you can! This is your time for crying!"

When I had talked him into a mood to let me feel if his feet were warm, I found that wounded limb dreadfully swollen, cold almost as death, stretched out as he lay on his back, and a cushion right under the heel. Had there been no wound the position must have been unendurable. Without letting him know, I drew that cushion up until it filled the hollow between the heel and calf of the leg, and supported the strained muscle, tucked a handful of oakum under the knee, moved the toes, brushed and rubbed the foot, until circulation started, sponged it, rolled it in flannel, of which I had a supply in my basket, washed the well foot, and put a warm woolen sock on it, arranged the cover so that it would not rest on the toes of the sore leg; told him to get the new surgeon next morning to make a large opening on the lower side of his thigh, where the bullet had gone out—to ask him to cut lengthwise of the muscle; get out everything he could, that ought not to be in there; keep that opening open with a roll of bandage, so that old Mother Nature should have a trap-door through which she could throw her chips out of that work-shop in his thigh; to be sure and not hint to the surgeon that I had said anything about it, and not fail to have it done.

18

I left him asleep, and the next day he told me the surgeon had taken a quart of pus and several pieces of woolen cloth out of his wound, and his recovery was rapid.

CHAPTER LX.

COST OF ORDER.

In making molds and rests for mangled limbs, I had large demands for little cushions, and without economy could not get enough. When one just fitted a place I wanted to keep it, and to do this, must have it aired, perhaps washed. To avoid lint dressings, I hunted pieces of soft, table linen, gave to patients pieces to suit, and as the supply was short they would get nurses and surgeons to leave their pieces of linen, after dressing their wounds until I should take charge, and have them cleansed for next time. To do all this, I must use the grass-plats and railings for airing and drying cushions and rags. These plats and railings were for ornament, and there was soon a protest against putting them to "such vile uses." I had gone into the hospital with the stupid notion that its primary object was the care and comfort of the sick and wounded. It was long after that I learned that a vast majority of all benevolent institutions are gotten up to gratify the asthetic tastes of the public; exhibit the wealth and generosity of the founders, and furnish places for officers. The beneficiaries of the institutions are simply an apology for their existence, and having furnished that apology, the less said about them the better.

The surgeons of Campbell did really want its patients to be happy and get well; but it was a model institution, with a reputation to sustain; was part of a system under general laws, which might not be broken with impunity. There was no law against a man dying for want of sleep from pain caused by misplaced muscle; but the statutes against litter were inexorable as those of the Medes and Persians. The Campbell surgeons winked at my litter, until one regular inspection day, when my cushions and rags, clean and unclean, those marked John Smith, and those labeled Tom Brown, were all huddled up and stuffed *en masse* into the pantry closet.

I used to wonder if the Creator had invented a new variety of idiot, and made a lot in order to supply the army with medical inspectors, or, if by some cunning military device, the Surgeon-General had been able to select all those conglomerations of official dignity and asinine stupidity, from the open donkey-market of the world. Inspecting a hospital was just like investigating an Indian fraud. The man whose work was to be inspected or investigated, met the inspector or investigator at the door, showed him all he wished him to see and examine witnesses wholly in his power— when the inspected and inspector, the investigated and investigator exchanged compliments, and the public were gratified to learn that all was in a most gratifying condition of perfect order.

One day we had a particularly searching inspection, and next day nurse told me of some four new cases which had been brought in a week before, one of whom the inspectors said was past hope. I found his feet and legs with a crust on them like the shell of a snail; had a piece of rubber cloth laid under them, and with tepid water, a good crash towel, and plenty of rubbing, got down to the skin, which I rubbed well with lard. Then with fresh towels and water at hand, I drew away the sheet in which the patient had rolled his head, and while I washed his head and arms and breast, I talked, and he tried to answer; but it was some time before he could steady his tongue and lips so as to articulate, and when he did, his first words were:

"Are you the woman that's been a-washin' my feet?"

"That is exactly what I have been doing, and much need they had of it. Do you not think you are a pretty fellow to have me come all the way from Minnesota to wash your feet?"

It was with much effort he could fix his dazed eyes on my face, and he made several pitiful attempts before he succeeded in saying:

"I think ye'r the best woman that ever I saw!"

"Ah, that is because you never saw much, away out there in Venango county, Pennsylvania, where you live. There are thousands of better women than I, running around hunting work, in this part of the country."

"Is there?"

"Yes, indeed; and nothing for them to do!"

"I never saw none uv 'em!"

"That is because you have had your head rolled up in that sheet. Just keep your head uncovered, so you can breathe this nice, fresh air; open your eyes every little while, and you will see a whole row of those women, all hunting work!"

He seemed quite interested, and when I had done washing and given directions to a nurse to cleanse the balance of his person, I asked if there was anything more I could do for him, when he stammered:

"Not unless you could get me a cup of tea—a cup of good green tea, 'thout any milk or sugar in it. If you do, I'll pay you for it."

"Pay me for it, will you? and how much will you give me—three cents?"

"Oh, I'll give you twenty-five cents."

"Twenty-five cents for a cup of good green tea, without any milk or sugar in it!"

I called the ward to witness the bargain, said I should grow rich at that rate, and hurried off for the tea.

I had a little silver tray and tea-set, with two china cups. Mrs. Gangewer, of the Ohio Aid Society, had sent me a tin tea-kettle and spirit-lamp; folks at a distance had sent plenty of the best tea; and that little tea-tray had become a prominent feature of Campbell long before this poor fellow specified his want. I made the tray unusually attractive that day, and fed him his tea from a spoon, while he admired the tiny pot, out of which, with the aid of the kettle, I could furnish twenty cups of good tea. When I had served all in that ward who wanted tea, the first one took a second cup, and while taking it his skin grew moist, and I knew he was saved from that death of misplaced matter vulgarly called "dirt," to which well-paid medical inspectors had consigned him, while giving their invaluable scientific attention to floor-scrubbing and bed-making, to whitewashing and laundry work.

I doubt if there were a Medical Inspector in the army who was not a first rate judge of the art of folding and ironing a sheet or pillow-slip; of the particular tuck which brought out the outlines of the corners of a mattress, as seen through a counterpane; and of the art and mystery of cleaning a floor. It did seem as if they had all reached office through their great proficiency as cabin-boys.

Next day I went to that ward with my tea-tray; and after learning that that man had been washed once more, asked him if he wanted another cup of tea.

"I'd like to have one," he stammered; "but I didn't pay you for the last one, and I can't find my wallet!"

I saw the debt troubled him, and took this as one more evidence that somewhere there were people who sold hospital stores to sick soldiers. So I took pains to explain that he owed me nothing; that the tea was his—ladies had sent it to me to give to him—and all the pay they wanted was for him to get well, and go home to his mother.

The idea that some one was thinking for him seemed to do him almost as much good as the tea.

I left Campbell next day, but on my first visit found him convalescing, and on the second visit he ran down the ward holding his sides and laughing, and I saw or heard of him no more.

CHAPTER LXI.

LEARN TO CONTROL PIEMIA.

About ten days after I went to Campbell, I was called at midnight to a death-bed. It was a case of flesh-wound in the thigh, and the whole limb was swollen almost to bursting, so cold as to startle by the touch, and almost as transparent as glass. I knew this was piemia and that for it medical science had no cure; but I wanted to warm that cold limb, to call circulation back to that inert mass. The first thought was warm, wet compresses, hot bricks, hot flannel; but the kitchen was locked, and it was little I could do without fire, except to receive and write down his dying messages to parents, and the girl who was waiting to be his wife.

When the surgeon's morning hour came he still lived; and at my suggestion the warm compresses were applied. He said, "they feel so good," and was quite comforted by them, but died about ten o'clock. I was greatly grieved to think he had suffered from cold the last night of life, but how avoid any number of similar occurrences? There was no artificial heat in any of the wards. A basin of warm water was only to be obtained by special favor of the cooks; but they had been very courteous. The third day of my appearance among them, one looked up over the edge of the tub over which he bent, washing potatoes, and said, as I stood waiting for hot water,

"Do you know what you look like going around here among us fellows?"

" No! but nothing dreadful I hope."

" You just look like an angel, and that's what we all think; we're ever so much better since you came."

The memory of this speech gave me courage to go and lay my trouble before the cooks, who gathered to hear me tell the story of that death, the messages left for the friends who should see him no more, and of my sorrow that I could not drive away the cold on that last, sad night.

They all wiped their eyes on their aprons; head cook went to a cupboard, brought a key and handed it to me, saying:

" There, mother, is a key of this kitchen; come in here whenever you please. We will always find room on the ranges for your bricks, and I'll have something nice in the cupboard every night for you and the nurses.

This proved to be the key to the situation, and after I received that bit of metal from cook, there was not one death from piemia in any ward where I was free to work, although I have had as many, I think, as sixty men struck with the premonitary chill, in one night. I concluded that "piemia" was French for neglect, and that the antidote was warmth, nourishing food, stimulants, friction, fresh air and cheerfulness, and did not hesitate to say that if death wanted to get a man out of my hands, he must send some other agent than piemia. I do not believe in the medical theory concerning it; do not believe pus ever gets into the veins, or that there is any poison about it, except that of ignorance and indifference on the part of doctors and nurses.

CHAPTER LXII.

FIRST CASE OF GROWING A NEW BONE.

I HAD searched for Minnesota men in Campbell, found none, and had been there a week, when Mrs. Kelsey told me there was one in ward ten, credited to a Wisconsin regiment; and from him I learned that he was a friend and neighbor of my friends, Mr. and Mrs. Bancroft, of Mantorville, and my conscience reproached me for not sooner finding him; but the second day Mrs. Gaylord came, as a messenger from the surgeons, to tell me I need not spend time and strength on him, as he could not be saved.

His was a thigh wound. They had thought to amputate, but found the bone shattered from joint to joint —had, with a chain saw, cut it off above the knee, and picked out the bone in pieces. There was a splinter attached to the upper joint, but that was all the bone left in the thigh, and the injury was one from which recovery was impossible. His father, a doctor, was visiting him, and knew he must die.

I went to the patient, who said:

" Dr. True, the ward surgeon has just been here, and tells me I must die!"

I sat by him fitting the measure I had been taking for two days to this new aspect of the case, and talking of death, and the preparation for it, until I thought I understood the case, when I said:

" Be ready for death, as every one of any sense should always be; but I do not intend to let you die."

"I guess you cannot help it! All the surgeons and father agree that there is no hope for me."

"But they are all liable to be mistaken, and none of them have taken into the account your courage and recuperative force; your good life and good conscience; your muscle, like a pine log; your pure breath; your clear skin and good blood. I do not care what they say, you will live; I will not let you die!"

I found Dr. Baxter, and said:

"I want you to save Corporal Kendall!"

"Corporal Kendall! who is he?"

"The man out of whose thigh you took the bone last week."

His face grew sad, but he said:

"Oh, we mean to save them all if we can."

"Doctor, that is no answer. I am interested in this man, know his friends and want to understand his case. If I can keep his stomach in good working order and well supplied with blood-making food, keep away chills and keep down pain, so that he can sleep, will he not get well?"

He laughed and replied:

"Well, I really never heard of a man dying under such circumstances."

"I can do that, doctor."

"If you can you will save him, of course, and we will give him to you."

"But, doctor, you must do all the surgery. I must not give him pain; cannot see that wound."

"Oh, certainly, we will do everything in our power; but he is yours, for we have no hope of saving him."

"Another thing, doctor; you will have him brought to Ward Four."

He gave the order at once, adding: "Put him to the right of Howard"—a young Philadelphian with a thigh stump, who was likely to die of hemorrhage, and whose jerking nerves I could soothe and quiet better than any one else.

By this arrangement the man minus a thigh bone was placed in the center of my field of labor, and under the care of Dr. Kelly; but full ten days after this arrangement was made, he came with a rueful face and said:

"We have consulted the Surgeon-General, Medical Inspector, and a dozen other surgeons outside the hospital, and they all agree that there is no hope for Kendall. The surgeons here have commissioned me to tell you, for we think you ought to know. We all appreciate what you are doing, and think you will save all your other men if you live, but you cannot stand this strain long. You do not know it; but there is a limit to your powers of endurance, and you are breaking. You certainly will die if you keep on as you have been going, and it is not worth your while to kill yourself for Kendall, for you cannot save him."

"What is the reason he cannot be saved?"

"Well, there are several reasons. First, I performed the operation, and did not do it as thoroughly as I wished. He was coming out from under the influence of the chloroform, and they hurried me. The case was hopeless, and no use to give him pain, so there are several pieces of bone which I failed to find. These are driven into the flesh, and nature in trying to get rid of them will get up such excessive suppuration that he must die of exhaustion. Then there is the thigh without a bone, and there is nothing in the books to warrant a hope that it could heal in that condition. We could not, in any case, hope for the formation of a new bone. There are re-sections of two inches, but this is the longest new formation of which we know anything, and in this case there can be no hope, because the periosteum is destroyed."

"Periosteum, doctor. What is that, again?"

"It is the bone-feeder; the strong membrane which incloses the bone, and through which it is made. In this case it is absolutely destroyed, removed, torn to shreds—gone. So there are several reasons why he cannot be saved."

"Doctor Kelly, do you intend to let him lie there and die?"

"Oh no! oh no! I will do all in my power for him. I am paid for that; it is my duty; but it is not your duty to sacrifice your own life in a vain effort to save another."

"Doctor Kelly, he *shall* not die; I will not let him. I know nothing about your books and bones; but he can live with one bone wanting, and I tell you he shall not die, and I will not die either."

It was a week or more after this conversation I found my patient, one morning, with blue lips and a pinched nose, and said to him:

"What is this?"

"Well, I had a chill last night."

"A chill and did not send for me?"

"You were here until after midnight, and must have some rest."

"Corporal Kendall, how *dare* you talk to me in that

manner? You promised to send for me if there were any change for the worse; and after this I cannot trust you. Now I must stay here. Do you think I am going to lose my investment in you? Do you suppose I would work over you as I have been doing, and then drop you for fear of a little more work?"

As I passed to the kitchen I found that blue lips and pinched noses had suddenly come into fashion; that there were more of them than I had time to count; but did not, for a moment, dream of letting a man get into the graveyard by that gate.

The merry, young Irishman who had volunteered as my orderly, had a period of active service; and no more willing pair of hands and feet ever were interposed between men and death. Hot bricks, hot blankets, bottles of hot water, hot whisky punch and green tea were the order of the forenoon, and of a good many hours of night and day after it; for that victory was won by a long struggle. For ten nights I never lay down in my room; but slept, all I did sleep, lying on a cot about the center of Ward Four, and two cots from the man minus a bone. I could drop asleep in an instant, and sleep during ordinary movements; but a change in a voice brought me to my post in a moment. I could command anything in the dispensary or store-rooms at any hour of the day or night, and carried many a man through the crisis of a night attack, when if he had been left until discovered in the morning, there would have been little hope for him; and when a surgeon could have done nothing without a key to the kitchen which none of them had.

I kept no secrets from any of them: told each one

just what I had done in his ward; thankfully received his approval and directions, asked about things I did not understand, and was careful that my nursing was in harmony with his surgery.

During that trial-time there was one night that death seemed to be gaining the victory in Corporal Kendall's case. Pain defied my utmost efforts and held the citadel. Sleep fled; the circulation grew sluggish, and both he and I knew that the result hung on the hour. It was two o'clock A. M., and from midnight I had been trying to bring rest. The injured limb was suspended in a zinc trough. I had raised, lowered it by imperceptible motions; cut bandage where it seemed to bind, tucked in bits of cotton or oakum, kept the toes in motion, irritated the surface wherever I could get the point of a finger in through the bandages; kept up the heat of the body, and the hope of the soul; and sat down to hold his hands and try mesmeric passes and sounds, when he turned his head on the pillow, and said:

"Even if I should get well, I'll never be fit for infantry service again."

"No, you never will."

"I might walk with that machine you talk of; but never could march and carry a knap-sack! But I have been thinking. I am a pretty good engineer. You know Secretary Stanton? You might get me transferred to the Navy, and I could run an engine on a gunboat."

"That is it, exactly! You will get over this! I will have you transferred to a gunboat, and next time you will go into the Rebellion prow foremost. You ought to be at work, in time to help take Charleston."

"I continued to talk, in a sing-song croone, to stroke his head, and hold his hand, until he slept, which was but a few moments after settling that transfer, and the last time I saw him, which was in '79, he got over the ground and up and down stairs, as fast as most people, his new bone being quite as good as any of the old ones, except being a little short and decidedly crooked, although the crook did not effect its usefulness or general appearance.

CHAPTER LXIII.

A HEROIC MOTHER.

JAMES BRIDE, who drew me to Campbell, by asking for "something to quench thirst," was one of the thousands who died of flesh-wounds, for want of surgical trap doors, through which nature might throw out her chips. His wound was in the hip, and no opening ever was made to the center of the injury, except that made by the bullet which had gone in and staid there.

His mother came three days before he died, and being minus hoops and finery, the ward surgeon was anxious she should remain with her son, and we arranged that she should sleep in my room. There was just space between the cot and wall for the breadth of a mattress, and when the door was shut, that space was long enough for me to lie between the door and the stand. I have never entertained a guest more cheerfully, or one by whose presence I felt more honored; yet the traveling costume was a short calico dress, strong leather shoes and blue woolen stockings, visible below the dress, a gingham sunbonnet and double-bordered cap tied under her chin.

Several richly dressed ladies came from Eastern cities to see dying relatives, but to none of them were the surgeons so thoroughly respectful, as to this plain, strong, clean, high-souled country-woman, who staid with her son, and was hailed with joy by all the men in his ward, to every one of whom she was sympathetic and helpful.

Her case was hard. She and her husband, who was old and feeble, had just three sons, two strong and vigorous, one a cripple. Their two vigorous sons enlisted together, and fell in the charge on Marie's Hill, within ten feet and ten minutes of each other. William was buried on the battle-field, and she had come to see James die in hospital.

When all was over and her boy was carried to the dead house, they brought her to me, and I have never heard such pathetic, eloquent expressions of grief as those she poured forth in that little, rough, barrack-room.

"Oh, William! William!" she sobbed, "You are lying, to-night, in your bloody grave, and your mother will never know where it is! and you, James! you were my first-born, but I cannot go to you now, where you lie in the darkness among the dead! Oh, but it is a sad story I must carry to your old father, to bring his gray hairs in sorrow to the grave. Who can we lean upon, in our old age? Who will take care of Johnny when we are gone? Oh, it is a hard, hard lot."

She wrung her hands, bowed over her knees, in a paroxysm of tears, then raised herself, threw back her head, and exclaimed.

"But oh! boys dear, would n't I rather you were where you are this night, than that you had thrown down your guns and run!"

CHAPTER LXIV.

TWO KINDS OF APPRECIATION.

Looking down the long vista of memory, to the many faces turned to me from beds of pain, I find few to which I can attach a name, and one I seem never to have looked upon but once. It is a long, sallow face, surmounted by bushy, yellow hair; it has a clear, oval outline, and straight nose, brown eyes and a down of young manhood on the wasted, trembling lips; I knew it then, as the face of a fever patient, but not one to whom I had rendered any special service, and felt surprised when the trembling lips said, in a pitiful, pleading way.

"We boys has been a talkin' about you!"

"Have you, my dear—and what have you boys been saying about me?"

"We've jist been a sayin' that good many ladies has been kind to us, but none uv 'em ever loved us but you!"

"Well, my dear, I do not know how it is with the other ladies, but I am sure I do love you very, very dearly! You do not know half how much I love you."

"Oh, yes, we do! yes, we do! we know 'at you don't take care uv us 'cause it's your juty! you jist do it 'cause you love to!"

19

"That is it exactly—just because I love to, and because I want you to get well and go to your mothers."

"Yes! but the boys says you don't care about 'em when they get well."

"They do not need to have me care for them when they are well."

"Oh, yes, they do! yes, they do! an' if that's the way you're a goin' to serve me, I'll stay sick a long time."

When hospital stores came to me so fast that there was great trouble in getting them wisely distributed, Campbell lent me an ambulance to go around, see where they were needed, and supply as many as I could. I had a letter from an old Pittsburg neighbor, asking me to see his brother in Douglas Hospital, and went in an ambulance well supplied with jellies and fruit.

Douglas Hospital was an institution of which the city was proud. It had much finer buildings than any other in the city, occupied the finest residence block in the city, and had a wide reputation for grandeur and beauty and superb management. I found the halls and rooms quite as elegant as I had any reason to expect, but was surprised to find that elegance undisturbed by the presence of sick or wounded men. In one back room a wounded officer looked lonely, and they said there were other rooms used for sick soldiers, but all I saw were parlors, reception rooms, offices and sleeping apartments for surgeons, and the Lady Abbess, with her attendant Sisters of Mercy or Charity.

After we had strolled through several sumptuous apartments, we were taken out into the adjoining square, where there were large barracks as white as lime and brushes could make them, and making a pretty picture among the trees. Inside, the walls were white as on the outside, and the pictures already up, as well as those just being put up, were bright as bright could be. Indeed, I do not know how pictures could have been greener or bluer or yellower or redder, and when the show-off man called my attention to them, as calculated to make the place cheerful; I recognized their merit, but suggested that some paper blinds might be desirable to keep the sun from shining into the faces of the men who lay on the cots.

The roof or walls did not seem well calculated to keep out wind or rain, but paper blinds would ward off sunshine. From the condition of the floor, it was evident that the demon of the scrubbing brush, which has possession of all model institutions, had full sway in Douglas barracks. Pine boards could not well have been made whiter. No laundry man need have feared to own to the doing up of the bed linen and counterpanes, and science had not discovered any mode of making a bed look more like a packing box, than those in that model hospital.

What an impertinence a sick or wounded man was, in one of those nice, square beds. He was almost certain to muss and toss it, and this must have been a crowning calamity.

After the showman had shown all he cared to have me see, I sat talking with the man I had come to visit, and he said, in a whisper:

" Are there lice in all the hospitals?"

" Lice? Why, certainly not."

"Well, there are plenty of them here, and they tell us they cannot be helped—that they have them in all the hospitals. Look here!"

He turned down the nice counterpane, and there, in the blanket, the disgusting creatures swarmed. I was shocked, and half rose, in the impulse to make an outcry, but he warned me not to let any one know he had told me, or it would be bad for him. I asked why he did not tell the surgeon.

"He knows all about them, and says they cannot be helped."

"You have Sisters of Charity here; tell them."

"Oh, they never do anything in the ward but walk around and talk nice, and pray with men who are going to die. They must know about them."

I walked around alone, and the show-man did not seem to like it, but I talked with the men in the cots, put my hand under the cover, found feet encrusted with the exudations of fever, until they were hard and dry as a bit of kindling wood; hair full of dust from the battle-field, and not one man who had been washed since being carried away from it; while there were vermin in every bed.

The ward-master objected to my leaving a jar of jelly with my friend. It would spoil the good order of the ward, and all delicacies were to be given into the care of the Sisters. I found one of them who was quite willing to take charge of anything I wished to leave, but was powerless in the matter of vermin. It was the ward master's business to attend to that. It was the business of the Sisters to look after the clothing when it came from the laundry, put it in order, and give it out when wanted.

My failure to get a bed for the man in the fort by applying to those in authority, made me feel that it would be useless to try that plan about the vermin; and, in my perplexity, I turned to my old friend and confidant, the public. To reach it, I wrote to the *New York Tribune*, giving a very mild statement of the case.

Two days after Surgeon Baxter came, with a copy of that letter, and told me he had been ordered to discharge me on account of it. I spoke of the men who must die if I left, and he was sorry but had no option. Then he bethought him that maybe I might get the Surgeon-General to permit me to remain, at least until the cases of my special patients were settled; otherwise I must leave the hospital that day. He was sorry I had dated the letter from Campbell, had it not been for this, he could use his influence to sustain me; but professional etiquette forbade him to harbor or countenance one who spoke unfavorably of a brother-surgeon. In other words, by living in a hospital I became one of a ring, bound to keep hospital secrets, and use only words of commendation in speaking or writing of anything I saw.

I took a street car and proceeded to the office of the Surgeon-General—saw the man who held the lives of my patients in his hands, ate the only piece of humble pie that ever crossed my lips, by apologizing for telling the truth, and got permission to go back to the men who looked to me for life.

I have felt that I made a great mistake—felt that if I had then and there made war to the knife, and the knife to the hilt, against the whole system of fraud and cruelty embodied in the hospital service, I should have saved many more lives in the end. Even while I talked to the head of that nest of corruption, and listened to his inane platitudes about my duty as an inmate of a hospital to report abuses to him, and "the regular way of proceeding," I did want to hurl the gauntlet of an irregular defiance into his plausible face, but the pleading eyes in Campbell held me; I could not let those men die, and die they must if I must leave them.

Nobody denied the truth of my statements about Douglas Hospital, and I never learned that any one objected to the facts or their continuance. It was only their exposure which gave offense.

This letter made me an object of dread. Folks never knew what I might see or say next; and there soon arose another trouble about my living in Campbell; for Miss Dix objected, claimed that it was an infringement on her authority. Then again, there were others who could not see why there should be but one female nurse in Campbell. Dr. Baxter, by admitting me, had abandoned his ground, acknowledged that men alone could not manage a first-class hospital; and having discovered his mistake, was bound to rectify it by admitting a corps of lady nurses. He was bombarded by Miss Dix's official power, pestered by the persistant appeals of volunteers; sneered and scoffed at and worried, until he fell back on his old position, and promptly dismissed me so soon as my patients were out of danger. He was always courteous to me as a visiter, and has my lasting gratitude and respect for breaking his rules and bearing the persecution he did, that I might do the work I did, and could not have done without his effective and generous co-operation.

The proportion of thigh stumps saved, was the test of a hospital's success; and the summer I was in Campbell, we saved nineteen out of twenty; next summer Chaplain Gaylord told me they lost nineteen in twenty, and added: "Piemia has literally swept our wards."

CHAPTER LXV.

LIFE AND DEATH.

WHEN released from the hospital, I had neither money nor clothes, and this is all the account I can render to the generous people who sent me hospital stores. I could not answer their letters. Some of them I never read. I could only give up my life to distributing their bounty, and knew that neither their money nor my own had remained in my hands when it was necessary for me to borrow two dollars to get a dress. My cloth traveling suit was no longer fit for use, and my platform suit too good. These were all I had brought to Washington; but the best men never refused me audience because I wore a shaker bonnet, a black lawn skirt and gray linen sack. Some thought I dressed in that way to be odd, but it was all I could afford.

The Quarter-Master-General had canceled my appointment, because I had not reported for duty, but Secretary Stanton reinstated me, and I went to work

on the largest salary I had ever received—fifty dollars
a month.   After some time it was raised to sixty, and
I was more than independent; but my health was so
broken that half a dozen doctors commanded me to
lie on my back for a month, and I spent every moment
I could in that position.

I had grown hysterical, and twice while at work in
the office, broke out into passionate weeping, while
thinking of something in my hospital experience,
something I had borne, when it occurred, without a
tear, or even without feeling a desire to weep.

In September I had twenty days' leave of absence to
go to St. Cloud, settle my business and bring my
household gods.   There were still no railroads in
Minnesota, and I was six days going, must have six to
return, and one to visit friends at Pittsburg, yet in the
time left, sold *The Democrat*, closed my home, and
met Gen. Lowrie for the first and last time.

He called and we spent an hour talking, principally
of the war, which he thought would result in two separate governments.   His reason seemed to be entirely restored; but his prestige, power, wealth and
health were gone.   I tried to avoid all personal matters, as well as reference to our quarrel, but he broke
into the conversation to say:

"I am the only person who ever understood you.
People now think you go into hospitals from a sense
of duty; from benevolence, like those good people who
expect to get to heaven by doing disagreeable things
on earth; but I know you go because you must; go
for your own pleasure; you do not care for heaven or
anything else, but yourself."

He stopped, looked down, traced the pattern of the carpet with the point of his cane, then raised his head and continued: "You take care of the sick and wounded, go into all those dreadful places just as I used to drink brandy—for sake of the exhileration it brings you."

We shook hands on parting, and from our inmost hearts, I am sure, wished each other well. I was more than ever impressed by the genuine greatness of the man, who had been degraded by the use of irresponsible power.

We reached Washington in good time, and I soon realized the great advantage of rest. Six hours of office work came so near nothing to do, that had I been in usual health I should probably have raised some disturbance from sheer idleness; but I learned by and by that the close attention demanded to avoid mistakes, could not well have been continued longer.

Several ladies continued distributing hospital stores for me all that fall and winter, and next spring I still had some to send out. When able I went myself, and in Carver found a man who had been wounded in a cavalry charge, said to have been as desperate as that of "the Light Brigade;" and who refused to take anything from me, because he had "seen enough of these people who go around hospitals pretending to take care of wounded soldiers."

I convinced him it was his duty to take the jelly in order to prevent my stealing it. Also, that it was for my interest to save his life, that I might not have to pay my share of the cost of burying him and getting a man in his place. Nay, that it was my duty to get

him back into the saddle as fast as possible, that my
government need not pay him for lying abed. He
liked this view of the case, and not only took what I
offered him, but next time I went asked for Jefferson-
tie shoes to support his foot, and when I brought them
said he would be ready for duty in a week.

In Judiciary Square, a surgeon asked me to give a
jar of currant jelly to a man in Ward Six, who was
fatally wounded.

I found the man, those in the neighboring cots and
the nurse, all very sad, talked to him a few moments,
and said:

"You think you are going to die!"

"That is what they all say I must do!"

"Well, I say you are not going to do anything of
the kind!"

"Oh! I guess I am!"

"Not unless you have made up your mind to it, and
are quite determined. Those hip wounds kill a great
many men, because folks do not know how to manage
them, and because the men are easy to kill; but it
takes a good deal to kill a young man with a good conscience, who has never drank liquor or used tobacco;
who has muscle like yours, a red beard and blue gray
eyes."

I summoned both his day and night nurse, told all
three together of the surgical trap-door that old Mother
Nature wanted made and kept open, clear up to the
center of that wound. The surgeon would always
make one if the patient wanted it. I told them about
the warmth and nourishment and care needed, and left
him and them full of hope and resolution.

Next time I was in Judiciary, a young man on crutches accosted me, saying :

"Were not you in Ward Six, about six weeks ago?"

"Yes!"

"Do you remember a man there, that every one said was going to die, and you said he would n't?"

"Yes."

"Well, I 'm the fellow."

I looked at him inquiringly, and said:

"Well, did you die?"

He burst into uproarious laughter, and replied:

"No, but I 'm blamed if I would n't, if you had n't come along."

I passed on, left him leaning against the wall finishing his laugh, and saw or heard of him no more.

It was but a few days after he passed out of my knowledge that news came of the death of Gen. Lowrie. It was the old story, "the great man down," for he died in poverty and neglect, but with his better self in the ascendent. His body lies in an unmarked grave, in that land where once his word was law.

Pondering on his death, I thought of that country boy going to his father's house, with the life restored by one he knew not, even by name, and the going home of that mature man, who thought he knew my inmost soul, and with whose political death I was charged. Only the wisdom of eternity can determine which, if either, I served or injured. To the one, life may lack blessing, to the other, death be all gain.

CHAPTER LXVI.

MEET MISS DIX AND GO TO FREDERICKSBURG.

I sat down stairs, for the first time after a two weeks' illness, when Georgie Willets, of Jersey City, came in, saying:

"Here is a pass for you and one for me, to go to Fredericksburg! A boat leaves in two hours, and we must hurry!"

For several days the air had shuddered with accounts of the terrible suffering of our men, wounded in the battle of the Wilderness; and a pall of uncertainty and gloom hung over the city.

I made a tuck in a queen's-cloth dress, donned it, selected a light satchel, put into one side a bottle of whiskey and one of sherry, half a pound of green tea, two rolls of bandage and as much old table-linen as packed them close; put some clothing for myself in the other side, and a cake of black castile soap, for cleansing wounds; took a pair of good scissors, with one sharp point, and a small rubber syringe, as surgical instruments; put these in my pocket, with strings attaching them to my belt; got on my Shaker bonnet, and with a large blanket shawl and tin cup, was on board with Georgie, an hour before the boat left.

It had brought a load of wounded from Belle Plain; some were still on board, and suffering intensely from thirst, and hard, dry dressings. It was a hot day, and we both went to work giving drinks of water, wetting wounds, and bathing hot heads and hands.

'As Georgie passed the foot of the cabin stairs, Miss Dix was coming down, and called to her, saying:

"What are you doing here?"

She made no reply, but passed on to her work, when the irate lady turned to where I was drawing water from a cooler, and asked, in a tone of high displeasure:

"Who is that young girl?"

"Miss Georgie Willets, of Jersey City," I replied.

"And where is she going?"

"To Fredericksburg."

"By whose authority?" she demanded.

"By authority of the Surgeon-General," I replied.

"The Surgeon-General has no authority to send a young girl down there alone."

"She is not going alone."

"Who is going with her?" she asked, tartly.

"I am."

"Who are you?"

I told her, and she ceased to be insulting long enough to expostulate on the great impropriety of the proceeding, as well as to explain the total lack of any need of help in Fredericksburg. She had just returned from that city, where she had arranged everything in the most satisfactory manner. Hospitals had been established, with surgeons and nurses. There was therefore not the slightest occasion for our going further; but she was about to organize relief for the men while waiting at the Washington wharf to be taken to hospitals. Here I might be useful, and here she would be glad to have me work; but as for that handsome young girl, she wondered at me for bringing her into such a place.

Georgie was not merely handsome.   She was grand, queenly; and I told Miss Dix that I differed with her about the kind of women who should go into such places. We wanted young, vigorous women—women whose self-respect and social position would command the respect of those to whom they ministered.   She grew angry again, and said:

" She shall not go to Fredericksburg; I will have her arrested!"

I was kneeling beside a man whose wounds I was bathing; for I had not suspended my work to talk with her, who stood, straight as a telegraph pole, holding a bottle which she ever and anon applied to her nose; but when she reached this climax, I raised my head, looked into her face, and said:

" I shall not be sorry Miss Dix, if you do; for then I shall apply to my friends, Mrs. Abraham Lincoln and Secretary Stanton, and have your authority tested."

I went on with my work; she growled something and left the boat, but did not disturb us further.

Going down the river I grew worse, and thought I might be obliged to return with the boat, and stay at home; but consulted a surgeon on his way to the front, who talked with another, and said:

" There is no immediate danger in your case.   It is only secondary hemorrhage; and with care you may go on, but must not attempt to do anything.   You can, however, be of incalculable service, simply by being in Fredericksburg; can sit down and see that people do their duty.   What our wounded need most, is people who have an interest in their welfare—friends. You can do a great deal toward supplying this want, this great need; but be careful and do not try to work."

After some time this surgeon brought, and introduced Col. Chamberlain, of Maine, evidently an invalid, and a man of the purely intellectual type. Two other surgeons were with him, and all three endeavored to persuade him to return to Washington, as his lack of health made it very dangerous, if not quite useless, for him to go to the front. I thought the surgeons right; and told him I feared he was throwing away his life, in an effort to do the impossible.

He explained that he was in command of a brigade of eight regiments; that in them were hundreds of his neighbors and pupils, for he had resigned a professorship in a college to enlist. Said he knew his own constitution better than any one else could know it; knew he would be stronger when he reached his post, and that the danger would be in any attempt to keep out of danger—the danger which his men must face. Turning to me he said:

"If you had eight children down there, you would go to them, if you could!"

We arranged that if he should be wounded so as to suffer a thigh amputation, he should let me know, that I might nurse him through.

At Belle Plaine, Georgie went to look for transportation, and I to the Sanitary Commission boat, where I was introduced to Mrs. Gen. Barlow and Miss Hancock, both busy furnishing hot coffee to those being embarked for Washington. Mrs. Barlow was a tall, superbly formed woman, very handsome, and full of health and spirits. She looked down on me compassionately, and said:

"Oh, you poor little thing! What ever brought you here? We have sick folks enough now! Do sit down until I get you a cup of tea!"

While I drank the tea, she stood looking at me, and said meditatively:

"Oh, you queer little thing," and hurried off to her work.

Soon a Colonel with a badly wounded head came on board, leaned against a post and groaned. I found a basin of water and a towel, and began bathing his head, wetting those torturing dressings and making him comparatively comfortable, when she stopped in her hurried walk, looked on an instant, and exclaimed:

"Oh, you nice little thing! Now I see what you are good for! I could not do that; but you will take care of their wounds and I will feed them! That will be grand!"

Soon Georgie came to say there was no transportation to be had, but she had found a Campbell surgeon in charge of a hospital tent, and he wanted me; said he was worn out, and had plenty of work for both of us. The doctor had a large tent, filled with wounded lying on loose hay. His patients seemed to want for nothing, but he must needs give so much time to receiving and forwarding those pouring in from the front, that he needed us. He had a little tent put up for us, and that was the only night I have ever slept in a tent.

Next morning while we were attending to a Colonel, and Lieutenant Colonel, both of the same regiment, and both badly wounded and just brought in, one said to the other: "My God, if our men in Fredericksburg

could have a little of this care!" "Why?" said I,
"I have heard that everything possible was being
done for them?"

"Everything possible!" exclaimed one, and both
together began the most terrible recital of the neglect
and abuse of the wounded in that horrible place—men
dying of thirst, and women spitting in their faces, kicking and spurning them." We set down our basins;
Georgie started in one direction and I in another, to
find transportation.

The surgeon in command of the station stood super-
intending the loading of oats while he looked at my
pass, and said he could not possibly send us, adding:
"Fredericksburg is no place for a lady. It is impossible to describe the condition of things there."

"But, Doctor, I am not a lady! I am a hospital nurse.
The place where men are suffering must be the place
for me. I do not look strong, but you cannot think
how much I can do.

"But, Madam, you forget that our army is cut off
from its base of supplies, and must be furnished with
subsistence, and that we have not half the transpor-
tations we need."

"Doctor, you are sending bags of oats in ambulances! I do not weigh much more than one, and
will be worth six when you get me there."

He promised to send me that afternoon, but I
doubted him; went to the Christian Commission tent,
found a man who knew me by reputation, and told
him they had better send me to Fredericksburg, or put
me under arrest, for I was in a mood to be dangerous.
He feigned fright, caught up his hat, and said:

20

"We'll get you out of this in the shortest possible space of time."

An hour after I was on the way, and Georgie a few moments in advance. I had seen bad roads in northern and western Pennsylvania, but this was my first ride over no road. We met a steady stream of such wounded as were able to walk, but comparatively few were brought in ambulances.

It was raining when we reached Fredericksburg, at four o'clock on Sabbath, and I went to the surgeon in command, reported, and asked him to send me to the worst place—the place where there was most need.

"Then I had better send you to the Old Theater, for I can get no one to stay there."

He gave me my appointment, and I went to a Corps Surgeon, who signed it, and advised me not to go to the theater—I could do nothing, as the place was in such dreadful condition, while I could be useful in many other places.

CHAPTER LXVII.

THE OLD THEATER.

THIS building was on Princess Ann street. The basement floor was level with the sidewalk, but the ground sloped upward at the back; so that the yard was higher than the floor. Across the front was a vestibule, with two flights of stairs leading up to the auditorium; behind the vestibule a large, low room, with two rows of pillars supporting the upper floor; and behind this three small rooms, and a square hall with a side entrance. The fence was down between the theater and Catholic church, next door. I stopped in the church to see Georgie, who was already at work there, came and left by the back door, and entered the theater by the side hall.

The mud was running in from the yard. Opposite the door, in a small room, was a pile of knapsacks and blankets; and on them lay two men smoking. To get into the large room, I must step out of the hall mud over one man, and be careful not to step on another. I think it was six rows of men that lay close on the floor, with just room to pass between the feet of each row; they so close in the rows that in most places I must slide one foot before the other to get to their heads.

The floor was very muddy and strewn with *debris*, principally of crackers. There was one hundred and eighty-two men in the building, all desperately wounded. They had been there a week. There were two leather water-buckets, two tin basins, and about every third man had saved his tin-cup or canteen; but no other vessel of any sort, size or description on the premises—no sink or cess-pool or drain. The nurses were not to be found; the men were growing reckless and despairing, but seemed to catch hope as I began to thread my way among them and talk. No other memory of life is more sacred than that of the candor with which they took me into their confidence, as if I had been of their own sex, yet ever sought to avoid wounding the delicacy they ascribed to mine.

I found some of the nurses—cowards who had run away from battle, and now ran from duty—galvanized

them into activity, invented substitutes for things
that were wanting—making good use of an old knapsack and pocket-knife—and had tears of gratitude
for pay.

One man lay near the front door, in a scant flannel
shirt and cotton drawers, his left thigh cut off in the
middle and the stump supported on the only pillow
in the house. It was six by ten inches, stuffed with
straw. His head was supported by two bits of board
and a pair of very muddy boots. He called me,
clutched my dress, and plead:

"Mother, can't you get me a blanket, I'm so cold;
I could live if I could get any care!"

I went to the room where the men lay smoking on
the blankets; but one of them wearing a surgeon's
shoulder-straps, and speaking in a German accent,
claimed them as his private property, and positively
refused to yield one. The other man was his orderly,
and words were useless—they kept their blankets.

Going into a room behind that, I found a man
slightly wounded sitting on the floor, supporting another who had been shot across the face, and was
totally blind. He called, and when I came and talked
with them, said:

"Won't you stay with us?"

"Stay with you?" I replied, "Well, I rather think
I will, indeed; I came to stay, and am one of the
folks it is hard to drive away!"

"Oh! thank God; everybody leaves us; they come
and promise, and then go off, but I know you will
stay; you will do something for us!"

It was so pitiful, that for an instant my courage
failed, and I said:

"I will certainly stay with you; but fear it is little I can do for you."

"Oh, you can speak to us; you do not know how good your voice sounds. I have not seen a woman in three months; what is your name?"

"My name is mother."

"Mother; oh my God! I have not seen my mother for two years. Let me feel your hand?"

I took between both of mine his hand, covered with mud and blood and smoke of battle, and told him I was not only going to stay with them, but was going to send him back to his regiment, with a lot more who were lying around here doing nothing, when there was so much fighting to be done; I had come on purpose to make them well, and they might make up their minds to it. My own courage had revived, and I must revive theirs; I could surely keep them alive until help should come. By softening the torturing bandages on his face, I made him more comfortable; and in an adjoining room found another man with a thigh stump, who had been served by field-surgeons, as the thieves served the man going from Jerusalem to Jericho: *i. e.*, "stripped him, left him naked and half dead." Those men surely did not go into battle without clothes; and why they should have been sent out of the surgeon's hands without enough of even underclothing to cover them, is the question I have never yet had answered. Common decency led to his being placed in the back room alone, but I shall never blush for going to him and doing the little I could for his comfort.

After I returned to the large room, I took notice

about clothing, and found that most of the men had on their ordinary uniform; some had two blankets, more had one; but full one-third were without any. There was no shadow or pretense of a bed or pillow, not even a handful of straw or hay! There was no broom, no hoe, or shovel, or spade to sweep or scrape the floor; and the horrors were falling upon me when the man of the blankets came, and said:

"Mattam, iv you are goin' to do any ding for tese men, you petter git dem someding to eat."

"Something to eat?"

"Yaas! mine Cot, someding to eat! De government petter leave dem to tie on de pattle field, nur do pring tem here to starve."

I looked at him in much surprise, and said:

"Who are you?"

"Vy, I am de surgeon. Tey send me here; put mine Cot, I cannot do notting. Tere ish notting to do mit!"

I called out: "Men, what have you had to eat?"

"Hard tack, and something they call coffee," was the response.

"Have you had no meat?"

"Meat? We have forgotten what it tastes like!"

In one corner, near the front door, was a little counter and desk, with a stationary bench in front. To this desk the surgeon gave me a key. I found writing material, and sent a note of four lines to the Corps Surgeon. Half an hour after, an irate little man stormed in and stamped around among those prostrate men, flourishing a scrap of paper and calling for the writer. His air was that of the champion who wanted to see "the man who struck Billy Patterson," and his fierceness quite alarmed me, lest he should step on some of the men. So I hurried to him, and was no little surprised to find that the offending missive was my note. I told him I had written it, and could have had no thought of "reporting" him, since I knew nothing about him.

After considerable talk I learned that he had charge of the meat, and that none had been issued to that place, because no "requisition" had been sent. I had never written a requisition, but found blanks in that desk, filled one, signed it and gave it to the meat man, who engaged that the beef should be there next morning.

It grew dark, and we had two tallow candles lighted! May none of my readers ever see such darkness made visible—such rows of haggard faces looking at them from out such cavernous gloom! I talked hopefully, worked and walked, while mentally exclaiming:

"Oh, God! What shall I do?"

About nine o'clock Dr. Porter, Division Surgeon, came with Georgie, to take us to our quarters. These were but half a block away, on the same side of the street, but on the opposite side, and corner of the next cross-street, in a nice two-story brick house, with a small yard in front. An old lady answered his summons, but refused to admit us: when he insisted and I interposed, saying the lady was afraid of soldiers, but would admit us. We would bid him good night, and soon our lodgings would be all right.

She was relieved, took us in, cooked our rations for herself and us, gave us a comfortable bed, and was

uniformly kind all the time we staid, and seemed
sorry to have us leave.

I spoke the first night to Dr. Porter about blankets
and straw, or hay for beds, but was assured that none
were to be had. Supplies could not reach them since
being cut off from their base, and the Provost Marshal,
Gen. Patrick, would not permit anything to be taken
out of the houses, though many of them were unoccu-
pied, and well supplied with bedding and other necessaries. I thought we ought to get two blankets for
those two naked men, if the Government should pay
their weight in gold for them; and suggested that the
surgeons take what was necessary for the comfort of
the men, and give vouchers to the owners. I knew
such claims would be honored; would see that they
should be; but he said the matter had been settled by
the Provost, and nothing more could be done.

It seems to me now that I must have been be-
numbed, or I could have done something to provide
covering for those men. I did think of giving one of
them my shawl, but I must have died without it. I
remembered my Douglas Hospital letter, and knew
that Gen. Patrick could order me out of Fredericksburg, and leave these men to rot in the old theater.
Already their wounds were infested by worms, which
gnawed and tormented them; some of those wounds
were turning black, many were green; the vitality of
the men was sinking for want of food and warmth.
I could not forsake them to look after reform; would
not fail to do what I could, in an effort to do what I
could not or might not accomplish.

In the morning I saw that the men had something

they called coffee, and found canned milk for it, which was nourishment; but a new difficulty arose. The men who brought the coffee would distribute it to those who had cups or canteens, and the others would get none. I had some trouble to induce them to leave their cans, until, with the two tin cups I could borrow, I could give about one-third the whole number the coffee they could not otherwise have.

Our cooking was done in the churchyard, with that of the church patients. A shed had been put up; but our cooking was an "uncovenanted mercy," and when our beef came there was a question as to how it could be cooked—how that additional work could be done.

I wrote to the Provost-Marshal, stating our trouble, and the extremity of one hundred and eighty-two men. Asked that we might take a cook-stove out of a vacant house near; promised to take good care of it and have it returned; and he wrote, for answer:

"I am not a thief! If you want a stove send to the Sanitary Commission!"

He must have known that the Commission was as pressed as the Government to conform its arrangements to the movements of an army cut off from its base of supplies, and that it had no stoves, so the plain English of his answer was:

"Let your wounded die of hunger, in welcome! I am here to guard the property of the citizens of Fredericksburg!"

I had already written to the Commission for blankets and a broom, but there were none to be had. It soon however sent a man, who cut branches off trees, and with them swept the floors.

CHAPTER LXVIII.

AM PLACED IN AUTHORITY.

On Monday morning I sent for Dr. Porter, and stated the trouble about nurses shirking. He had them all summoned in the front end of the large room, and in presence of the patients, said to them:

"You see this lady? Well, you are to report to her for duty; and if she has any fault to find with you she will report you to the Provost-Marshal!"

I have never seen a set of men look more thoroughly subdued. There were eleven of them, and they all gave me the military salute. The doctor went off, and I set them to work. One middle-aged Irishman had had some experience as a nurse; could dress wounds—slowly, but very well—was faithful and kind; and him I made head-nurse up stairs, where there were fifty-four patients, and gave him three assistants, for whom he was to be responsible. After Patrick's note, I calculated my resources, and got ready for a close siege. As I sat on that little stationary bench, making an inventory, I heard shrieks, groans and curses, at the far end of the room; ran to the place, and got there in time to see the surgeon of the blankets tearing the dry dressings off a thigh stump! Coming up behind him, I caught him by both ears, and had my hands full, ordered him to stop, and said:

"You had better go back to your room and smoke."

Again I sent for Surgeon Porter, and in less than two hours that little wretch, with his orderly, packed up his blankets and I saw him or them no more. I had never dressed a thigh stump, but must dress a good many now; I rolled that one in a wet cloth, and covered it carefully, to let the man get time to rest, while I got rid of his horrid tormentor. When there was so much to be done, I would do the most needful thing first, and this was ridding the wounds of worms and gangrene, supporting the strength of the men by proper food, and keeping the air as pure as possible. I got our beef into the way of being boiled, and would have some good substantial broth made around it. I went on a foraging expedition—found a coal-scuttle which would do for a slop-pail, and confiscated it, got two bits of board, by which it could be converted into a stool, and so bring the great rest of a change of position to such men as could sit up; had a little drain made with a bit of board for a shovel, and so kept the mud from running in at the side door; melted the tops off some tin cans, and made them into drinking cups; had two of my men confiscate a large tub from a brewery, set it in the vestibule to wash rags for outside covers to wounds, to keep off chill, and had others bring bricks and rubbish mortar from a ruin across the street, to make substitutes for pillows.

I dressed wounds! dressed wounds, and made thorough work of it. In the church was a dispensary, where I could get any washes or medicines I wished, and I do not think I left a worm. Some of them were over half an inch long, with black heads and many feet, but most were maggots. They were often deeply seated, but my syringe would drive them out, and twice a day I followed them up. The black and green places grew smaller and better colored with every dressing. The men grew stronger with plenty of beef and broth and canned milk. I put citric acid and sugar in their apple sauce as a substitute for lemons. I forget how many thigh stumps I had, but I think as many as twelve. One of them was very short and in a very bad condition. One morning when I was kneeling and dressing it, the man burst into tears, and said:

"You do not seem to mind this, but I know you would not do it for anything but the love of God, and none but He can ever reward you; but if I live to see my wife and children, it will be through what you have done for me, and I will teach them to bless your name!"

He quite took me by surprise, for I seemed to have forgotten any other life than that I was then living; and dressing the most frightful wounds was as natural as eating. I felt no disgust, no shrinking, and mere conventional delicacy is withdrawn when the Angel of Death breathes upon it.

The man we stepped over at the back door, proved to be a student from the Pennsylvania Agricultural College, shot through the alimentary canal, near the base of the spine. For him there was no hope, but I did what I could to make him less uncomfortable, and once he said:

"This is strange work for a lady."

"You forget," I said, "that I am surgeon in charge, that you and I were made of the same kind of clay, in much the same fashion, and will soon turn into just the same kind of dust."

How my heart was wrung for him, with his refined face, dying for a country which sent its bayonets to stand between him and the armful of straw, with which I might have raised him above that muddy floor. He had no knapsack to serve as a pillow, no blanket, no cup, and his position across the doorway was cold and uncomfortable; but even after I had made a better place for him, he objected to leaving two companions, who lay next to him, and I could not find room for all three together, even on that dirty floor. He himself always dressed the wound where the bullet entered, and was most grateful for the means of doing so. I cared for that one through which Death's messenger made its exit, and although he knew its condition, he did not know the certainty of a fatal result, and resented any intimation that he should not recover.

CHAPTER LXIX.

VISITERS.

THE second morning of my work in the old theater, Miss Hancock came to see how I got along. She was thoroughly practical, and a most efficient laborer in the hospital field, and soon thought of something to better the condition of the man minus clothes, who lay quite near my desk and the front door, and caught my dress whenever he could, to plead for a blanket. She could get no blanket; but was stationed in the Methodist Church, where there was a surgeon in charge, and everything running in regular order. In a tent adjoining, this man could be laid out of the draught and chill of that basement, and she would do her best to get some clothing for him. She sent two men with a stretcher, who took him to the church tent, where I fear he was not much better provided for than in the place he left.

After some days, Mrs. Gen. Barlow came to see the men who all belonged to her husband's division, and were rejoiced to see her; and to express a general fear for my life. I was to die of overwork and want of sleep, "and then," she exclaimed, "what will become of these men? No one but you ever could or would have done anything for them. Do you know there were three surgeons detailed for duty here, before you came, and none of them would stay? Now if you die, they will. Do take some rest!"

I listened and looked at her flushed face, while she talked, and said:

"Mrs. Barlow, I am not going to die—am in no danger whatever, and will hold out until help comes. This cannot last; Government will come to the rescue, and my men will be here when it comes. After all is over, I will fall to pieces like an old stage coach when the king-bolt drops out; will lie around as lumber for a while, then some one will put me together again, and I will be good as new. It is you who are killing yourself. You must change your arrangements or you will take typhoid fever, and after such a strain, recovery will be hopeless. I take nobody's disease—am too repellant; but you will catch contagion very readily. Keep away from fever cases and rest; you are in imminent peril."

She hurried away, laughing at the idea of one in her perfect health being injured by hard work; but my heart was full of evil omen. I had talked with Mrs. Senator Pomeroy, on her way from her last visit to the Contraband camp, where she gave her life in labor for the friendless and poor, and she had looked very much as Mrs. Barlow did that day.

Soon after this, I was made glad by the sight of my friend, Mrs. Judge Ingersol. People say her daughter, Mrs. Gov. Chamberlain, is a beauty, but she is not old enough ever to have been as beautiful as her mother, that day, in her plain widow's dress, walking among the wounded, with her calm face so full of strength and gentleness.

She and Mrs. Barlow had hatched a rebellion. In the city was a barn containing straw, for want of which our men were dying. It was guarded by one of Gen. Barlow's men. Mrs. Barlow took two others, went with them, placed herself in front of the guard, told them to break open the barn and carry out the straw, and him to fire, if he thought it is duty; but he must reach them through her. The man's orders were to guard the barn; with the straw out of it he had nothing to do. The men moved side and side, going in and out, and she kept in range to cover them until the last armful had been removed. It was taken away and was to be distributed; but there was still so little compared to the need, that there must be consultation about the manner of using it. Mrs. Ingersol thought it should be made into small pillows, and volunteered to undertake that work; as the Commission could furnish muslin, I thought this best. She found

a loft, and engaged several Fredericksburg women to
work for pay. They worked one day, but did not return on the second. There were a good many Union
women there by this time, who should have helped,
but few could confine themselves to obscure work in
a loft, when there was so much excitement on the
streets. There was no authority to hold any one to
steady employment; and so about two-thirds the help-
ers who reached Fredericksburg, spent a large part of
their time in an aimless wandering and wondering,
and finding so much to be done, could do nothing.

So, most of the time Mrs. Ingersol was in her loft
alone, except the orderlies who stuffed her slips, sewed
up the ends and carried them off to the places she
designated; but she had nimble fingers, and sleight-of-
hand, and turned out a surprising number of small
straw pillows.

As my allowance came, the question was what to do
with them. They were too precious for use. What
should I do with those scraps of white on that field of
grime? Our gaunt horror became grotesque, in view
of such unwonted luxuries. What! A whole dozen
or two little straw pillows among one hundred and
sixty men! Who should elect the aristocrats to be
cradled in such luxury amid that world of want?

When my aristocrat was elected, how should his
luxury be applied? Would I put it under his head
or mangled limb? I think I never realized our destitu-
tion until those little pillows came to remind me that
sometimes wounded men had beds! Oh, God! would
relief never come? Like the Scotch girl in the besieged
fortress of India, I felt like laying my ear to the ground,

to harken for the sound of the bagpipes, the tramp of the Campbells coming. It did seem that, without surgical aid or comforts of any kind, my men must soon be all past hope; but a surgeon came, and I hailed him with joy, thinking him the advance guard of the army of relief. Half an hour after his appearance I missed him, and saw him no more; and this was the fourth which left those men, after being regularly detailed to duty among them—left them to die or live, as they could.

Soon after this we had an official visit from one of those laundry critics, called "Medical Inspectors." As there were no sheets or counterpanes to look after, he turned his attention to a heap of dry rubbish in the vestibule, which gave the place an untidy appearance, as seen from the street. To remove this eyesore he had one of my nurses hunt up a wheel-barrow, and two shovels—shovels were accessible by this time—and ordered him and another to wheel that rubbish out into the street. The wheel-barrow coming in the door called my attention, when I learned that we were going to be made respectable. I sent the wheel-barrow home, gave the shovels to two men to dig a sink hole back in the yard, and forbade any disturbance of the dry, harmless rubbish in the vestibule. I would not have my men choked with dust by its removal, and set about getting up false appearances. No medical inspector should white that sepulchre until he cleared the dead men's bones out of it. He had not looked at a wound; did not know if the men had had any dinner. A man did not need a medical diploma to clear up after stage carpenters. If the Government wanted

21

322

that kind of work done, it had better send a man and cart with its donkey.

CHAPTER LXX.

WOUNDED OFFICERS.

In Washington, I had done nothing for any wounded officer, except a captain who was brought to our ward when all the others were taken away, and in Fredericksburg I began on that principle. I found twenty in the Old Theater, and had them removed to private houses, to make room for the men, and that they might be better cared for. Officers could be quartered in private houses, and have beds, most of those taken out of the theater were put into houses between it and our quarters, so that I could see them on my way to and from meals. Among them was the blind man, who still craved to hear me speak and feel my hand, and I kept his face in a wet compress until a surgeon was dressing it and found the inflammation so gone that he drew the lid of one back, and the man cried out in delight: " I can see! I can see! now let me see mother." I stood in his range of vision, until the surgeon closed the lids, when he said: " Now, mother, I shall always remember just how you look."

I found in my visit to those men that some orderlies needed some one to keep them in order, and that a helpless man is not always sure his servant will serve him. Often the orderlies themselves were powerless, and those men would have suffered if I had not cared for them. More than once some of them said: " I wish, mother, we were back with you in the Old Theater?"

There was a captain whose stump I must fix every night before he could sleep, and when his wife came I tried to teach her, but she was so much afraid of hurting him she could do nothing.   I learned in time that officers quartered in private houses, even with the greater comforts they had, often suffered more than the men in all their privations.   Mrs. Barlow came for me to see one given up to die, and I found him in a large handsome room, on the first floor of an elegant residence, absolutely hopeless, but for years have not been able to recall the trouble in his case.

It must have been easy to set right, for he began at once to recover, and I felt that people had been very stupid, and that there was an unreasonable amount of wonder and gratitude over whatever it was I did. It was often so easy to save a life, where there were the means of living, that a little courage or common sense seemed like a miraculous gift to people whose mental powers had been turned in other directions.

But I found another side to looking after officers in private quarters.   One evening after dark, Georgie called to tell me of a dreadful case of suffering which a surgeon wished her to see.   He was there to accompany her, but she declined going without me, and I went along, walking close behind them, as the pavement was narrow.   He did not seem to notice that I was there, was troubled with the weight of his diploma and shoulder-straps, and talked very patronizingly to the lady at his side, until she turned, and said to me:

"Do you hear that?"

"Oh, yes," I replied, "and feel very grateful to the young man for his permission to do the work he is paid for doing, but if he had reserved his patronage until some one had asked for it, it would have had more weight."

"Your friend is sarcastic," was his reply to her; and I said no more until we reached the case of great distress, which was on the second floor of a vacant house, and proved to be a colonel in uniform, seated in an easy chair, smoking, while his orderly sat in another chair, on the other side of the room.

Georgie stood looking from one man to the other in speechless surprise; but I spoke to the man in the chair, saying:

"How is it, sir, that you, an officer, in need of nothing, have trespassed upon our time and strength, when you know that men are dying by hundreds for want of care?"

He began to apologize and explain, but I said to Georgie:

"Come, Miss Willets, we are not needed here."

As we passed from the room, the surgeon took his cap to accompany us, when I stopped, made a gesture, and said:

"Young man! stay where you are! Your friend must be too ill to do without you. I will see the young lady to her quarters. The vidette is on the corner, and we do not need you!"

We came away filled with wonder, but we did not for some time realize the danger. We came to know that Miss Dix's caution was not altogether unwise; that women had been led into traps of this kind, when it would have been well for them had they died there, and when duty to themselves and the public required them to get one or more doctors ready for dissection. After that lesson, however, I did not fear to leave Georgie, who remained with the army, doing grand work, until Richmond fell, but laying the foundation of that consumption, of which she died.

Of all the lives which the Rebellion cost us, none was more pure, more noble, than that of this beautiful, refined, strong, gentle girl.

CHAPTER LXXI.

"NOW I LAY ME DOWN TO SLEEP."

THE Sanitary Commission soon got a supply of clothing, and sent two men to wash and dress my patients. These, with the one sweeping floors with branches, were an incalculable help and comfort; but these two did their work and passed on to other places. One of the men they had dressed grew weak, and I was at a loss to account for his symptoms, until by close questioning, I drew from him the answer,

"It is my other wound!"

These words sounded like a death-knell, but I insisted on seeing the other wound, and found four bullet holes under his new clothes. From the one wound, for which I had been caring, he might easily recover; but with four more so distributed that he must lie on one, and no surgeon to make trap doors, no bed—there was no hope. He was so bright, so good, so intelligent, so courageous, it was hard to give him up. Ah, if I had him in Campbell, with Dr. Kelly to use the knife! How my heart clung to him!

He lay near the center of the room, with his head close to a column; and one night as I knelt giving him drink, and arranging his knapsack and brick pillow, making the most of his two blankets, and thinking of his mother at home, I was suddenly impressed by the beauty and grandeur of his face;—his broad, white brow shaded by bushy, chestnut hair, half curling; the delicate oval of his cheeks; the large, expressive grey eyes; the straight nose and firm chin and lips!—he could not have been more than twenty-two, almost six feet high, with a frame full of vigor. How many such men were there in this land? How many could we afford to sacrifice in order to preserve a country for the use of cowards and traitors, and other inferior types of the race?

The feeble light of my candle threw this picture into strong relief against the surrounding gloom, and it was harder than ever to give him up, but this must be done; and I wanted to extract from that bitter cup one drop of sweetness for his mother; so I said to him:

" Now, George, do you think you can sleep?" He said he could, and I added:

" Will you pray before you sleep?" He said he would.

" Do you always pray before going to sleep?" He nodded, and I contined:

" Let us pray together, to-night, just the little prayer your mother taught you first."

He clasped his hands, and together we repeated

"Now I lay me down to sleep," to the end; when I said:

"Do you mean that, George? Do you mean to ask God to keep your soul, for Christ's sake, while you are here; and, for His sake, to take it to Himself when you go hence, whenever that may be?"

The tears were running over his cheeks, and he said, solemnly:

"I do."

"Then it is all well with you, and you can rest in Him who giveth his beloved sleep."

There was no time for long prayers, and I must go to another sufferer.

A kind, strong man, from the Michigan Aid Society, came and worked two days among my men, and said:

"If I only had them in a tent, on the ground; but this floor is dreadful!"

Up stairs were some wounds I must dress, while a corpse lay close beside one of the men, so that I must kneel touching it, while I worked. It lay twelve hours before I could get it taken to its shallow, coffinless grave; and while I knelt there, the man whose wound I was dressing, said:

"Never mind; we'll make you up a good purse for this!"

He had no sooner spoken than a murmur of contemptuous disapproval came from the other men, and one said:

"A purse for her! She's got more money than all of us, I bet!"

Another called out:

"No, we won't! Won't do anything of the kind! We 're your boys; ain't we, mother? You 're not working for money!"

"Why," persisted the generous man, "we made up a purse of eighty dollars for a woman t' other time I was hurt, and she had n't done half as much for us!"

"Eighty dollars!" called out the man who thought me rich; "eighty dollars for her! why I tell you she could give every one of us eighty dollars, and would not miss it!"

Another said:

"She is n't one of the sort that are 'round after purses!"

Why any of them should have thought me rich I cannot imagine except for the respect with which officers treated me. To veil the iron hand I held over my nurses, I made a jest of my authority, pinned a bit of bandage on my shoulder, and played commander-in-chief. Officers and guards would salute when we passed, as an innocent joke, but the men came to regard me as a person of rank.

Citizens of Fredericksburg, who at first insulted me on the street, as they did other Yankee nurses, heard that I was a person of great influence, and began to solicit my good offices on behalf of friends arrested by order of Secretary Stanton, and held as hostages, for our sixty wounded who were made prisoners while trying to pass through the city, before we took possession.

So I was decked in plumes of fictitious greatness, and might have played princess in disguise if I had had time; but I had only two deaths in the old theater—

this man up stairs, and the man without clothes, who
lay alone in that back room, and after the amputa-
tation of his thigh, had no covering until government
gave him one of Virginia clay.

CHAPTER LXXII.

MORE VICTIMS AND A CHANGE OF BASE.

ONE day at noon, the air thrilled with martial music
and the earth shook under the tramp of men as seven
thousand splendid troops marched up Princess Ann
street on their way to reinforce our army, whose rear
was about eight miles from us. They were in superb
order, and the forts around Washington had been
stripped of their garrisons, and most of their guns, to
furnish them; but the generalship which cut our
army off from its base of supplies, and blundered
into the battle of the Wilderness, like a blind horse
into a briar patch, without shelling or burning the dry
chapperal in which our dead and wounded were consumed together, after the battle, had made no arrangements for the safe arrival of its reinforcements.
So they were ambushed soon after passing through
Fredericksburg; and that night, before ten o'clock, all
the places I had succeeded in making vacant were
filled with the wounded from this reinforcement. How
many of them were brought to Fredericksburg I do
not know; but it must have been a good many, when
some were sent to my den of horrors.

One evening, after dark, I went to the dispensary,
and found a surgeon just in from the front for sup-

plies.   While they were being put up, he told us of
the horrible carnage at Spottsylvania that day, when
the troops had been hurled, again and again, against
impregnable fortifications, under a rain of rifle balls,
which cut down a solid white oak tree, eighteen inches
in diameter.

The battle had ceased for the night, and it was
not known whether it would be renewed in the
morning.

"But if it is," said the speaker, "it will be the
bloodiest day of the war, and we must be whipped,
routed.   The Rebels are behind breastworks which
cannot be carried.   Any man but Grant would have
known that this morning, but he is to fight it out
on this line, and it is generally thought he will try
it again in the morning.   If he does, it will be a
worse rout than Bull Run."

No one was present but the surgeon in charge of
the church, the dispensary clerk, and myself; so he
was no alarmist, for when he had done speaking, he
took his package, mounted his horse and left.   People
had said, through the day, that the roar of guns was
heard in the higher portions of the city, but no news
of the battle seemed to have reached it during all the
next day.

I spent it in preparing for the worst, warned Georgie, and tightened the reins on my nurses.   I had had
no reason to complain of any, and felt that I should
hold them to duty, even through a rout.   It also
seemed well to know where our wounded were located,
in that part of the city, so that if an attempt were
made to remove them, in a hurry, there might not
be any overlooked.

At half-past eleven that night I had heard nothing from the front, and went to sleep, with heavy forebodings.   At two o'clock I was aroused by the sounds of a moving multitude, rose and looked out to see, under the starlight, a black stream pouring down the side street, on the corner of which our quarters were situated, and turning down Princess Ann, toward the river landing.   To me, it was the nation going to her doom, passing through the little period of starlight, on into the darkness and the unknown.

In Louisville, I had learned to believe that the Eternal verities demanded the destruction of our Government.   True, the South had beaten the North in her bloody struggle for the privilege of holding her slaves while she flogged them; but I could see, in this, no reason why that North should be chosen as Freedom's standard-bearer!   Our ignoble Emancipation Proclamation had furnished no rock of moral principle on which to plant her feet while she struggled in that bloody surf.   God was blotting out our name from among the nations, that he might plant here a government worthy of such a country.

I calculated there was a rear guard that would hold the enemy back until morning, and did not wake Georgie, who needed sleep; but I must be with my men, who would be alarmed by the unusual sounds; must see that those nurses did not run away.

To get to my post, I must cross that stream, and as I stood waiting on the bank, could see that it was not composed of men in martial array.   It met exactly all my previous conceptions of a disorderly flight.   There were men in and out of uniform, men rolled in blankets, men on horseback and men on foot, cannon, caisons, baggage wagons, beef cattle, ambulances and nondescripts, all mixed and mingled, filling the street from wall to wall; no one speaking a word, and all intent on getting forward as fast as possible. So thickly were they packed that I waited in vain, as much as twenty minutes, for some opening through which I might work my way to the other side, and at last called the vidette, who came and helped me over.

Reaching the theater, I found many of the men awake and listening; went among them and whispered, as I did something for each, that there was some movement on the street I did not understand, but should probably know about in the morning. During the suspense of those dark hours, and all the next day I was constantly reminded of the Bible metaphor of "a nail fastened in a sure place." The absolute confidence which those men reposed in me, the comfort and strength I could give them, were so out of proportion to my strength that it was a study. I was a very small nail, but so securely fastened in the source of all strength, that they could hold by me and hope, even when there seemed nothing to hope for. As for me, all the armies of the world, and the world itself might melt or blow away, but I should be safe with God, and know that for every creature He was working out some noble destiny. All the pain, and sorrow, and defeat, were rough places—briars in an upward path to something we should all rejoice to see.

All day that dark stream surged around that corner, and I took heart that the flight was not disorderly, since I heard of none coming by any other street. All day the work went on as usual at the old theater, and I made short excursions to other places. Up that street in one end of an engine house, up a narrow, winding stair, I found a room full of men deserted, and in most pitiable condition. They were all supposed to be fever cases, but one young man had an ankle wound, in which inflammation had appeared. I hurried to the surgeons, stationed in the far end of the building, and reported the case. They sent immediately for the man, and I knew in two hours that the amputation had been successful, and barely in time.

As I went on that errand, I met two Christian Commission men walking leisurely, admiring the light of the rising sun on the old buildings, and told them of the urgent demand for help, and chicken broth or beef broth and water up in that room. They were polite, and promised to go as soon as possible to the relief of that distress; but when I returned and up to the last knowledge I had of the case, they had not been there.

I secured a can of cooked turkey, the only one I ever saw, and a pitcher of hot water, and with these made a substitute for chicken broth; gave them all drinks of water, bathed their faces, found one of their absent nurses, made him promise to stay, and went back to the main building to have some one see that he kept his word.

Here was a large floor almost covered with wounded, and among them a woman stumbled about weeping, wailing, boo-hooing and wringing her hands; I caught her wrist, and said:

" What *is* the matter?"

"Oh! oh! oh! Boo-hoo! boo-hoo! the poor fellow is goin' to die an' wants me to write to his mother."

"Well, write to her and keep quiet! you need not kill all the rest of them because he is going to die."

"Oh! boo-hoo! some people has no feelin's; but I have got feelin's!"

I led her to the surgeon in charge, who sent her and her "feelin's" to her quarters, and told her not to come back.

She was the only one of the Dix' nurses I saw in Fredricksburg, and her large, flat, flabby face was almost hideous with its lack of eye-brows and lashes; but this hideousness must have been her recommendation, as she could not have been more than twenty years old.

From the engine house I went to the Methodist church. Miss Harcock had been detailed to the General Hospital, just being established, and I found a house full of men in a sad condition. Nine o'clock, on a hot morning, and no wounds dressed; bandages dry and hard, men thirsty and feverish, nurses out watching that stream pouring through the city, and patients helpless and despondent.

I got a basin of water and a clean rag, never cared for sponges, and went from one to another, dripping water in behind those bandages to ease the torment of lint splints, brought drinks and talked to call their attention from the indefinite dread which filled the air, and got up considerable interest in—I do not remember what—but something which set them to talking.

Some wounds I dressed, and while engaged on one, a man called from the other side of the house to know what the fun was all about, when the man whose wound I was attending placed a hand on each of his sides, screamed with laughter, and replied:

"Oh, Jim! do get her to dress your wound, for I swear, she'd make a dead man laugh!"

I found some of the nurses; a surgeon came in who would, I thought, attend to them, and I went back to my post to find every man on duty.

It was near sundown when we heard that this backward movement was a "change of base;" but to me it seemed more like looking for a base, as there had been none to change. The stream thickened toward nightfall, and continued until two o'clock next morning; so that our army was twenty-four hours passing through Fredericksburg; and in that time I do not think a man strayed off on to any other street! All poured down that side street, turned that corner, and went on down Princess Ann.

CHAPTER LXXIII.

PRAYERS ENOUGH AND TO SPARE.

The next evening, after hearing of the battle of Spottsylvania, and while waiting to know if it had been renewed, I sat after sundown on the door-step of our quarters, when an orderly hurried up and inquired for the Christian Commission. A lieutenant was dying, and wanted to see a preacher. I directed the messenger, but doubted if he would find a preacher, as I had seen nothing of any save a Catholic priest, with whom I had formed an alliance; and I went to stay with the dying man, who was alone.

I found him nervous and tired, with nothing to hinder his return to his regiment inside of a month. He had been converted, was a member of the Methodist church, and seemed an humble Christian man. I told him he was getting well, had seen too much company, and must go to sleep, which he proceeded to do in in a very short time after being assured that that motion was in order.

He had slept perhaps five minutes when the messenger returned, followed by six preachers! I made a sign that he slept and should not be disturbed, but they gathered around the bed with so much noise they waked him.

There seemed to be a struggle for precedence among his visitors, but one gained the victory. They all wanted to shake hands with the man in the bed, but his left arm was off, and I objected; whereupon the head spokesman groaned a good solid groan, to which the others groaned a response. He stood at the foot foot of the bed, spread his chest, and inquired:

"Well, brother, how is your soul in this solemn hour?"

The answer was such as a good Christian might make; and I told the gentleman that the lieutenant had been unnecessarily alarmed; that he had seen too much company, was weary and excited, needed rest, and was rapidly recovering; that he ought to go to sleep; but they all knelt around the bed, and the first prayed a good, long, loud prayer; talked about "the lake that burneth," and other pleasant things, while I held the patient's hand, and felt his nerves jerk.

I thought it would soon be over; but no sooner had

this one finished than the next fell to, and gave us a prayer with more of those sobs made by hard inhalation than his predecessor, and a good deal more brimstone. No sooner had he relieved his mind than a third threw back his head to begin, and I spoke, quietly as possible; begged they would let the lieutenant sleep; told them that down in the old theater was a man in a back room, alone and dying. I had tried to get some one to sit with him and pray with him, and hoped one or two of them would go to him at once, as every moment might make it too late. A man was also dying in the engine-house, who ought to have some Christian friend with him as he crossed the dark valley.

They listened impatiently; then the man whose turn it was to ventilate his eloquence, pushed his sleeves up to the elbows, rubbed his hands as if about to lift some heavy weight, and exclaimed:

"Yes, sister! Yes. We'll attend to them; but, first, let us get through with this case!"

Then he went to work and ladled out groans, sobs and blue blazes. The other three followed suit, and when they had all had a good time on their knees, each one gave a short oration, and when they got through I reminded them again of the two dying men; but like the undutiful son, they said, "I go! and went not!"

It was two of the six whom I met next morning, and asked to go to the relief of those poor patients, who promised and went not.

22

CHAPTER LXXIV.

GET OUT OF THE OLD THEATER.

I DO not know how long I was in charge of the old theater, but remember talking to some one of having been there ten days, and things looking as usual. It was after the change of base, that one afternoon I got eight hopeful cases sent to the General Hospital, where they would have beds. That night about ten o'clock the vidette halted a man, who explained that he was surgeon in charge of that institution, and when he got leave to go on, I caught him by the lapel of his coat, and said:

"If you are Surgeon—what is the reason that the eight men I sent you this afternoon had had no supper at nine o'clock?"

He promised to attend to them before he slept, and on that we parted. Soon after this, Dr. Childs, of Philadelphia, and a regular army surgeon, came to the old theater, hung their coats and official dignity, if they had any, on the wall—never said a word about the rubbish in the hall, but fastened up their sleeves and went to work. When they came, I felt as if I could not take another step, went to my room and lay down, thinking of Raphael's useless angels leaning their baby arms on a cloud. My angels wore beards, and had their sleeves turned up like farm laborers, as they lifted men out of the depths of despair into the light and warmth of human help and human sympathy.

In sending the men away, they sent the amputation cases and George to the church, and sent for me to go to them there.

Georgie had gone to the General Hospital, and there was no surgeon in charge at the church when I went to it. So, once more, I set about doing that which was right in my own eyes. I could have a bale of hay, whipped out my needle and thread, and for several bad cases who had two blankets converted one into a bed tick, had it filled with hay, and a man placed on it; but three were sadly in need of beds, and had no blankets; and to them I alloted the balance of my precious bale, had it placed under them loose, and rejoiced in their joy over so great a luxury. My theater men had been laid in a row close to the wall, next to the late scene of their suffering; and about midnight of the first night there, a nurse asked me to go to a man who was dying. I found him in front of the altar. The doors and front panels of the pews had been fastened V shape to the floor, and he lay with one arm over this, and his head hanging forward. He had been shot through the chest, was breathing loud and in gasps, worn out for want of support, and to lay him down was to put out his lamp of life instantly. What he needed was a high-backed chair, but General Patrick's sense of duty to the citizens of Fredericksburg left no hope of such a support. As the only substitute in my reach, I sat on the edge of the pew door and its panel, drew his arm across my knee, raised his head to my shoulder, and held it there by laying mine against it. In this way I could talk in a low monotone to him, and the hopes to which the soul turns when about to leave the tenement of clay. He gasped acquiescence in these hopes, and his words led several men near to draw their sleeves across their eyes; but they all knew he was dying, and a little sympathy and sadness would not injure them.

He reached toward the floor, and, the man next handed up a daguerreotype case, which he tried to open. I took and opened it; found the picture of a young, handsome woman, and held it and a candle, so that he could see it. His tears fell on it, as he looked, and he gasped,

"I shall never be where that has been."

I said:

"Is it your wife?" and he replied,

"No! but she would have been."

I always tried to avoid bringing sadness to the living on account of death; but it must have been hard for men to sleep in sound of his labored breathing; and to soften it I began singing "Shining Shore." He took it up at once, in a whisper tone, keeping time, as if used to singing. Soon one, then another and another joined, until all over the church these prostrate men were singing that soft, sad melody. On the altar burned a row of candles before a life-sized picture of the Virgin and Child. The cocks crew the turn of the night outside, and when we had sung the hymn through, some of the men began again, and we had sung it a second time when I heard George call me. I knew that he, too, was dying, and would probably not hear the next crowing of the cock. I must go to him! how could I leave this head unsupported? Oh, death where is thy sting? I think it was with me that night; but I went to George, and when the sun arose it looked upon two corpses, the remains of two who had gone from my arms in one night, full of hope in the great Hereafter.

CHAPTER LXXV.

TAKE BOAT AND SEE A SOCIAL PARTY.

Next morning a new surgeon took charge, and ordered that hay to be removed.   The men clung to their beds and sent for me; I plead a respite, in hopes of getting muslin to make ticks; but was soon detected in the act of taking a bowl of broth to one of my patients. This the surgeon forbade on the ground that it was not regular meal time. I said the man was asleep at meal time. This he would not permit, men must be fed at regular hours, or not at all, and the new authority informed me that

" More wounded soldiers had been killed by women stuffing them than by anything else."

He had just come from Massachusetts, and this was his first day among the wounded.   I set my bowl down before the altar, found a surgeon who ranked him, and stated the case, when the higher authority said:

" Give every man an ox, every day, if he will take it in beef tea."

" But, Doctor, there is nothing in beef tea.   I give broth."

" Very good, give them whatever you please and whenever you please—we can trust you."

The new surgeon was promptly dismissed, and when next I saw him he was on his way back to Massachusetts.

That night a nurse came for me to go to the theater which had been vacated, and once more almost filled with men who lay in total darkness, without having any provision made for them. I got them lights, nurses and food, but could not go back for another siege in that building—could not leave my present post, but the city was being evacuated. Both theater and church were emptied, and I went to the tobacco warehouse, where Mrs. Ingersol was perplexed about a man with a large bullet in his brain. When I had seen him and assured her that another ounce of lead in a skull of that kind was of no consequence, she redoubled her care, and I have no doubt he is living yet. But there was one man in whom I felt a deep interest and for whom I saw little hope. He had a chest wound, and had seemed to be doing well when there was a hemorrhage, and he lay white and still almost as death. He must not attempt to speak, and I was a godsend to him, for I knew what he needed without being told, and gave him the best care I could. He was of a Western State, and his name Dutton, and when I left him I thought he must die in being moved, as he must be soon; but I must go with a boat-load of wounded.

This boat was a mere transport, and its precious freight was laid on the decks as close as they could well be packed, the cabin floor being given up to the wounded officers. There were several surgeons on board who may have been attending to the men, but cannot remember seeing any but one engaged in any work of that kind. There were also seven lady nurses, all I think volunteers, all handsomely if not elegantly dressed. Of course they could do nothing there, and I cannot see how they could have done anything among the wounded in any place where there were no bedsteads to protect the men from their hoops. They had probably been engaged in preparing food, taking charge of, and distributing supplies and other important work, for personal attendance on the men was but a part of the work to be done.

Surgeons could do little without soiling their uniforms, but my dress had long been past soiling or spoiling; my old kid slippers without heels, could be slid, with the feet in them, quite under a man, and as I stepped sideways across them, they took care that my soft dress did not catch on their buttons. When I sat on one heel to bathe a hot face, give a drink or dress a wound, some man took hold of me with his well hand and steadied me, while another held my basin. I had half of an old knapsack to put under a wound, keep the floor dry and catch the worms when I drove them out—and no twenty early birds ever captured so many in the same length of time. I became so eager in the pursuit that I kept it up by candle-light, until late midnight, when I started to go to my stateroom.

Entering the cabin, I came upon a social party, the like of which I trust no one else will ever see. On the sofas sat those seven lady nurses, each with the arm of an officer around her waist, in full view of the wounded men on the floor, some of whom must go from that low bed, to one still lower—even down under the daisies.

I stopped, uttered some exclamation, then stood in speechless surprise. Three surgeons released the ladies they were holding, came forward and inquired if there was anything wanted. I might have replied that men and women were wanted, but think I said nothing. When I reached my room I found in the berth a woman who raised up and said:

"The stewardess told me this was your room; will you let me stay with you?"

She was another Georgie—young, calm, strong, refined, was Miss Gray of Columbia Hospital, and staid with me through a long hard trial, in which she proved that her price was above rubies.

Next morning I found on one of the guards, young Johnson, the son of an old Wilkinsburg schoolmate, Hoped I had so checked the decay and final destroyers which had already taken hold of him, that he might live. Wrote to his people, and saw him at noon transferred with the other patients, the surgeons and stylish lady nurses, to a large hospital boat; when Miss Gray and I returned in the transport to Fredricksburg.

CHAPTER LXXVI.

TAKE FINAL LEAVE OF FREDERICKSBURG.

I CANNOT remember if our boat lay at the Fredricksburg wharf one day or two; but she might start any moment, and those who went ashore took the risk of being left, as this was the last boat. The evacuation was almost complete, and we waited the result of expeditions to gather up our wounded from field hospitals at the front. We were liable to attack at any moment, and were protected by a gunboat which lay close along side.

There was plenty to do on board, but in doing it I must see the piles of stores on the wharf brought there too late to be of service to our wounded, and now to be abandoned to the Rebels. There were certainly one hundred bales of hay, which would have more than replaced all that was withheld by United States bayonets from our own men in their extremity. I soon learned after entering Fredericksburg, that our Commissaries were issuing stores without stint to the citizens; went and saw them carry off loads of everything there was to give; and when those one hundred and eighty-two Union soldiers were literally starving in the old Theater, Union soldiers were dealing out delicacies to Rebels, while others guarded the meanest article of their property, and kept it from our men, even when it was necessary to save life.

I consulted several old Sanitary Commission men, who told me it was always so when Grant was at the front; that he was then in absolute command; that Patrick, the Provost Marshal, was his friend, and would be sustained; and that we must be quiet or we would be ordered out of Fredericksburg.

Gen. Grant may have been loyal to the Union cause, but it has always seemed to me that in fighting its battles, he was moved by the pure love of fighting, and took that side which could furnish him the most means to gratify his passion for war. His Generalship was certainly of a kind that would soon have proved fatal to our cause in the war of the Revolution, and only succeeded in the war of the Rebellion, because the resources at his command were limitless, as compared with those of the enemy. It was late in the afternoon when our boat shoved off, and as we steamed away we saw the citizens rush down and take posses-

sion of the stores left on the wharf. During the
evening and night we were fired into several times
from the shores, but these attacks were returned from
the gun-boat, which kept our assailants at such distance that their shots were harmless. We must have
no lights that night, and the fires were put out or concealed, that they might not make us a target. So I
slept, as there was nothing to be done, but in the morning was out early in search of worms, and was having
good success, when two richly, fashionably dressed
ladies came to tell me there was to be nothing to eat,
save for those who took board at the captain's table.
They had gone to the kitchen to make a cup of tea for
a wounded officer, and were ignominiously driven off
by the cook. What was to be done? We might be
ten days getting to Washington.

I went in search of a surgeon in charge, and found
one in bed, sick; waited at his door until he joined me,
when together we saw the captain of the boat. There
were two new cook-stoves on board, but to put one
up would be to forfeit the insurance. There were
plenty of commissary stores. The surgeon went with
me, ordered the commissary to give me anything I
wanted, and went back to bed. Our stores consisted
of crackers, coffee, dried-apples, essence of beef, and
salt pork in abundance, a little loaf bread, and about
half a pound of citric acid. Of these only the crackers
and bread could be eaten without being cooked.
There were four hundred and fifty wounded men—all
bad cases, all exhausted from privation. How many
of them would live to reach Washington on a diet of
crackers and water? I went to the cook, a large, sen-

sible colored woman, and stated the case as well as I could. After hearing it she said:

"I see how it is; but you see all these officers and ladies are agoin' to board with the captain, an' I'll have a sight o' cooking to do. I can't have none of those fine ladies comin' a botherin' around me, carryin' off my things or upsettin' 'em. But I'll tell you what I'll do; I'll hurry up my work and clare off my things; then you can have the kitchen, you an' that young lady that's with you; but them women, with their hoops an' their flounces, must stay out o' here!"

It was hard to see how two of them would get into that small domain, a kitchen about ten feet square, half filled by a cook-stove, shelves, and the steep, narrow, open stairs which led to the upper deck; but what a kingdom that little kitchen was to me! All the utensils leaked, but cook helped me draw rags through the holes in the three largest which I was to have, and which covered the top of the stove. There were plenty of new wooden buckets and tin dippers on board as freight, some contraband women, and an active little man, who had once been a cook's assistant. He and the women were glad to work for food. He was to help me in the kitchen. They worked outside, and must not get in the way of the crew. They washed dried apples and put them to soak in buckets, pounded crackers in bags and put the crumbs into buckets, making each one a third full and covering them with cold water. I put a large piece of salt pork into my largest boiler, added water and beef essence enough to almost fill the boiler, seasoned it, and as soon as it reached boiling point had it ladled into the buckets with the cracker-crumbs, and sent for distribution. The second boiler was kept busy cooking dried apples, into which I put citric acid and sugar, for gangrene prevailed among the wounds. In the third boiler I made coffee; I kept it a-soak, and as soon as it boiled I put it strong into buckets, one-third full of cold water. I kept vessels in the oven and on the small spaces on top of the stove. My little man fired up like a fire-king, another man laid plenty of wood at hand; and I think that was the only cook-stove that was ever "run" to its full capacity for a week. By so running it, I could give every man a pint of warm soup and one of warm coffee every twenty-four hours. To do this, everything must "come to time."

When one piece of pork was cooked, it was cut into small pieces and distributed, and another put into the boiler. During our cooking times I usually sat on the stairs, where I could direct and be out of the way; and to improve the time, often had a plate and cup from which I ate and drank. Cook always saved me something nice, and I made tea for myself. I was running my body as I did the cook stove, making it do quadruple duty, and did not spare the fuel in either case. Around each foot, below the instep, I had a broad, firm bandage, one above each ankle and one below each knee. If soldiers on the march had adopted this precaution, they would have escaped the swollen limbs so often distressing. I also had each knee covered by several layers of red flannel, to protect them while I knelt on damp places. Soon after going into Campbell, I discovered that muscles around the bone will do double service if held firmly in place, and so was enabled in all my hospital work, to do what seemed miraculous to the most experienced surgeons.

I rested every moment I could, never stood when I might sit, made no useless motions, spent no strength in sorrow, had no sentiment, was simply the engineer of a machine—my own body; could fall asleep soon as I lay down, and wake any moment with my senses all alert, outlived my prejudice about china cups, and drank tea from brown earthen mugs used for soup, and never washed save in cold water; often ate from a tin plate with my left hand, while my right held a stump to prevent that jerking of the nerves which is so agonizing to the patient, many a time eating from the same tin plate with my patient, and making merry over it; and think I must have outstanding engagements to dance cotillions with one hundred one-legged men.

One day while I sat eating and watching, that just enough cans of beef were put into each boiler of broth, and no time wasted by letting it stand after reaching boiling point, a surgeon asked to see me at the kitchen door. He informed me that up on the forecastle, some men had had soup twice while those in some other place had had none. He evidently wished to be lenient, but felt that I had been guilty of great neglect. I heard his grievance, and said:

" Doctor, how many of you surgeons are on this boat?"

After some consideration he answered:

" Four!"

" Four surgeons!" I repeated, " beside the surgeon in charge, who is sick! We have four hundred and fifty wounded men! I draw all the rations, find a way to cook them, have them cooked and put into the buckets, ready for distribution. Do you not think that you four could organize a force to see that they are honestly distributed—or do you expect me to be in the kitchen, up in the forecastle, and at the stern on the boiler deck, at one and the same time? Doctor, could you not take turns in amusing those ladies? Could they not spare two of you for duty?"

I heard no more complaints, but left Miss Grey more in charge of the kitchen, and did enough medical inspecting to know that I had been unjust. Some of the surgeons had been on duty, and the men were not so much neglected as I had feared. As for the ladies, I do not know how many there were of them, but they were of good social position—quite as good as the average of those whose main object in life is to look as much better than their neighbors as circumstances will admit. There was on board one of those folks for whose existence Christianity is responsible, and which sensible Hindoos reduce to their original elements, viz.: a widow who gets a living by being pious, and is respectable through sheer force of cheap finery; one who estimates herself by her surroundings, and whose every word and look and motion is an apology for her existence. She was a Dix, or paid nurse. The ladies snubbed her; we had no room for her hoops; and she spent her time in odd corners, taking care of them and her hair, and turning up her eyes, like a duck in a thunder-storm, under the impression that it looked devotional. If I had killed all the folks I have felt like killing, she would have gone from that boat to her final rest.

One night about eleven o'clock a strange surgeon, who had just come aboard with twenty wounded, came to the kitchen door, and handed in a requisition for tea and custard and chicken for his men. The man told him he could have nothing but cracker-broth or coffee. He was very indignant, and proceeded to get up a scene; but the man said, firmly:

"Can't help it, Surgeon! That's the orders!"

"Orders! Whose orders?"

I got down from my perch on the stairs, came forward and said:

"It is my orders, sir, and I am sorry, but this is really all we can do for you. If your men have tin cups, each one can have a cup of warm soup—it will not be very hot—or a cup of warm coffee. Those who get soup will get no coffee, and those who get coffee can have no soup. You can get tin cups from the commissary, and should have them ready, so that the food will not cool."

While I made this statement he stood regarding me with ineffable disdain, and when I was through inquired:

"Who are you?"

"I am the cook!"

"The cook!" he repeated, contemptuously. "I will report your insolence when we reach Washington!"

"That may be your duty; but I will send up the coffee and soup, and do you get the tin cups."

He stamped off in dudgeon, and others who heard him were highly indignant; but I was greatly pleased to find a surgeon who would get angry and raise a disturbance on behalf of his patients. I never knew his name, but if this should meet his eye I trust he will accept my thanks for his faithfulness to his charge.

On the lower deck, behind the boilers, lay twenty wounded prisoners, who at first looked sulky; but as I was stepping over and among them, one caught my dress, looked up pleadingly, and said:

"Mother, can't you get me some soft bread? I can't eat this hard-tack."

He was young, scarce more than a boy; had large, dark eyes, a good head—tokens of gentle nurture—and alas! a thigh stump. He told me he was of a Mississippi regiment, and his name Willie Gibbs. I bathed his hot face, and said I would see about the bread; then went to another part of the deck, where our men were very closely packed, and stated the case to them. There was very little soft bread—it was theirs by right; what should I do? I think they all spoke at once, and all said the same words:

"Oh, mother! give the Johnnies the soft bread! we can eat hard-tack!"

I think I was impartial, but there was a temptation to give Willie Gibbs a little more than his share of attention. His face was so sad, and there was so little hope that he would ever again see those who loved him, that I think I did more for him than for any other one on board. His companions came to call me "mother," and I hope felt their captivity softened by my care; and often rebel hands supported me while I crouched at work.

When we approached Washington, I proposed rewarding the cook for the incalculable service she had rendered, but she replied:

" No, ma'am, I will not take anything from you,
'cept that apron!   When we get to Washington, you
will not want it any more, an' I'll keep it all my life
to remember you, and leave it to my children!   Lord!
there isn't another lady in the world could 'a done
what you've done; an' I know you're a lady!   Them
women with the fine clothes is trying to pass for
ladies, but, Lord!   I know no lady 'u'd dress up that
way in a place like this, an' men know it, too—just
look at you, an' how you do make them fellers in
shoulderstraps stand 'round!"

Her observation showed her Southern culture, for
whatever supremacy the North may have over the
South, Southern ladies are far in advance of those of
the North in the art of dress.   A Southern lady seldom commits an incongruity, or fails to dress according to age, weather, and the occasion.   I do not think
any one of any social standing would have gone
among wounded men, with the idea of rendering any
assistance, tricked out in finery, as hundreds, if not
thousands, of respectable Northern women did.

The apron which I gave to my friend the cook, was
brown gingham, had seen hard service, and cost, originally, ten cents, and half an hour's hand-sewing;
but if it aids her to remember me as pleasantly as I
do her, it is part of a bond of genuine friendship.

23

CHAPTER LXXVII.

TRY TO GET UP A SOCIETY AND GET SICK.

AFTER two days in bed at home, I was so much better, that when Mrs. Ingersol came with a plan for organizing a society to furnish the army with female nurses, I went to see Mrs. Lincoln about it. She was willing to coöperate, and I went to Secretary Stanton, who heard me, and replied:

"You must know that Mrs. Barlow and Mrs. Ingersol and you are not fair representatives of your sex," and went on to explain the embarrassment of the Surgeon-General from the thousands of women pressing their services upon the Government, and the various political influences brought to bear on behalf of applicants, and of the well grounded opposition of surgeons to the presence of women in hospitals, on account of their general unfitness. Gen. Scott, as a personal friend of Miss Dix, had appointed her to the place she held, and it was so convenient and respectful to refer people to her, that the War Department would not interfere with the arrangement. In other words, she was a break-water against which feminine sympathies could dash and splash without submerging the hospital service.

After what I had seen among the women who had succeeded in getting in, I had not much to say. A society might prescribe a dress, but might be no more successful than Miss Dix in making selections of those who should wear it.

I asked the Secretary how it came that no better

provision had been made for our wounded after the battle of the Wilderness, and tears sprang to his eyes as he replied:

"We did not know where they were. We had made every arrangement at the points designated by Gen. Grant, but he changed his plans and did not notify us. The whole army was cut off from its base of supplies and must be sustained. As soon as we knew the emergency, we did everything in our power; but all our preparations were lost. Everything had to be done over again. You cannot regret the suffering more than I, but it was impossible for me to prevent it."

I never saw him so earnest, so sorrowful, so deeply moved.

That effort seemed to be the straw which broke the camel's back, and I was so ill as to demand medical attendance. For this I sent to Campbell. Dr. Kelly came, but his forte was surgery, and my case was left with Dr. True, who had had longer practice in medicine. They both decided that I had been inoculated with gangrene while dressing wounds, and for some weeks I continued to sink. I began to think my illness fatal, and asked the doctor, who said:

"I have been thinking I ought to tell you that if you have any unsettled business you should attend to it."

I had a feeling of being generally distributed over the bed, of being a mass of pulp without any central force, but I had had a letter that day from my daughter, who was with her father and grandmother in Swissvale, and wanted to come to me, and the thought came: "Does God mean to make my child an orphan, that others may receive their children by my death?" Then I had a strange sensation of a muster, a gathering of scattered life-force, and when it all came together it made a protest; I signed to the doctor, who put his ear to my lips, and I said:

"Doctor True, I shall live to be an hundred and twenty years old!"

He took up the lamp, threw the light on my face, and peered anxiously into it, and I looked straight into his eyes, and said:

"I will!"

He laughed and set down the lamp, saying:

"Then you must get over this!"

"You must get me over it. Bring Dr. Kelly!"

Next morning, I had them carry me into a larger room, where the morning sun shone on me, and ten days after, started for Pennsylvania, where I spent three weeks with my old Swissvale neighbors, Col. Hawkins and Wm. S. Haven.

When I returned to Washington, I found an official document, a recommendation from the Quarter-Master General, of my dismissal for absence without leave. It was addressed to Secretary Stanton, who had written on the outside:

"Respectfully referred to Mrs. Swisshelm, by Edwin M. Stanton."

I went back to work, and learned that Mrs. Gen. Barlow had died of typhoid fever, in Washington. No man died more directly for the Government. Thousands who fell on the battle-field, exhibited less courage and devotion to that service, and did less to to secure its success. I know not where her body lies, but wherever it does, no decoration-day should pass in which her memory is not crowned with immortelles.

She died at a time when my life was despaired of, and when Mrs. Ingersol wrote to a Maine paper of my illness, adding:

"I hope the Lord will not take her away, until He has made another like her."

She told me afterwards that just then she held the world at a grudge; but it must have been relieved of my presence long ere this, if I had not found in homœopathy relief from pain, which for eight months made life a burden, and for which the best old-school physicians proposed no cure.

CHAPTER LXXVIII.

AN EFFICIENT NURSE.

To show the capabilities of some of the women who thought they had a mission for saving the country by acting as hospital nurses, I give the history of one.

While I lay ill, a friend came and told of a most excellent woman who had come from afar, and tendered her services to the Government, who had exerted much influence and spent much effort to get into a hospital as nurse, but had failed.

Hearing of my illness, her desire to be useful led her to tender her services, so that if she could not nurse wounded soldiers she could nurse one who had. The generous offer was accepted, and I was left an afternoon in her care.

I wanted a cup of tea. She went to the kitchen to

make it, and one hour after came up with a cup of tea, only this and nothing more, save a saucer. To taste the tea I must have a spoon, and to get one she must go along a hall, down a long flight of stairs, through another hall and the kitchen, to the pantry. When she had made the trip the tea was so much too strong that a spoonful would have made a cup. She went down again for hot water, and after she had got to the kitchen remembered that she had thrown it out, thinking it would not be wanted. The fire had gone out, and she came up to inquire if she should make a new one, and if so, where she should find kindling? She had spent almost two hours running to and fro, was all in perspiration and a fluster, had done me a great deal of harm and nobody any good, had wasted all the kindlings for the evening fire, enough tea to have served a large family for a meal, and fairly illustrated a large part of the hospital service rendered by women oppressed with the nursing mission.

My sense of relief was inexpressible when Mrs. George B. Lincoln returned from her visit to the White House, sent my tea-maker away and took charge of me once more.

CHAPTER LXXIX.

TWO FREDERICKSBURG PATIENTS.

SOME months after leaving Fredricksburg, I was walking on Pennsylvania avenue, when the setting sun shone in my face, and a man in uniform stopped me, saying:

"Excuse me! you do not know me, but I know you!"

I turned, looked at him carefully, and said:

" I do not know you!"

" Oh, no! but the last time you saw me, you cut off my beard with your scissors and fed me with a teaspoon. When you left me you did not think you would ever see me again."

" Oh!" I exclaimed joyfully, "you are Dutton."

He laughed, and replied, "That's me. I have just got a furlough and am going home."

He was very pale and thin, but I was so glad to see him and shake hands, and wish him safely home with his friends.

During the great review after the war, I had a seat near the President's stand. There was a jam, and a man behind me called my attention to a captain, at a short distance, who had something to say to me, and passed along the words:

" You took care of me on the boat coming from Fredericksburg."

Looking across, I could see him quite well, but even when his hat was off could not recognize him; and this is all I have ever heard from or of the men with whose lives mine was so knit during that terrible time.

I fear that not many survived, and doubt if a dozen of them ever knew me by any other name than that of " Mother."

CHAPTER LXXX.

AM ENLIGHTENED.

WHEN Early appeared before Washington, we all knew there was nothing to prevent his coming in and taking possession. The forts were stripped. There were no soldiers either in or around the city. The original inhabitants were ready to welcome him with open arms. The departments were closed, that the clerks might go out in military array, to oppose; but of course few soldiers were sitting at desks at that stage of the war. The news at the Quartermaster's office one morning was that the foreign ministers had been notified, and that the city would be shelled that afternoon. We lived on the north side of the city; and when I went home, thousands of people were on the streets, listening to the sound of guns at Fort Reno.

So far as I knew, there was a universal expectation that the city would be occupied by rebel troops that night. As this was in harmony with the general tenor of my anticipations for a quarter of a century, I readily shared in the popular opinion, and for once was with the majority.

Among the groups who stood in the streets were many contrabands, and their faces were pitiful to see. One scantily-clad woman, holding a ragged infant, and with two frightened, ragged children clinging to her skirts, stood literally quaking. Her black face had turned gray with terror, and she came to me and asked:

" Oh! Missus! does ye tink dey will get in?"

Suddenly my eyes were opened, like those of the prophet's servant when he saw the horses and chariots of fire, and I replied:

"No! never! They will come no nearer than they now are! You can go home and rest in peace, for you are just as safe from them as if you were in heaven!"

She was greatly comforted; but a gentleman said, as she moved away:

" I wish I could share your opinion; but what is to hinder their coming in?"

" God is to hinder! He has appointed us to rescue these people. They are collected here in thousands, and the prayers of centuries are to be answered now!"

I myself went home feeling all the confidence I spoke, and wondering I could have been so stupid as to doubt. Our Government and people were very imperfect, but had developed a sublime patriotism— made an almost miraculous growth in good. Ten righteous men would have saved Sodom. We had ten thousand; and I must think there are few histories of supernatural interference in the affairs of the Jews more difficult to account for, on merely natural grounds, than the preservation of Washington in that crisis.

CONCLUSION.

DECEMBER 6th, 1865, the fiftieth anniversary of my birth, found me in Washington, at work in the Quarter-Master's office, on a salary of sixty dollars a month, without any provision for support in old age; and so great a sufferer as never to have a night of rest unbroken by severe pain, but with my interest in a country rescued from the odium of Southern slavery, and a faint light breaking of the day which is yet to abolish that of the West.

In the summer of '66, Dr. King, of Pittsburg, came to know what I would take for my interest in ten acres of the Swissvale estate, which he had purchased. My deed had presented a barrier to the sale of a portion of it, and he was in trouble:

I consulted Secretary Stanton, who said:

"Your title to that property is good against the world!"

It had become valuable and the idea of its ownership was alarming! I had made up my mind to poverty, had been discharged from the Quarter-Master's office by special order of President Johnson, " for speaking disrespectfully of the President of the United States!"— *Washington Star*—was the first person dismissed by Mr. Johnson; was without visible means of support, could not suddenly adjust my thought to anything so foreign to all my plans as coming into possession of a valuable estate, and said:

"Oh, Secretary Stanton, how shall I ever undertake such a stewardship at my time of life?" He looked sternly at me, and replied:

"Mrs. Swisshelm, don't be a fool! take care of yourself! It is time you would begin. The property is yours now. You are morally responsible for it, and can surely make some better use of it than giving it away to rich men around Pittsburg. Go at once and attend to your interests."

This was our last interview. I instituted the suit he advised, and he would have plead my cause before the Supreme Court, but when it came up he was holding possession of the War Department to defeat President Johnson's policy of making the South triumphant. However, the decree of the court was in my favor, and through it I have been able to rescue the old log block-house from the tooth of decay, and to sit in it and recall those passages of life with which it is so intimately connected.